KANT'S NONIDEAL THEORY OF POLITICS

KANT'S NONIDEAL THEORY OF POLITICS

Dilek Huseyinzadegan

Northwestern University Press
Evanston, Illinois

Northwestern University Press
www.nupress.northwestern.edu

Copyright © 2019 by Northwestern University Press.
Published 2019. All rights reserved.

Printed in the United States of America

10 9 8 7 6 5 4 3 2 1

ISBN 978-0-8101-3987-9 (paper)
ISBN 978-0-8101-3988-6 (cloth)
ISBN 978-0-8101-3989-3 (ebook)

Cataloging-in-Publication Data are available from the Library of Congress.

Anneme

Contents

Acknowledgments		ix
List of Abbreviations		xi
Introduction. Locating a Nonideal Theory in Kant's Political Thought: A Systematic Approach		3

Part I. History and Politics: Political History and Cosmopolitanism

1	A Matter of Orientation	27
2	Historical Patterns, Political Aims	43

Part II. Nature, Culture, and Politics: Political Anthropology and Cosmopolitanism

3	Organisms, Bodies Politic, and Progress	67
4	Political *Zweckmässigkeit*, or From Nature to Culture	87

Part III. Nature and Politics: Political Geography and the Cosmopolitan Right

5	Teleology and Peace on Earth	117
6	Peace, Hospitality, and the Shape of the Earth	137
	Conclusion. Theorizing the Lawfulness of the Contingent in Politics: A Defense of Teleology	159
	Notes	169
	Bibliography	189
	Index	199

Acknowledgments

This book would not have been possible without the help and support of many people and institutions. The Department of Philosophy at Emory University provided a comfortable and supportive environment, together with its fantastic team of faculty, staff, and students. Special thanks go to the Emory University Research Committee and the College of Arts and Sciences, which allowed me to spend the Fall Semesters of 2016 and 2017 revising and editing chapters of the book for a timely submission, and the Center for Faculty Development and Excellence, which provided writing groups, meet-the-editor sessions, and book proposal workshops along the way. I am grateful to my writing group friends Tanine Allison, Zach Ludington, and Dan Reynolds for reading and commenting on drafts of various chapters from an interdisciplinary perspective, and to the graduate students in my Kant seminars, especially Jordan Leah Daniels and Omar Quiñonez, for their enthusiasm and intellectual vivacity.

I would also like to extend my gratitude to Tina Chanter, Avery Goldman, Namita Goswami, Rick Lee, Elizabeth Millán, Darrell Moore, and Kevin Thompson for their mentorship and friendship at various stages of my academic career. This project benefited immensely from various conversations I have had with amazing colleagues, especially the participants of the Institute for the History of Philosophy Seminar in summer 2016: Lisa Ellis, Rachel Jones, Larry Krasnoff, Jennifer Mensch, Elaine Miller, Pablo Muchnik, Angelica Nuzzo, Jameliah Shorter-Bourhanou, Kristi Sweet, Joseph Trullinger, and Donald Wilson, as well as Rudi Makkreel, who has also been a valuable resource in Atlanta.

I would not be where I am and who I am right now without my Chicago family members Andrew Dilts, Marie Draz, Emily García, Sina Kramer, Jana McAuliffe, Jeff Pardikes, H. Rakes, and Perry Zurn, who have shown me that one can find a home away from home and that friends are the family we choose. Suffice it to say that their undying solidarity and unmatched intellectual brilliance are continuing sources of inspiration. Argyle and Grafton also provided much needed perspective for the past few years—I think that they are happy to see this book to its completion. My family back in Istanbul had to put up with seeing me only once a year for fourteen years and still provided enthusiasm and encouragement for my academic career. I dedicate this work to my mother, whose unconditional support made it possible for her daughters to achieve higher education degrees and to pursue fulfilling careers.

I owe particular thanks to my partner Jeremy Bell, who read through the manuscript in various stages and gave innumerable helpful suggestions for revisions and edits in addition to putting up with me through anxious and stressful periods of research, writing, and revision. There are in fact no words to fully and adequately express the depth of my gratitude, admiration, and love for Jeremy.

Finally, I wish to thank the editors of the following journals for granting permission to reprint versions of previously published materials: a shorter version of chapter 3 appears as "Does Kant Have an Organic Theory of State?" in *Natur und Freiheit: Akten des XII. Kant-Kongresses*, ed. Violetta Waibel and Margit Ruffing (Berlin: Walter de Gruyter, 2018), 2557–64; and a section of chapter 4 appears as "Kant's Political *Zweckmässigkeit*," in *Kantian Review* 20, no. 3 (2015): 421–44. Reprinted with permission of the publisher.

Abbreviations

Throughout the text and notes, all abbreviated references to Kant's works will refer first to German editions. There will be no reference to the English pagination when the English translators include pagination from the original edition in their translations. Unless otherwise noted, I use *The Cambridge Edition of the Works of Immanuel Kant* for English translations. Numbers following the abbreviations refer to volume numbers.

All references to Kant's works will cite *Kants gesammelte Schriften*, traditionally referred to as the Academy Edition (*Akademieausgabe*; *AA*). English translations cite the *Cambridge Edition of the Works of Immanuel Kant*, unless noted otherwise.

AA	*Kants gesammelte Schriften: Akademieausgabe* (Berlin: Walter de Gruyter, 1902–).
	The Cambridge Edition of the Works of Immanuel Kant, edited by Paul Guyer and Allen Wood (Cambridge: Cambridge University Press, 1992–).
Anth	*Anthropologie in pragmatischer Hinsicht* (*AA* 7:117–333)
	Anthropology from a Pragmatic Point of View, in *Anthropology, History, and Education*, edited and translated by Robert B. Louden and Günter Zöller, 2007.
GMS	*Grundlegung zur Metaphysik der Sitten* (*AA* 4:385–463)
	Groundwork of the Metaphysics of Morals, in *Practical Philosophy*, edited by Mary J. Gregor, 1996.
"IaG"	"Idee zu einer allgemeinen Geschichte in weltbürgerlicher Absicht" (*AA* 8:15–32)
	"Idea for a Universal History with a Cosmopolitan Aim," in *Anthropology, History, and Education*, edited and translated by Robert B. Louden and Günter Zöller, 2007.
KpV	*Kritik der praktischen Vernunft* (*AA* 5:19–164)
	Critique of Practical Reason, in *Practical Philosophy*, edited by Mary J. Gregor, 1996.

ABBREVIATIONS

KrV   *Kritik der reinen Vernunft* (*AA* 3 and 4)

Critique of Pure Reason, edited and translated by Paul Guyer and Allen W. Wood, 1998.

KU   *Kritik der Urteilskraft* (*AA* 5 and 20)

Critique of the Power of Judgment, edited and translated by Paul Guyer and Eric Matthews, 2000.

MS   *Metaphysik der Sitten* (*AA* 6:203–494)

The Metaphysics of Morals, in *Practical Philosophy*, edited by Mary J. Gregor, 1996.

PG   *Physische Geographie* (*AA* 9)

Physical Geography, in *Natural Science*, edited by Eric Watkins, 2012.

Rel   *Die Religion innerhalb der Grenzer der blossen Vernunft* (*AA* 6:1–102)

Religion within the Boundaries of Mere Reason, in *Religion and Rational Theology*, edited and translated by Allen W. Wood and George di Giovanni, 1996

"RezHerder"   *Recensionen von J. G. Herders Ideen zur Philosophie der Geschichte der Menschheit* (*AA* 8:43–67)

"Review of J. G. Herder's *Ideas for the Philosophy of the History of Humanity*," in *Anthropology, History, and Education*, edited and translated by Robert B. Louden and Günter Zöller, 2007.

"WA"   "Beantwortung der Frage: Was ist Aufklärung?" (*AA* 8:33–42)

"An Answer to the Question: What Is Enlightenment?" in *Practical Philosophy*, edited by Mary J. Gregor, 1996.

"WDO"   "Was heisst: Sich im Denken orientieren?" (*AA* 8:131–48)

What Does It Mean to Orient Oneself in Thinking? in *Religion and Rational Theology*, edited and translated by Allen W. Wood and George di Giovanni, 1996.

"ZeF"   "Zum ewigen Frieden: Ein philosophischer Entwurf" (*AA* 8:341–86)

"Toward Perpetual Peace: A Philosophical Sketch," in *Practical Philosophy*, edited by Mary J. Gregor, 1996.

KANT'S NONIDEAL THEORY
OF POLITICS

Introduction

Locating a Nonideal Theory in Kant's Political Thought: A Systematic Approach

Despite the systematic rehabilitation that Kant gives to the principle of purposiveness in the *Critique of Judgment*, Kant's teleological arguments in political philosophy have a bad reputation. Political philosophers are especially uneasy with the teleological language found in Kant's historico-political writings; most recently Elisabeth Ellis dubbed teleology "the straitjacket of Kant's political thought" and urged us to omit teleological arguments from our reconstructions of his politics.[1] There are three main reasons for this discomfort: first, teleology seems to presuppose an outdated metaphysics, a hand of God in human affairs; second, the epistemic status of regulative teleology in Kant seems to be too tentative to be of practical use in any political discourse; and third, Kant's recourse to teleology more often than not seems to justify the most unpleasant aspects of his political thought, namely, his gendered and racially hierarchical view of human beings and a Eurocentric vision of history. In response to this general uneasiness, in this book I show that teleology makes an important systematic contribution to Kant's political thought and our understanding of it. Regulative teleology, or what Kant comes to call in the *Critique of Judgment* the principle of "the lawfulness of the contingent" (KU/AA 5:404), is the guiding thread of his nonideal theory of politics.

I start with the premise that, as a systematic thinker, Kant must have a systematic political philosophy. If we follow this premise further, we see that Kant's well-known philosophical dualisms exhibit themselves in his political thought as two complementary yet distinct guiding threads and two types of theoretical endeavors. Accordingly, I will argue that when we are trying to reconstruct Kant's political thought, we have, systematically speaking, two interpretive keys: on the one hand, we have the principle of *Recht*, or right, firmly anchored in Kant's practical philosophy, providing us with *a priori* norms and allowing us to identify ideal political goals; on the other hand, we have the regulative principle of *Zweckmässigkeit*, or purposiveness, anchored in Kant's philosophy of nature, allowing us to produce tentative pictures of the politically salient features of history,

3

culture, and nature as a whole. The former path is well trodden. Indeed, the familiar view of Kant's most important legacy for political thought today is often construed as a version of an ideal theory of politics, mainly of cosmopolitanism, grounded in the principle of *Recht* as a discourse on rights and institutions. This legacy is based on *The Doctrine of Right* and is in line with Kant's own definition of politics in that work as a limited domain of *Recht*, a narrow branch of moral philosophy. In this book, I aim to show that Kant also deals with the contingent variables of politics—namely, history, culture, and geography—in each and every political text that he wrote; furthermore, I argue that the systematic ground of his treatment of these variables is the regulative principle of teleology. I then classify a set of questions in these texts—those that he asks and answers by means of a regulative teleology—as belonging to a nonideal theory of politics. Thus, my goal is to develop a different approach to his political thought, a road less travelled, which I label "Kant's nonideal theory."

The present study is inspired in part by the recent movement in Kant scholarship that focuses on the empirical dimensions of Kant's works, specifically those of his practical philosophy.[2] In line with these recent books on the second part of Kant's ethics or transcendental project, my aim here is to identify and develop *the second part of his political philosophy*. To this end, I take a systematic approach to Kant's political thought and locate the underlying unity of the presuppositions and methodology of a nonideal theory of politics in the critical-regulative principle of teleology. Through this systematic investigation of the place of teleology in Kant's political thought, I accomplish three related yet distinct interpretive tasks. First, I show that we find in Kant a hitherto underappreciated nonideal theory of politics, which gives us a broader conception of his political legacy than one of mere variations on an ideal theory of cosmopolitanism. Second, I show that Kant's idea of a cosmopolitan world order is not directly a transhistorical or transcultural goal; rather, it is informed by quite specific views of history, culture, and nature and thus has historical, anthropological, and geographical foundations. Finally, I show that making a distinction between Kant's ideal and nonideal theories of politics allows us to acknowledge the historical, cultural, geographical assumptions that any political theory, whether implicitly or explicitly, has to make.

Ideal and Nonideal Theory in Political Thought: Content, Method, Questions

The distinction between ideal and nonideal theories in political philosophy is rather recent, most importantly drawn by John Rawls, John

Simmons, Laura Valentini, Zofia Stemplowska, Adam Swift, and Charles Mills. It is a distinction that, in Valentini's terms, originates out of a "methodological debate on the proper nature of political philosophy and its ability to guide action in real-world circumstances."[3] There are various ways to draw this distinction, but in broad strokes, we can say that an "ideal theory" is "more-or-less a utopian theory" which provides "the blue print for a perfectly just society," whereas a "nonideal theory" focuses on the feasibility constraints that may matter to normative political theorizing and thus provides a "transitional theory."[4] If ideal theory attempts to work out the principles that characterize "a well-ordered society under favorable circumstances,"[5] then nonideal theory might be seen as "filling the gap between the theoretical ideal and political reality."[6] Relatedly, the distinction between ideal and nonideal theories of politics can refer to the structure and content of two different forms of theorizing,[7] or to the distinct methodologies employed by each.[8] I will give a brief overview of this distinction to point out the features that I take to be relevant for reconstructing Kant's political thought and its nonideal part. My wager is that, when mapped onto his political philosophy overall, this distinction enhances and deepens our understanding of Kant's contemporary political legacy.

Ideal Theory of Politics

Rawls writes that ideal theory "works out the principles that characterize a well-ordered society under favorable circumstances . . . [and this] ideal part presents a conception of a just society that we are to achieve if we can. Existing institutions are to be judged in light of this conception."[9] In his view, an ideal theory identifies the long-term goals that we want to achieve and explores the basic features and institutions that an ideal society ought to have.

Furthermore, as Mills points out, ideal theory operates with *an idealized social ontology*, a notion of human agents with *idealized capacities*, and an *idealized version of social institutions*, and, in this sense, it can also be seen as a methodological strategy.[10] Mills contends that all political philosophy is ideal in the sense of ideal-as-normative.[11] However, the distinction between ideal and nonideal theory lies in the difference between the starting points and aims of any given theoretical approach to politics, that is, between various methodological strategies.[12] Thus, when we begin with an ideal-as-normative model with the aim of articulating a set of normative political ideals, we are proceeding from the top down, from the ideal to the real: we are doing ideal theory. Here, we ask what the ideal institutions under favorable circumstances *ought to* look like or what our ultimate goal in organizing or reorganizing a society *ought to* be.

Kant's Ideal Theory of Politics

Such brief definitions will suffice for outlining the structure, content, and methodology of any ideal theory of politics. According to these definitions, *The Doctrine of Right* incorporates a number of the distinguishing features of an ideal theory methodology and exemplifies a predominantly ideal and formal theory of politics. First, in *The Doctrine of Right* Kant begins with the external and practical *form* of the relation of one person to another (*MS/AA* 6:230). Thus, the entire doctrine of right is dedicated only to the *form* of the interaction among individuals in a lawful state, not to the actual *matter* of relations of free choice. In fact, the very idea of the doctrine of right requires us to focus only on the *form* of these relations and to work out the formal, ideal principles and institutions of right. Second, Kant claims that there is only one innate right, namely, "the freedom or independence from being constrained by another's choice"; this entails an innate equality, hence "a human being's quality of being his own master" (*MS/AA* 6:237). These are admittedly all *idealized attributes* that a majority of the world's population, then and even now, cannot really take for granted as innate or actual. More explicitly, Kant writes that the doctrine of duties represents the human being "in terms of his capacity for freedom, which is wholly supersensible," and this being's personality "independent of physical attributes" (*MS/AA* 6:239). These explicitly *idealized capacities* are not concerned with and therefore should not refer to the sensible qualities of human beings. Third, the *Doctrine of Right* is concerned not with the existing civil condition but with the rightful one—that is, it is not about what is the case but *what ought to be the case*. In this regard, the private right to own something external as my own, for instance, is provisional upon the rightful civil condition (*MS/AA* 6:256–66).

Furthermore, the highest-order ideal of Kant's political philosophy is peace. He calls establishing universal and lasting peace "the entire final end of the doctrine of right," and calls peace "the highest political good [*das höchstes politisches Gut*]" (*MS/AA* 6:355). Insofar as an ideal theory is understood as a more or less utopian theory, the Kantian utopia that we locate in *The Doctrine of Right* and other political writings is one of perpetual peace—which means that Kant's ideal theory of politics is an ideal theory of peace. For Kant the idea of peace constitutes the ideal conception of justice, which in turn provides the highest-order ideal around which all the rules and structures governing our collective lives ought to be organized.

Rather than giving an exhaustive account of what I call Kant's ideal theory of politics, here I merely wish to clarify its relevant features: it works with idealized and formal notions of personhood, rights, social interactions, and institutions, and it represents an ideal theory of peace. We find most of these features represented in *The Doctrine of Right*, which I therefore interpret *in large part if not fully* as a treatise on Kant's ideal theory of politics. This is also consistent with the Rawlsian characterization of ideal theory outlined above, since such a theory lays out "a perfectly just basic structure," where a conception of justice must be the ideal form for background institutions.[13]

Nonideal Theory of Politics

A nonideal theory of politics designates an approach that theorizes the nonideal, or actual, conditions of our social world. A nonideal theory—as Simmons points out, drawing on Rawls—will be broadly concerned with working out how we can gradually achieve our political ideals given our natural limitations and historical contingencies.[14] Simmons writes that, "where ideal theory dictates the objective, nonideal theory dictates the route to that objective (from whatever imperfectly just condition a society happens to occupy)."[15] Structurally speaking, therefore, a nonideal theory is about the principles of gradual achievability or feasibility of our ideal goals, and thus provides us with specific policies and courses of action toward these goals.[16] It is a transitional theory that aims to provide guidance for our actions here and now.[17]

Simmons adds that since nonideal theory will require us to determine the "political possibility" and "likely effectiveness" of these policies and courses of action, it will need reasonably specialized knowledge of the structure and workings of a particular society.[18] In other words, it will require us to have a sense of the politically salient facts about such things as human nature, history, or geography. In the realm of nonideal theory, then, we find a greater concern for facts than we did in ideal theory, as well as a pressing need to determine how this concern might be incorporated into normative theorizing.[19]

In Mills's terms, nonideal theory is also a methodological strategy: we begin with the less-than-ideal actual workings of the world and try to come up with conceptually adequate renderings of these conditions.[20]

INTRODUCTION

If we are constructing such specialized knowledges of the world or the knowledge of our empirical conditions, then we are using what Mills calls the ideal-as-descriptive model.[21] In this model, our aim is not immediately or directly normative; it is to come up with a politically salient description of reality. We are proceeding from the bottom up, from the real to the ideal, and we are doing nonideal theory.

Kant's Nonideal Theory of Politics

Kant's political thought cannot be construed exclusively as an ideal theory, since we find a considerable amount of empirical detail regarding *how* we ought to accomplish peace throughout his political writings, including in parts of *The Doctrine of Right* but also in "Idea for a Universal History with a Cosmopolitan Aim," in parts of the *Critique of Judgment*, and in "Toward Perpetual Peace." When we take a broader view of Kant's political thought, in other words, we find Kant both addressing questions belonging to nonideal theory and using the methodology of nonideal theory. Thus, we will see that with his nonideal theory Kant attempts to provide an overview of the feasibility constraints affecting his ideal theory and to bridge the gap between theoretical ideals and practical reality.

Valentini points out that a successful nonideal theory will need to address two things: first, it needs "to make sure that its factual input is in some sense 'appropriate' to the particular question it aims to answer," and second, it needs to "come up with a general rule prescribing what the correct level of idealization in normative theorizing should be."[22] She contends that figuring out what types of idealizations are appropriate or what facts ought to be taken into account in political theorizing will depend on the question that the theory itself is meant to answer.[23] As I have pointed out, the overall question that ought to frame Kant's entire political philosophy, the highest political good as he sees it, is peace. As I will argue in this book, Kant deems the regulative principle of purposiveness to be the appropriate rule of generalization, and deems history, anthropology, and geography to be the politically salient facts. Thus, in Kant's political philosophy we find both a general rule for the correct level of idealization and a preliminary list of the kinds of facts that ought to be taken into account in our pursuit of peace.

If, as Stemplowska and Swift argue, we want nonideal theory to guide our actions in our current circumstances,[24] then Kant provides such a theory—or so I will argue. In order to orient this kind of a theoretical inquiry within what is possible and feasible here and now, Kant uses the regulative principle of purposiveness as a guiding principle. By means of this regulative principle, he is able to orient his reflections on history and conclude that its direction must be a cosmopolitan world order; he is able to orient his reflections on cultural production and conclude that our ultimate goal must be one of developing our skills completely in a cosmopolitan world; and he is able to orient his reflections on nature and conclude that its primary means of putting us in contact with one another must be through hospitable commerce.

Kant reminds us repeatedly in the *Critique of Judgment* that we employ the principle of purposiveness to name the relationship between what is objectively *contingent* and what is subjectively *lawful: Zweckmässigkeit* thus refers to *the lawfulness of the contingent* (*KU/AA* 20:204, 20:243, 5:180, 5:184, 5:404). In the language of the *Critique of Pure Reason*, purposiveness is a guiding principle that is needed by an intellect like ours in order to orient itself and to make sense of what remains, to a large degree, objectively contingent. This regulative principle, when used in his political writings, allows him to produce a theory that speaks to feasibility concerns, a theory of transition from nonideal to ideal conditions, and concrete proposals to guide our action here and now. Therefore, regulative teleology is the principle of what I will term Kant's nonideal theory.

I do not wish to repudiate an ideal theory of politics or its place altogether in Kant's thought. There are important methodological reasons why Kant thinks that the normativity or justification of *Recht* must be construed independently of empirical reality and prior to the question of its applications.[25] Ideal theory, oriented by *a priori* laws and principles of pure reason, has a priority in the Kantian system; as Zammito aptly puts it in another context, "without this *a priori* commitment to 'pure' reason, Kant becomes unrecognizable."[26] My point is that we find in Kant's political writings also the complementary approach of a nonideal theory at work. In these writings, he reflects on the contingent element of our collective lives more broadly, providing us with theorizations of history, culture, and nature as they pertain to politics.

While Kant himself did not distinguish between his ideal and nonideal theories of politics, I introduce this distinction here in order to make sense of his use of teleology in his historico-political writings and to uncover the political salience of his claims about history, anthropology, and geography. When we map this distinction onto Kant's political thought, I argue that the main principle of Kant's ideal theory of politics is that of *Recht,* whereas the principle of his nonideal theory of politics is that of *Zweckmässigkeit.* A systematic investigation of the use of teleology in Kant's political philosophy allows me to incorporate his reflections on history, culture, and nature into political discourse. Thus, the theoretically important upshot of introducing a distinction between his ideal and nonideal theories is that we get a broader conception of politics in Kant than a set of ideal theories of rights, league of nations, or hospitality. Lastly, introducing this distinction to Kant's political philosophy offers methodological clarity regarding the levels of abstraction and idealization that we find in his thought, and more importantly, it deepens and enhances our view of his contemporary political legacy by uncovering his sensitivity to and regard for the contingent variables of our collective lives.

Because my main goal is to articulate in broad strokes the systematic place and contribution of a nonideal theory in Kant's political thought, in the book I limit my analyses to the political writings and focus on the use of the regulative principle of teleology in these texts. My claim is not that only the writings with which I explicitly engage belong to his nonideal theory of politics. On the contrary, if I am right about this systematic overview and division of his political thought, and specifically about his nonideal theory of politics and the role of teleology therein, then it would mean that his other writings on history, culture, race, sex and gender, nationality, anthropology, and geography could also be incorporated into his critical system and into his political philosophy, by means of the regulative principle of teleology, as elements of his nonideal theory.

The Relationship between Ideal and Nonideal Theories in Kant's Political Thought

Broadly speaking, the relationship between ideal and nonideal theory must be configured as one of *complementarity.* While an ideal theory of politics governs the nonideal theory of history, culture, and geography, the nonideal theory of politics provides a theoretical map of the world in which we find ourselves, and in this way, it bears on, shapes, and concretizes how we can bring about our political goals. If ideal theory provides the normative foundations of politics from the top down, then nonideal theory deals with its historical, anthropological, and geographical foundations from the bottom up. My claim, therefore, is not that Kant's nonideal theory is more important than, has primacy over, or destroys the normative claims of his ideal theory, or even that it can work independently of the formal aspects of his political thought. Rather, I consider ideal and nonideal theory as they are figured in Kant's political thought to be two complementary approaches to and methodologies of politics.[27]

We can think of these two approaches to politics as operating at two different levels of abstraction, following the renewed interest in Kant's writings on anthropology and history spearheaded most notably by Robert Louden, Holly Wilson, Patrick Frierson, and Alix Cohen.[28] These authors argue that in addition to the all-too-familiar picture of Kant's moral philosophy and its pure *a priori* principles, in Kant's philosophical system we also find (qua Louden) an "impure ethics," including the fields of education, anthropology, art, religion, and history,[29] or (qua Cohen) a pragmatic theory of the human sciences, namely, biology, anthropology, and history, as a counterpart to the transcendental project.[30] Thus, on the one hand we have a highly abstract pure ethics, and on the other hand we have an impure or pragmatic moral theory.

Accordingly, I suggest that we make a parallel division in Kant's political philosophy. At the highest level of abstraction, we have the ideal of peace, the highest political good. We then need a set of normative principles to guide our pursuit of peace. On the one hand and still at a high level of abstraction—the level of Kant's ideal theory of politics—we have a large part of *The Doctrine of Right*, where he provides us with the rules and institutions that ought to govern our collective lives, deduced from the *a priori* principle of *Recht*. On the other hand and at a lower level of abstraction, we have a nonideal theory of politics, which consists of his arguments about political history, political anthropology, and political geography, all of which are oriented by the regulative principle of teleology, or *Zweckmässigkeit*.

The ideal of peace helps us to guide our actions in the real world to a limited extent; Kant writes that morally practical reason gives us "its irresistible *veto: there is to be no war* . . . for war is not the way in which everyone should seek their rights" (*MS/AA* 6:354). Thus, the ideal of peace does not give us empirical details, but constitutes the overall condition and the highest objective of political organization—no peace, no relations of right. I am suggesting that in Kant's work we have two principles that help us to further specify how we must go about working toward peace. First, we have the principle of *Recht*, which helps us to "derive, *a priori* by reason from the ideal of a rightful association of human beings under public laws as such" (*MS/AA* 6:355). This principle allows us to ask what norms ought to govern the organization of our collective lives such that we remain on the path of peace. Kant's answers include an innate right to equality, a republican constitution, rightful relations of property, a federation of free states, and so on. These considerations operate at a higher level of abstraction, since they relate to the *form* of our interactions with each other, as I mentioned above. Second, at a lower level of abstraction, we have the principle of *Zweckmässigkeit*, which allows us to ask after the feasibility of our political ideals and about how we can organize our collective lives here and now toward a better political condition. Here, Kant specifically tells us to study history, cultural development, and geopolitics, and he produces tentative universal theories for understanding them. These tentative pictures of universal history, anthropology, geopolitics in turn bear on how we ought to understand and work toward a cosmopolitan ideal, a suitable means for establishing the highest political good, peace on earth.

Peace, Cosmopolitanism, and Ideal Theory: Reframing the Contemporary Legacy of Kant's Political Thought

Most contemporary reconstructions of Kant's political thought traffic in ideal theory in that they deal with the principles and institutions of a well-ordered society. That is, they are concerned with theorizing the ideal conditions of justice at the national, international, and global levels, and they put forth ideal political theories of liberalism and cosmopolitanism. Diverse examples of such scholarship on Kantian political thought include Arthur Ripstein, Onora O'Neill, Garret W. Brown, Seyla Benhabib, John Rawls, David Held, and Jürgen Habermas.[31] These ideal theory reconstructions of Kant's political thought often take the principle of *Recht*, the ideal of the Kingdom of Ends, or the idea of cosmopolitanism as their focal points. When we think of Kant's contribution to political thought today, then, we tend to think of variations of ideal theories of a morally-grounded liberal cosmopolitanism.

As James Ingram points out, Kant is the most common source of the key elements of nearly any contemporary cosmopolitanism.[32] There is also sufficient textual evidence in Kant to justify an ideal theory approach that focuses on *Recht*, moral ideals, and especially cosmopolitanism: Kant himself construes politics as the limited domain of *Recht* under his broader doctrine of morals in *The Metaphysics of Morals* (MS/AA: 6:205), and the moral ideals of the Kingdom of Ends or the Ethical Commonwealth found in the *Groundwork of the Metaphysics of Morals* and *Religion within the Limits of Mere Reason* provide plenty of material for configuring Kant's idea of a cosmopolitan world order as a transhistorical, transcultural moral ideal with universalistic aspirations (*GMS/AA* 4:433; *Rel/AA* 6:95).

However, I believe that this picture of Kant's contemporary legacy for political thought with its exclusive reliance on an ideal theory is incomplete at best and misleading at worst, on at least two counts: first, it tends to conflate the ideal of peace with the ideal of cosmopolitanism; second, and more importantly, it tends to erase Kant's sensitivity to the politically salient features of history, culture, and geography that we find in his political writings. I will briefly explain each of these two points, which articulate my primary motivations for recovering a nonideal theory of politics in Kant's thought.

First, systematically speaking, it is the idea of peace, and not that of a cosmopolitan world order, that constitutes the highest order ideal of Kant's political philosophy: peace is the "highest political good" (*MS/AA* 6:355). As I show throughout the book, Kant claims in his political writings that we ought to establish a cosmopolitan world order, not because such an order is the ultimate *end* of politics, but because it provides a promising *means* for approximating the final goal of the doctrine of right, establishing the highest political good: peace. Relatedly, I will point out that in a significant number of Kant's historico-political writings, the very idea of a cosmopolitan world order refers not to an unconditional moral or political ideal as we today might understand it. Rather, cosmopolitanism is posited as the aim of history (as in "Idea for a Universal History with a Cosmopolitan Aim"), as the culmination of our cultural activities (as in the *Critique of Judgment*), or as a specific type of right to hospitality (as in "Toward Perpetual Peace" and *The Doctrine of Right*). In each case, it is proposed out of a certain tentative and teleological picture of history, cultural development, or geopolitics. In this sense, we can say that a cosmopolitan world order is not an end-in-itself for Kant's political thought; the ultimate end goal of politics, as he understands it, is peace, and so we might rather characterize Kant's political thought as an ideal theory of peace.

Second, and relatedly, contemporary Kantian scholarship on politics that operates at the level of ideal theory and focuses on *Recht*, moral ideals, or cosmopolitanism, tends to underestimate the role that a developmental view of history, culture, and nature plays in Kant's political thought, as well as how particular pictures of these variables shape and inform his conceptualization of a cosmopolitan world order. This underestimation is misleading, since when we look at Kant's cosmopolitanism with the benefit of "two hundred years' hindsight," in Habermas's terms, we tend to think that all that cosmopolitanism needs today is a quick update regarding the contingent, politically salient variables of our own time.[33] We do not, however, ask how these contingent variables of politics, history, culture, or geography, are themselves constellated by Kant, or how they informed his very idea of a cosmopolitan world.

I suggest that asking these questions grants us an important theoretical advantage: it will allow us to acknowledge the unsavory aspects of Kant's claims regarding history and anthropology, and in doing so will open up his political philosophy to alternative political constructions that may be informed by different and diverse views of history, culture, and geography. Attending to Kant's nonideal theory of politics reminds us that the idea of a cosmopolitan world order as it is figured in his work is inflected by and rooted in European conceptions of history, culture, and geography. Furthermore, a systematic consideration of the whole of Kant's political philosophy makes it clear that any construction of a universal purpose as an ideal cannot feign disinterest in or independence from the contingent elements of our lives. Thus, I take it as a hitherto unremarked-upon Kantian lesson that the contingencies of history, culture, and nature do matter to politics and that they matter a great deal—a lesson that we miss if we follow only the ideal theory reconstructions of Kantian political thought.

Let me circle back to the tentative nature of the notion of purposiveness that is at play in Kant's historico-political writings for a moment. This notion is critical and regulative—that is, it always comes with epistemic cautions and caveats. We begin to see the development of the principle of teleology in the Appendix to the Dialectic of the *Critique of Pure Reason*, in "What Does It Mean to Orient Oneself in Thinking?," and most explicitly in the Critique of Teleological Judgment in the *Critique of Judgment*. Insofar as these teleological arguments in Kant's political philosophy are not meant to replace the arguments from pure or formal principles, and insofar as they are not simply telling us naïvely empirical stories about the world, we must understand them not as dogmatic but always as critical and regulative. Thus, Kant's regulative teleology reminds us that the lawfulness that we presuppose in the world is bound to remain contingent from an absolute point of view.

While we do not in fact gain actual full-blown cognition from teleological arguments in the Kantian system, we do recover guiding threads of narratives that are nevertheless useful for our purposes. The fact that such knowledge of history, culture, or geography is admittedly weak or tentative arising out of regulative and hypothetical grounds is something to be celebrated. This is one place where a Kant-inspired humility would in fact be an advantage for political theory, for it would mean that his constructions of history, culture, and geography can be reconfigured, originating as they do from hypothetical assumptions. Thus, Kant's teleological principles give us a significant nonideal theory of politics, and attending to this body of theory reminds us that we need to have a working knowledge, however tentative, of history, human nature and development, and geography, insofar as these stories or knowledges bear on the conceptualization and accomplishment of our ideals. Kant's recognition that such knowledge always has pragmatic grounds represents an important Kantian insight and one that I want to recover here.

Teleology and Its Discontents

It may (rightly) be objected that the validity of the pure and formal *a priori* principles of *Recht* does not depend on historical, cultural, or geographical factors, and that these political principles are therefore unaffected by Kant's specific view of these factors. Indeed, this would be the main defense of the normative (as opposed to descriptive) model of ideal theory: it is undeniable that everyone *ought to* be equal, independent, and free, even if this is not the case at any given time. Why then would one want to trace or rescue Kant's teleological story, especially when we consider that the writings with which I deal here exemplify gendered, racialized, and Eurocentric views of the world? While a fuller response unfolds over the remainder of this book, this is a good place to begin to address this question, one that represents a pressing issue for any Kant scholar working on moral and political philosophy.

For starters, it is important to note that in his 1784 essay on a cosmopolitan world order Kant does not consider nonwestern and non-European peoples to have a role in world history, except as narrated by "more civilized" cultures, and he does not take the development of the innate capacities of nonwhites and women to be relevant to the aim of history, predicting that Europe will one day legislate for the entire world.[34] Similarly, in his writings on human cultural production, he proposes Europe as the model of labor and industry and prioritizes European lifestyles over others.[35] Finally, his cosmopolitan right of universal hospitality is closely linked to a paradigmatically Western and European form of commercial interaction.[36]

This means that Kant takes European history to be *the* universal or world history, the European mode of life and cultural activity to be *the* paradigm of human cultural production as such, and the European way of interacting with the world to be *the* primary model for all global relationships. In other words, his views of history, culture, and nature are further inflected by how he construes the "universal" element in each of these: as a result, his stated vision of a cosmopolitan world order has a distinctly European bent while masquerading as a universal ideal.

I do not want to enter into the particular debates regarding if and when Kant might have changed his views about racial hierarchies among human beings, or whether or not his sociopolitical philosophy can accommodate cultural difference.[37] My reconstruction of his nonideal theory of politics will show that his *actual* views on history, cultural development, and geography are sexist, racist, and Eurocentric. Furthermore, these problematic claims seem to originate out of a developmental, or teleological, conception of history and humanity. Thus, I agree that the historical-anthropological-geographical foundations of Kant's cosmopolitanism are suspect to say the least.[38]

My question in the first instance then is not whether Kant himself held racist or Eurocentric beliefs simultaneously with his formulation of a cosmopolitan world order; the answer to that is quite obvious. Rather, I ask: On what systematic grounds did he employ a view of universal history, cultural development, and geographical analysis in his political thought, and how did he construct the idea of "universality" in these analyses? That is, I suggest that if we want to have a better and more nuanced understanding of the relationship between the supposedly universal ideal of cosmopolitanism and such distorted views about historical and cultural development, we cannot either excuse Kant for being a man of his time or attribute to him progressive views that are more appropriate to our contemporary situation. Rather, we need to investigate the systematic reasons why he is led to the views that he held, and how and to what extent these views about history, culture, and geography bear on and inform his political thought. One way to do so will be to separate ideal and nonideal theories and then assess the complementary relationship between the two in systematic terms. This assessment will then help us to spell out how we may better construct political ideals that truly represent the world in all its contingency and diversity.

In sum, what we uncover in light of the teleological arguments in Kant's political theory, first and foremost, is that Kant pays specific attention to the contingent variables of history, culture, and geography. The theoretical advantage of attending to Kant's nonideal theory by tracing the teleological arguments in his political writings is that this new orientation to Kant's political thought will offer an opportunity to recognize and perhaps correct a number of misguided judgments found in most contemporary universalistic and ideal theory reconstructions of his cosmopolitanism: most importantly, the tendencies to view history as told from the perspective of the victors, to cast cultural differences in superficial terms, and to render the world metaphorically flat.

My reading in a broader sense should therefore be seen as a rescue operation intended to salvage what is useful in Kant for contemporary political thought; to this extent, my endeavor can be construed along the lines of what Mills calls a "retrieval project."[39] My approach differs from ones that focus only on the useful parts of Kant's philosophy, however, in that I do not undertake this rescue operation at the expense of what is allegedly useless or unseemly (such as the ethnic, gendered, and racial hierarchies in his philosophy). On the contrary, I argue that we may only rescue the useful Kantian insight—namely, the necessity of a nonideal theory that pays attention to contingencies or particularities of history, culture, and nature—*if* we examine its allegedly useless or outdated content and understand its systematic place in Kant's political thought.

Chapter Overview

In order to locate Kant's nonideal theory of politics and tease out the significance of teleology as its orienting, regulative principle, this book focuses on those unambiguously political writings in which Kant employs the principle of purposiveness. In three sections and six chapters, I identify how Kant uses the regulative principle of the purposiveness of nature in political philosophy: first, in reflections on history as a whole; second, in reflections on human nature and culture as a whole; and third, in reflections on geography as a whole.

The first section begins with the role of history in Kant's political thought. Chapter 1 looks at the Appendix to the Transcendental Dialectic of the *Critique of Pure Reason* as well as "What Does It Mean to Orient Oneself in Thinking?" and lays the groundwork of how Kant employs the regulative principles of teleology in forming rational hypotheses and imaginary focal points as well as in orienting his thought about history as a whole. In chapter 2 I reconstruct the main argument of his 1784 essay "Idea for a Universal History with a Cosmopolitan Aim" in terms of Kant's emphasis on a particular view of history. In my methodological analysis in this chapter, I show that underlying his formulation of a cosmopolitan intent of history in the "Idea" essay is a teleological way of orienting oneself in thinking about world history. Here, a "cosmopolitan world order" is *not* first and foremost articulated as a transhistorical or transcultural ideal or political goal as we would think of it today. Rather, this term is originally a tentatively universal concept that Kant deems appropriate for world history thanks to his regulative principle of teleology. The concept of a cosmopolitan world order is supposed to capture, hypothetically, the narrative of actual history. Although in the end his specific notion of world history encompasses only certain—namely, Western and European—parts of the world, focusing on the systematic and methodological underpinnings of the "Idea" essay in light of the first *Critique* and

INTRODUCTION

the "Orientation" essay allows me to discover a nonideal theory at work in Kant, specifically in his attention to history and his proposed philosophy of history. Thus, I conclude that an important Kantian lesson is that history, or a particular orientation toward history, matters to politics.

The next section of the book turns to cultural development and anthropology. In chapter 3 I look at the organic metaphors that Kant uses in political contexts, specifically in §65 of the *Critique of Judgment*, in "What Is Enlightenment?," and in §52 of *The Doctrine of Right*. I argue that these metaphors give us an interpretive clue to the significance of nonidealized notions of human beings and of cultural and social processes in Kant's political thought. I begin with a brief sketch of Kant's reflective teleological judgments in the *Critique of Judgment* and enumerate the reasons why he finds a similarity between the ways we must judge an organism and judge an ideal body-politic. I then show that the "What Is Enlightenment?" essay is not only a defense of the public use of reason for the progress of humankind, but also proposes an organic and teleological understanding of political progress. Here, Kant theorizes agents of the public as parts of an organic cosmopolitan whole and agents of any private commonwealth as parts of a machine. This allows us to articulate a more earthbound view of human beings and a holistic, quasi-organic picture of cosmopolitanism in his political philosophy. Another organic metaphor that he uses in §52 of *The Doctrine of Right* further supports this interpretation; here, he likens political reform to a metamorphosis, the slow transformation of an organism, once again resorting to teleological language to draw parallels between an organism and an ideal state, between organic growth and political progress. In chapter 4 I show that this teleological perspective of development culminates in §§82–84 of the *Critique of Judgment*, where he further emphasizes the natural embeddedness of human beings in politics, rather than taking them as idealized rational agents. Here, I show that the term "cosmopolitan world-whole" embodies Kant's regulatively teleological way of thinking about human nature and cultural production. This term, to be clear, is *not* proposed as a transhistorical moral or political ideal but as a concept referring to the ultimate purpose of our cultural activities. While his particular construction of the ultimate end of cultural production prioritizes a certain, European way of life and work, I show that with the help of a regulatively teleological view of the earthbound nature of human beings, Kant begins to develop what we might call a political anthropology. Thus, I conclude that Kant's use of organic language in his political writings, together with his formulation of cosmopolitanism as the ultimate goal of cultural development, show us that for Kant a notion of cultural production, or anthropology, matters to politics.

The third and final section analyzes Kant's theorization of nature outside us (i.e., geography) in his political writings. Chapter 5 looks at "Toward Perpetual Peace," where I find not only a set of principles and institutions that we ought to adopt in order to establish peace, but also a teleological way of thinking about nature outside us. This way of thinking about nature also attends to the question of the feasibility of these principles and institutions. It is to answer the question of feasibility, I argue, that the First Supplement of the essay employs a regulatively teleological view of nature and sets forth a preliminary political geography. In chapter 6 I return to the two principles of Kant's political philosophy, *Recht* and *Zweckmässigkeit*, and show in concrete terms how these two principles complement each other. Here, I look at the "Public Right" section of *The Doctrine of Right* and identify the principle of purposiveness as the material principle of Kant's politics by contrasting it with the formal principle of *Recht*. I show that in this text Kant not only gives us an ideal theory of peace but also a quasi-geographical argument for the cosmopolitan right of universal hospitality, locating its foundations in the spherical and limited shape of the earth. This geographical argument from his nonideal theory complements the rights argument from his ideal theory by providing it with further geopolitical specificity. While Kant's articulation of the best way to live peaceably on a sphere prioritizes a Western way of interacting with the world (i.e., commerce), I take his central insight to be about the geopolitical rootedness of any cosmopolitan right. For Kant, that is, geography matters to politics, and following this insight can lead us to propose geographically-informed solutions to current global political issues. The book concludes with a few brief sketches of what it looks like to develop nonideal political theories with reference to a Kant-inspired methodology.

In Defense of Political *Zweckmässigkeit*

What provides a nonideal theory of empirical and politically-relevant details in the Kantian system is the regulative principle of *Zweckmässigkeit*, or "purposiveness"; I therefore name Kant's deployment of teleology in the service of political theoretical pursuits the principle of "political *Zweckmässigkeit*." If the conception of peace, together with the *a priori* principle of *Recht*, provide the ideal rules of interactions and institutions governing our collective lives, the principle of *Zweckmässigkeit* gives us an overview of the politically salient facts regarding history, culture, and nature. This latter principle therefore helps us to identify the constraints that we may face in implementing our ideals and allows us to theorize how we may best transition from where we are to where we ought to be. It is worth noting here that throughout this book I focus on the *theoretical* benefits of the principle of *Zweckmässigkeit* for politics—that is, on what this principle contributes to our theoretical understanding of politics or of politically salient aspects of our world—rather than on its utility for practical or moral considerations. This has important methodological implications for the present work. Rather than focusing exclusively on the understanding of teleology developed in the third *Critique*, I instead develop a narrative beginning with the account of the hypothetical use of reason offered in the first *Critique* that is later configured as a type of a theoretical orientation in the "Orientation" essay and finally as the regulative principle of reflective teleological judgments in the third *Critique*. Accordingly, I find the intermediate concepts of "hypothesis" and "orientation" useful for highlighting the theoretical—that is, the epistemological and metaphysical—significance of the principle of purposiveness for political thought. As such, this work is also a contribution to political epistemology.

Through an appeal to the principle of political *Zweckmässigkeit*, I demonstrate that teleology plays three related roles in Kant's political thought: 1) systematically speaking, it constitutes the material principle of Kant's political philosophy in general and the guiding normative principle of what I call his nonideal theory of politics in particular; 2) it orients his portrayal of the contingent elements of politics and allows Kant to develop preliminary notions of political history, political anthropology, and political geography; and 3) it subtends theories of history, culture, and nature that, either implicitly or explicitly, bear upon how political ideals are formed or pursued in Kant's political philosophy. Thus, I defend teleology by restoring it to its systematic place in Kant's political thought.

Part I

History and Politics
Political History and Cosmopolitanism

History is one of the contingent variables of politics that Kant addresses in his political writings. Here I analyze his view of history and show how this view figures in the rest of his political thought. Paying attention to the underlying epistemological commitments of his historico-political writings allows us to uncover an important connection between history and politics in Kant's works. It is this very connection, prefigured in terms of teleology, that I want to recover from his essay "Idea for a Universal History with a Cosmopolitan Aim"—interpreted in light of the *Critique of Pure Reason* and "What Does It Mean to Orient Oneself in Thinking?"—for this connection gives us the first hint about a nonideal theory of politics in Kant's thought.

Kant's "Idea" essay makes a claim about universal history, that is, about the history of the world as a whole. While various scholars, most notably Kleingeld, Allison, and Wood, have recently taken up the nature of the epistemic and metaphysical commitments of such a teleological or goal-oriented claim about history,[1] the question of what these commitments might entail for Kant's cosmopolitan political agenda has not been addressed. It is my aim in the following two chapters to begin to explore this connection between teleology and politics and to show that a certain picture of history is what directs and orients Kant's proposed political goals. More broadly, I argue that a cosmopolitan political agenda is embedded in a certain orientation toward, and a particular understanding of, empirical history as Kant develops it here. This particular philosophy of history, I will show, must be construed as a part of Kant's nonideal theory of politics.

In his recent book *Grounding Cosmopolitanism: From Kant to the Idea of a Cosmopolitan Constitution*, Garrett W. Brown argues that while Kant's political theory does evolve from his more complex philosophical principles, "there is no simple way to summarize or encapsulate Kant's critical philosophy and the transition to his political theory."[2] It is of course true that there is no simple way to summarize the entire critical system and how it relates to politics; the relationship between the two is complex. Because of this complexity, Brown chooses to limit his analysis of Kant's cosmopolitan theory to his political philosophy only, in order "not to get bogged down in Kant's more technical philosophical principles."[3]

This is in fact common practice: current interpreters of Kant's political thought, specifically those of his ideal theory, want to salvage his idea of cosmopolitanism but do not want to deal with the heavy baggage of the specific methodological or metaphysical arguments that come with it. It might be this supposed difficulty, coupled with Kant's own contention that pure practical philosophy must abstract from all contingencies of human condition (including history), that has led many scholars working on Kantian cosmopolitanism to interpret it as a set of moral and institutional guidelines for ideal global justice theory. As a result, when we look at the majority of works on Kant's political thought, we tend to think of cosmopolitanism as a part of Kant's ideal theory of politics and as morally grounded: thus Kant's cosmopolitanism is taken up as a transhistorical normative moral and legal ideal—a practical postulate, as it were—and at best loosely related to his picture of history.[4]

I challenge the idea that it is too difficult to determine the connection between Kant's critical philosophy and political theory; what is more, articulating this connection gives us a startlingly new picture of Kant's political thought and reveals a nonideal theory of history as informing and orienting his politics. This new picture may even lead us to rearticulate or revise what we mean by an ideal cosmopolitan world order. In the next two chapters I show that it is a mistake to think of Kant's notion of cosmopolitanism merely as an extension of his ideal moral philosophy or as a part of his ideal theory of politics. In fact, a closer investigation of the theoretical justification of the idea of a cosmopolitan world order in the "Idea" essay demonstrates that this notion originates as a problematic concept of world history, and thus as a part of Kant's philosophy of history. The cosmopolitan political agenda that is often attributed to this essay in fact refers to an overarching pattern and aim of history that can only be posited as a hypothesis. In this essay Kant is not searching for or offering a universal moral grounding for our collective lives; rather, in the process of trying to adequately describe empirical history as a whole under an umbrella concept, he proposes cosmopolitanism as the appropriate aim of universal history.

No matter how we define it—whether as a moral, cultural, or political attitude, as a normative ideal of global justice, or in terms of world citizenship—it is undeniable that modern cosmopolitanism has roots in Kant's thought, specifically in his 1784 essay, "Idea for a Universal History with a Cosmopolitan Aim." This is one of the first essays in which Kant uses the term cosmopolitan in a quasi-political context; interestingly enough, however, the essay primarily addresses the philosophy of history. In other words, Kant was not in the first instance trying to ground cosmopolitanism as a political or moral ideal but providing a guiding thread for our reflections on history as a whole. A cosmopolitan world order is posited, tentatively, as a guiding concept for the philosophy of history and as the final aim of world history. What do we then make of this connection between history and politics?

I argue that Kant's overall political commitment to a cosmopolitan agenda has an important link to history. I do not mean that cosmopolitanism was a popular idea in Kant's time or that he changed his mind about it at various points throughout his career, although that is also true.[5] Rather, my argument is that a specific picture of world history, which Kant put forth in the "Idea" essay by means of a regulatively teleological view, informs his cosmopolitan politics. Instead of dismissing the epistemic-metaphysical commitments of this picture of history as too complicated or messy, as Brown and other ideal theorists I have mentioned might prefer, I suggest that we shift our attention to the very principles that underlie Kant's methodology here. My aim is in part to show that the connection between Kant's critical philosophy—with all its technical concepts and principles—and his political theory is too important to be ignored. More importantly, I argue that this connection in the "Idea" essay reveals that the ability to articulate a specific political agenda requires a certain theoretical orientation toward history. This orientation is a normative one, provided by the regulative principle of teleology, the main principle of what I will develop throughout the book as Kant's nonideal theory of politics.

In the first chapter, I frame larger commitments of Kant's thoughts on history in terms of the *Critique of Pure Reason* and the "Orientation" essay. I show that, systematically considered, Kant's argument about history and politics boils down to this: in order to identify a viable political goal for ourselves, we need a specific view of the overall pattern of history. In order to have such a view of history, however, we first need to orient our thinking about history hypothetically, by means of what Kant calls a rational hypothesis concerning God and purposiveness. The way in which a theoretical orientation toward interpreting history is justified goes back to what Kant, in the *Critique of Pure Reason*, calls "the hypothetical use of reason" and in the "Orientation" essay calls "orientation in thinking." As O'Neill points out, because for Kant reason's fundamental task is normative, orientation by means of regulative principles will also be a normative endeavor.[6] I argue that this notion of orientation in thinking is particularly useful for parsing out the epistemic-metaphysical commitments of Kant's philosophy of history in the "Idea" essay. Based on an explanation of these commitments, in the second chapter I recast the status of cosmopolitan aim of history as a matter of orientation toward empirical reality.

Both of these technical ideas, originally developed in the context of Kant's critical philosophy—namely, the hypothetical use of reason and orientation in thinking—show us that we cannot avoid a certain epistemic uncertainty when we reflect on empirical history as a whole and that we must nonetheless orient our thinking by means of regulative principles and produce tentatively universal concepts of history. My analysis shows that the only way we can tentatively overcome epistemic uncertainties with respect to theoretical questions is by means of rational hypotheses. Focusing on how Kant arrives at the idea of a cosmopolitan world order in this essay, therefore, demonstrates that the idea of cosmopolitanism itself has tentative and hypothetical origins.

Furthermore, Kant here exemplifies a methodology of nonideal theory, one that begins with as adequate a description as possible of existing nonideal circumstances under a hypothetical guiding thread, and from there prescribes a future goal. I will show that it is out of a certain fallibilistic picture of history that Kant comes to propose cosmopolitanism as our collective political goal in the "Idea" essay, and that this picture of history must be understood as a part of Kant's nonideal theory of politics. The "Idea" essay deals with questions of whether or not we can discern a pattern in history, and if we can do so, then how we should direct our political efforts toward the culmination of such a pattern. Kant's philosophy of history proposes neither a random collection of empirical facts nor an account of Providence as it unfolds on earth. In his terms, human affairs as a whole require a narrative that mediates the necessity of the causally determined laws of nature with the contingency of our often capricious free decision-making. If there were a picture of historical events as a whole, it would have to be supplied by us, not by events themselves or by their random connections. In short, Kant argues that we need to construct a historical narrative, oriented by the principle of purposiveness and organized under a hypothetically universal concept, i.e., a cosmopolitan world order, that weaves together seemingly unconnected occurrences and tells a coherent story of humanity as a whole.

While in what follows I do deal with the question of whether or not the picture of universal history provided by the "Idea" essay is grounded theoretically or practically, I am in fact asking a different question of Kant, the question of what significance a certain orientation toward and a particular narrative of history hold for his political philosophy. A historical narrative of our less-than-ideal conditions matters to and will be useful for political decisions in two senses, theoretical and practical: first, such a story will provide a compass for navigating our ever-changing historical circumstances in that it will give us a hypothetical and yet reliable political *description* of reality (this is its theoretical utility); and second, the unifying pattern of the story can point to an aim that will give us a political *prescription* for changing reality (this is its practical utility).[7]

Finally, I investigate whether or not Kant's own, universal philosophy of history can still orient us in the development of a desirable and achievable political agenda today. While Kant's portrayal of universal history and his notion of cosmopolitanism—while meant to capture the overall telos of particular historical realities—are yet distinctly Eurocentric, as I will show, my claim is that his underlying methodological or meta-theoretical point, that a particular view of history is crucial for developing a political agenda, is still valid and useful for contemporary political thought. This is a legacy of Kant's nonideal theory of politics that starts with the actual conditions in which we find ourselves and attempts to produce an adequate concept. We only uncover this important methodological point about his nonideal theory, however, if we turn our attention to the ways in which he justifies his particular claims about history and politics in light of his larger epistemology and metaphysics—that is, to the rather complex technical principles of his critical philosophy, and most importantly, to teleology.

1

A Matter of Orientation

I identify two key methodological points in Kant's critical philosophy that make visible the epistemological and metaphysical commitments of his universalizing claims regarding history. First, when we are reflecting on empirical history as a whole, we are in effect aiming to group together a number of particular events under a hypothetical universal narrative. The procedure for projecting such a unity onto particular realities is what Kant calls, in the Appendix to the Transcendental Dialectic of the *Critique of Pure Reason* (1781), "the hypothetical use of reason."(KrV, A646–47/B674–75) Here, he also dubs the origin of such a hypothetical unity "an imaginary focal point."(KrV, A644/B673) Second, in his essay "What Does It Mean to Orient Oneself in Thinking?" (1786), he develops this procedure further and formulates our need to subjectively guide our thinking by means of such imaginary focal points as "a need of reason" and as a matter of orientation in thinking. (WO, AA 8:142) In this essay, the idea of God and its corollary maxim of purposiveness allow us to orient ourselves in systematic thinking in general, as well as, I argue, in systematic thinking about history and politics in particular. Thus, the maxim of a purposive unity is a compass that renders a diverse array of empirical things intelligible; thanks to this compass, we are able to posit an imaginary focal point according to which various components of our thinking about the world connect and make sense together.

Teleology in the *Critique of Pure Reason*

Kant's idea that a cosmopolitan world order is the overall aim of historical progress stems from the guiding thread that history as a whole can be viewed as a purposive unity. In his critical philosophy, we find the first systematic exploration of such a purposive unity in the *Critique of Pure Reason*, specifically, in the Appendix to the Transcendental Dialectic. It is important to remember that for Kant such a unity will always remain *hypothetical*. Kant makes purposiveness a subjective or regulative maxim of the hypothetical use of reason, a principle that guides our inquiry into diverse particulars by allowing us to hypothesize in advance that these particulars will merge in an imaginary focal point. His coinage of the term "the hypothetical use of reason" originates from the inability of the human intellect to arrive at exact normative universals or a systematic theory from a mere survey of a diverse array of particulars. In order to proceed from such particulars to universal claims with some sense of assurance, then, Kant allows us to presuppose a hypothetical unity. This hypothesis is useful, for it points the way toward an imaginary focal point at which our particular cognitions may come together purposively.

A major question of the Appendix is just how we can have unified knowledge or knowledge of the world as a whole, how we can know everything, including what is already given to experience and what is not yet and perhaps never can be given to it. Kant tells us that these questions about systematicity are the task of *reason*, as opposed to the *understanding*: while the understanding synthesizes given sensible intuitions with its concepts and yields theoretical cognition, reason's job is to organize these theoretical cognitions into a systematic and unified whole. Reason presupposes an idea

> [that] postulates complete unity of the understanding's cognition, through which this cognition comes to be not merely a contingent aggregate but a system interconnected in accordance with necessary laws. One cannot properly say that this idea is the concept of an object, but only that of the thoroughgoing unity of these concepts, insofar as the idea serves the understanding as a rule. (*KrV*, A644–45/B673–74)

In the Kantian system, the faculty of understanding provides us with rules for the judgments we make about our experience. These rules of the understanding, however, remain too broad, because they provide only the rules for the possibility of experience in general and do not furnish us with particular empirical concepts or rules for everything that we may encounter in experience. When we encounter a new animal, for instance, we may want to know under which rules we can call it a "mammal." These rules are constructed empirically and by means of the guiding idea of the unity of the genus "animal" and the species "mammal." We presuppose that there must be a sufficient amount of affinity between various species of animals such that we can group some of them under the empirical concept or genus of "mammal." Kant calls the guiding presupposition behind this constructed empirical concept "the idea of a systematic unity."

This idea of a systematic unity is far from being an arbitrary assumption for Kant. If such a unity of all of our cognitions is not presupposed as a higher-order rule, then the totality of our empirical concepts risks becoming a haphazard collection, an aggregate or a merely contingent and conditional mass of information (*KrV*, A645/B673). Without the idea of a unity, we would have no basis for presupposing a unity of all animals as a species, as in my example above, nor would we be able to generalize from particulars that exhibited significant affinities. Presupposing such a unity then becomes a rule of systematic research, and this rule originates from what Kant calls the ideas of reason. This systematic unity, however, will be hypothetical and only subjectively and indirectly valid for our cognitions, because it is provided by the ideas of reason and does not apply directly to our experience (*KrV*, A665–66/B693–94). It is the kind of guiding thread that can provide higher-order reflections on our experience and concepts, because reason's job is to guide the understanding.

Ideas of Reason as Hypotheses

In these sections of the *Critique of Pure Reason* Kant assigns ideas of reason an important function in his critical system. Ideas of reason, such as the world-whole, the soul, or God, can never become objects of experience or knowledge, nor can they refer to anything that we find in our experience. They do not have any direct use for our experience in the sense that they do not have any experiential content. They do, however, have an indirect use, since they can function as *loci* of a hypothetical unity of our cognitions. When we reflect on a set of diverse particulars and wonder if and how they come together, we are permitted to assume that they are hypothetically united. Kant dubs this procedure, one which starts with particulars and tries to find a universal, "the hypothetical use of reason" (*KrV*, A646–47/B674–75).[1]

Consider again the example of the classification of a mammal that I gave above. Unlike what Kant calls the apodictic use of reason, according to which we subsume particular objects under given universal concepts or rules of the understanding (such as causality or substance), the hypothetical use of reason starts with the particulars for which no specific universal concept is given. In this case, our thinking about these particulars needs to be guided by a general hypothetical unity of such particulars, and from there we posit a *problematic* empirical concept that should bring them together in a meaningful whole. The empirical concept of "mammal," then, is a problematic universal concept which we obtained as a result of the procedure of the hypothetical use of reason. It is now a tentatively universal and normative concept, for it will also provide a rule for judging other similar particulars that we may come across. All investigations aimed at such a systematic unity or at the creation of a universal empirical concept in this way involve the hypothetical use of reason.

CHAPTER 1

Imaginary Focal Points

The hypothetical use of reason means that the overarching concept we project onto a handful of particulars will remain problematic or open to revision. This use of reason is nevertheless beneficial for theoretical inquiries, as ideas of reason provide us with an *imaginary focal point*. Kant writes,

> [Ideas of reason] have an excellent and indispensably necessary regulative use, namely that of directing the understanding to a certain goal respecting which the lines of direction of all its rules converge at one point, which, although it is only an idea (*focus imaginarius*)—i.e., a point from which the concepts of the understanding do not really proceed, since it lies entirely outside the bounds of experience—nonetheless serves to obtain for these concepts the greatest unity alongside the greatest extension. (*KrV*, A644/B672)

The hypothetical unity of all of our cognitions tells us that we should not be discouraged by the seeming infinitude and diversity of the sensible content that we encounter in the world; we are allowed to proceed *hypothetically* or *as if* all these diverse particulars merged in or originated from an imaginary focal point. The chief use of the ideas of reason, then, is to direct us toward such an imaginary focal point. This focal point allows us to produce an umbrella term, a problematic universal concept, which brings together our seemingly disparate particular concepts and cognitions.

One such imaginary focal point of theoretical inquiry, for Kant—namely, the idea that we have to consider the unity of all possible experience "*as if* the sum total of all appearances (the world of sense itself) had a single supreme and all-sufficient ground outside its range . . . *as if* the objects themselves had arisen from that original image of all reason" (*KrV*, A672–75/B700–703)—is the idea of God.[2] While God can never become an object of knowledge or refer directly to experience, the very idea of God can serve as a unifying focal point for us, providing us with the principle of the purposiveness of the world as a whole. This means that we are allowed to view the world as a purposive and interconnected unity, as if it were to originate from one original point.

The use of the idea of God and the principle of purposiveness has important caveats in the Kantian system, however. Any empirical claim based on such an imaginary focal point will be of a weak epistemic status and of regulative use only. Therefore, the purposiveness of the world can only be assumed as a subjective heuristic maxim of research, and not as an ontologically thick principle constitutive of reality as such, as I show below.

Purposiveness as a Regulative Maxim of Theoretical Inquiry

While its referent cannot be proven necessarily to exist (since there is no sensible intuition corresponding to it), the idea of God gives us the principle of purposiveness, that is, the principle "to regard all combination in the world *as if it* arose from an all-sufficient necessary cause" (*KrV*, A619/B647). According to Kant, the idea of God:

> means nothing more than that reason bids us to consider every connection in the world according to principles of a systematic unity, hence *as if* they had all arisen from one single all-encompassing being, as supreme and all-sufficient cause.... This highest formal unity that alone rests on concepts of reason is the *purposive* [*zweckmässige*] unity of things; and the *speculative* interest of reason makes it necessary to regard every ordinance in the world as if it had sprouted from the intention of a highest reason. (*KrV*, A686–87/B714–15)

The mere idea of God provides us with the principle of purposiveness, which must then direct our systematic inquiries regarding nature as a whole. Because we have no insight into the existence of God as the intelligent ground of nature, we cannot use purposiveness as a *constitutive principle* by means of which to conclude that God created everything for a purpose. Instead, reason makes God into the principle of a systematic unity and order, and therefore we make the purposiveness (*Zweckmässigkeit*) of the world's arrangement into a *regulative principle* of our investigation of nature (*KrV*, A697/B725). In other words, we cannot prove, either *a priori* or *a posteriori*, that nature itself is governed by this teleological principle; however, the principle of purposiveness as a regulative principle can still be useful for us, as it opens up the possibility of "connecting up things in the world in accordance with teleological laws, thereby attaining the greatest systematic unity among them" (*KrV*, A687/B715). Therefore, it is *useful* to assume such purposiveness in nature as a heuristic maxim of research based on the hypothetical use of reason. To return to my previous example, the concept of "mammal" is a useful universal concept for describing certain animals and it also provides us with a rule for the judgment of other similar particulars, though we do not (and cannot) claim to have revealed the essential constitution of these particulars, as God intended them, when we use the concept. This is what it means to make use of a *regulative* as opposed to a *constitutive* principle of reason.

We can see the usefulness of the maxim of purposiveness more clearly when we look at how our systematic research would fare without the idea of God used as an imaginary focal point. Kant argues that we naturally strive after a systematic and unconditioned completion of all of our cognitions, all the while knowing that we cannot find anything unconditioned in our experience (*KrV,* A307/B364). In other words, we want to know about things even if they are not found in our experience and even when they can never be given to experience—things like the beginning of the world, the existence of God, and the purpose or interconnectedness of the natural formations in the world. These are the objects of inquiry of a *metaphysica specialis,* which for Kant is a precritical metaphysics—as he puts it in the Preface to the first *Critique,* a pointless battlefield of concepts without reference to experience, "a groping among concepts" (*KrV* Bxv). The pointless battle of the concepts is this: when we pursue thoughts and concepts as objects of knowledge, we are led to make contradictory claims—such as, "Everything in the world must have a purpose," and, "Everything in the world exists without purpose"; or, "God exists," and, "God does not exist." Such contradictions cannot be resolved through an appeal to experience; evidence could point either way, depending on how it is construed. Either claim could plausibly be justified, because in the terrain of precritical metaphysics we do not need to make reference to objects or experience: mere conceptual grounds will suffice to prove that something unconditioned exists or does not exist.

Here, Kant's critical philosophy and especially its notion of imaginary focal points offers a productive and pragmatic compromise regarding these questions. The idea of God taken as merely an imaginary focal point provides us with the heuristic maxim of purposiveness and obviates the pointless battle about whether or not God exists. If, as Kant claims, all that the idea of God means for theoretical inquiry is that we must assume the purposiveness of nature in our systematic inquiries—without turning this principle into an objective or constitutive principle of nature itself—then not only are we safe from error and contradiction, but our inquiry is empirically sound. We will neither dogmatically assert that nature is created purposively by an intelligent author nor skeptically refrain from making any judgments regarding its possible purposive unity. We will be able to construct a regulative concept of the mammal based on certain empirical affinities that we find among animals, even if we are not able to claim that God must have created animals with such a classification in mind. The maxim of purposive unity among animals provides our empirical research with a guiding principle. This is what Kant's imaginary focal points grants us, thereby saving us from falling into pointless disputes.

Kant summarizes the uses of this maxim in the following way: for every cognition we have, we must search for something at a higher level, a universal concept or explanation that makes it necessary, and for the sake of unity must keep searching for a complete *a priori* explanation—as he puts it, "you should philosophize about nature *as if* there were a necessarily first ground for everything belonging to existence, solely in order to bring systematic unity to your cognition by inquiring after such an idea, namely an *imagined first ground*" (*KrV*, A616/B644, emphases added).[3] If and when our aim is systematic unity, we treat the imagined first ground of reality, God, as a rational hypothesis. We can then orient our research by such an imagined first ground as long as we do not turn that into a sure thing. This principle only tells us to proceed *as if* there were an unconditional first ground of all things in the world and gives us a hypothesis to connect various cause-effect relationships in the world into a single first cause *as if* they all stemmed from it. In other words, such a principle allows us to explain natural phenomena as a whole, hypothetically and in purposive terms: this is the hypothetical use of reason in action.

If we take this principle too far and claim that God did in fact create all natural phenomena in a purposive way, we are claiming something that we have no way of experiencing. This goes against the limitations of knowledge that Kant specified in the first half of the *Critique of Pure Reason*, in which each unit of cognition must contain both a concept and a spatio-temporally given intuition (*KrV*, A51/B75). If we then proceed to claim that God exists, we become disoriented and entangled in word games, trying to prove God's existence in terms of logic or by means of mere thought or idea of it, committing various fallacies and ending up once again embroiled in pointless battles.[4]

Kant's claim about the hypothetical use of reason boils down to this: in order not to get disoriented claiming to know more than we can possibly know, we need to limit the claims and domains of our principles to what we can experience and their possible unity. This allows us to see that some regulative principles are useful for certain inquiries, as in the case of the principle of purposiveness. The principle regarding the purposive unity of nature provides a nontrivial hypothesis about our systematic research, for it presupposes that there is a continuity and homogeneity among the diversity and multiplicity of the particulars that we encounter in the world. Insofar as we do not claim that this presupposition is *constitutive* of nature or that this is how nature *actually is*, we can always use it to subjectively orient our thought and systematic research. This means that the ideas of reason are not just empty formulas about objects that we can never experience; rather, they give us heuristic maxims for research by means of which we can guide our theoretical inquiries "better and further" (*KrV*, A329/B385).

We can investigate nature all we want, in the most granular manner possible, in order to determine its ultimate aims or whence these aims originate; this would be in vain, according to Kant, unless we first orient ourselves in a certain way by means of a specific nondogmatic principle. In other words, a hypothetical unity together with the maxim of purposiveness of nature, while they are not given to us by experience or observation, are productive for orienting, guiding, and advancing our empirical inquiries. The principle that allows us to view nature as a systematic and purposive order is "a legitimate and excellent regulative principle of reason, which however, as such, goes much too far for experience or observation ever to catch up with it; without determining anything, *it only points the way toward systematic unity*" (*KrV*, A668/B696, emphasis added).

Subjective and Indirect Validity of the Hypothetical Use of Reason

Ideas of reason as imaginary focal points do not relate to our experience directly and as a result only have "indeterminate objective validity" or *subjective validity* with respect to experience (*KrV*, A664–67/B692–95). Kant uses the term "subjective" here not in the sense of "particular to each individual" but in the sense of pertaining to the cognitive capacities of the thinking subject. This means that when we are given a diverse array of particular experiences and aim for a universal theory or a concept with which to bring them together, we can hypothesize that they merge in an imaginary focal point but we cannot assume that this focal point fully determines the diversity of our experience or that this unity is objectively valid for our experience. Rather, such a focal point will merely be helpful for imagining how and where our inquiries merge. From this assumption, we will be able to produce a problematic, universal, and yet empirical concept that hypothetically captures all the particulars under investigation. In the example of animals and mammals, the principle of purposive unity, used hypothetically, led us to posit a problematic empirical concept of the "mammal" to bring together the affinities among particular animals. In the "Idea" essay about universal history, we will see that "a cosmopolitan world order" functions as such a problematic, universal, and yet empirically useful concept, one which originates out of the hypothetical use of reason and aims to capture all particular historical events in the world, bringing together the affinities among these events considered on a large scale.

The methodologically important argument of the Appendix to the Transcendental Dialectic, one that I want to underscore here, is the following: Kant argues that our claims about the purposive unity of nature always have a hypothetical and subjective basis, for these claims are justified by means of the imaginary focal points provided by the hypothetical use of reason. The idea of God, when taken in the way that Kant intends here, is nothing more than a subjective and regulative principle of purposiveness for our theoretical inquiries. Our need to use such maxims is subjective, and indeed, it is for this reason that such compasses or guidelines are called "maxims [and] not principles" (*KrV*, A666–68/B694–66).

Next I will argue that Kant further clarifies the epistemic and metaphysical status of such maxims in the "Orientation" essay, where he defines the purposiveness of nature as a subjective maxim originating from the rational hypothesis of the existence of God. Here, he shows that it is only thanks to this hypothesis and to its corollary maxim of purposiveness that we are able to orient our thinking. While contributing to a public debate on the uses and abuses of reason in the "Orientation" essay, therefore, Kant finds another opportunity to discuss the subjective maxims and hypotheses that we can use to orient ourselves in our systematic theoretical inquiries. The notion of disorientation and orientation in thinking will prove useful when we turn to Kant's reflections on history.

Teleology in "What Does It Mean to Orient Oneself in Thinking?"

Entering into the so-called *Pantheismusstreit*,[5] Kant aims to demonstrate in his "Orientation" essay that reason, rather than superstition or hearsay, must be the final touchstone of all inquiries. I argue that he also introduces here a new way of talking about the regulative maxims of reason: what in the first *Critique* he had called the hypothetical use of reason, in this essay he calls orienting oneself in thinking by means of a rational hypothesis. I therefore frame my analysis of the "Orientation" essay in terms of its argument regarding general systematic and procedural questions that relate to questions arising from the hypothetical use of reason.

These questions include the following: How do we make generalizing or universalizing claims about diverse particulars among which we do not immediately see a regularity or connection? With what do we even begin our theoretical inquiries in such circumstances? What can provide and justify a solid unifying starting point that does not lead us to dogmatic or unwarranted claims? In short, what does it mean to orient oneself in thinking, and how does the critical philosopher do it? When translated into the domain of the philosophy of history, I argue that these questions ask after the overall pattern of history and how we can justify our claims about such a pattern. They help us to understand how we orient ourselves in thinking about history as a whole.

Why We Need to Orient Our Thought

In order to talk about the significance of orienting ourselves in theoretical inquiries, we need to understand why our thinking might be disoriented in the first place. As the famous line in the Preface to the *Critique of Pure Reason* reminds us, for Kant, "thoughts without content are empty, intuitions without concepts are blind" (*KrV*, A51/B75). Valid theoretical or speculative claims about experience require both a thought (a concept) and its content (namely, a spatio-temporal or sensible intuition). Having repeated this dictum in the first few sentences of the "Orientation" essay, Kant proceeds to discuss some cases in which no sensible intuition is readily available for a given concept, and the need to proceed by means of hypotheses or principles in such cases. In other words, our thinking may get disoriented if one of the two necessary elements of cognition—either a concept or an intuition—is missing from our inquiry, and this lack necessitates our use of a set of maxims or principles. Such guidelines help us to mark out in advance how far and in which direction we can go in our claims. In short, in the absence of objective answers based on experience, such guidelines can provide an orientation for our thinking. As O'Neill points out, Kant's aim in this essay is to "show how we can orient ourselves in thought without relying on dogmatic claims about the powers of reason."[6]

As I have argued above, we cannot expect objective answers to all of our inquiries, especially when it comes to questions of the unity and the interconnectedness of things in the world, but we are allowed to use subjective maxims to guide such inquiries. This was the outcome of the use of ideas in the Appendix in the *Critique of Pure Reason*, and in the "Orientation" essay Kant further elaborates on such subjective principles. Starting from orienting oneself in a particular space (geographical orientation) and in any space in general (mathematical orientation), he concludes that to orient ourselves in thinking in general (logical orientation) we must be allowed to use subjective maxims in certain crucial inquiries where no objective principles are available ("WDO"/*AA* 8:137). In addition, we must use these maxims in order not to fall into dogmatism or skepticism about important theoretical and practical questions. Let me briefly turn to the different types of orientation in Kant's account to clarify why and in which cases we need to orient ourselves in thinking by means of subjective principles.

In orienting ourselves in a particular physical space, we need both an unchanging reference point and a subjective distinction. In order to find our way in a geographical area, for instance, in addition to all the objective data in the sky (such as the sun or the North Star) we still need to feel a subjective distinction between our right and left so that we may conclude that to our right is the east and to our left is the west ("WDO"/ *AA* 8:135). In mathematical orientation, or orienting ourselves in analytic space, we make use of both an unchanging fixed space, such as the coordinate system, and a subjective distinction, a distinction between where things are placed in relation to us and to each other ("WDO"/*AA* 8:135). In short, one's orientation requires a subjective feeling or a feeling within the subject, even when there are objective markers.

The cases of geographical and mathematical orientation are similar to the case of orienting oneself in thinking, Kant argues, because our thought too needs both an anchor and a compass. He writes,

> By analogy [with mathematical and geographical orientation] one can easily guess that it will be a concern of pure reason to guide its use when it wants to leave familiar objects (of experience) behind, extending itself beyond the bounds of experience and finding no object of intuition at all, but merely space for intuition; for then it is no longer in a position to bring its judgments under a determinate maxim according to objective grounds of cognition, but solely to bring its judgments under a determinate maxim *according to a subjective ground of differentiation* in the determination of its own faculty of judgment. ("WDO"/*AA* 8:136, emphases added)

In other words, when we are concerned with objects that are not directly given to experience, we do not have objective markers in front of us but find only a fixed space, a rational or reasonable space, in which to operate. In this operation we *need* subjective markers, a compass, to orient ourselves so that we do not get disoriented or make unwarranted claims about reality or the powers of our reason. As Kant adds in a footnote immediately following the passage above, "to orient oneself in thinking in general means: when objective principles of reason are insufficient for holding something true, to determine the matter according to a subjective principle" ("WDO"/*AA* 8:136n).

I have shown above that, according to the Appendix to the *Critique of Pure Reason*, subjective maxims originating in reason are legitimate as long as we do not attempt to apply them to experience directly and as long as we do not take them to be objective. Here, in orienting ourselves in thinking about objects that we do not directly experience, we use subjective maxims as our compasses in any given space of rational inquiry and we apply these maxims to experience indirectly, that is, based on subjective grounds. This makes it clear that what Kant in the first *Critique* calls the hypothetical use of reason, whereby we use ideas of reason as subjective maxims or imaginary focal points for certain inquiries, is now in the "Orientation" essay recast as a means of *orienting oneself in thought*. Although we cannot presuppose that God exists (on objective grounds), we can presuppose it, because it is a "need" (*Bedürfnis*) of reason. That is, we can presuppose it on subjective grounds and as a maxim or signpost. It will be useful and, in some instances, necessary to orient ourselves by means of such maxims.

Orientation in Theoretical Questions

According to Kant, our need to orient ourselves in thinking manifests itself in two types of inquiries. On the one hand, we have what Kant designates *practical* or *moral* inquiries, or inquiries which concern questions that we *must* ask, such as those regarding the highest good of morality and its causes. When we attempt to answer them, however, we may become disoriented because the answers do not seem to fall within the limits of our experience. It becomes too easy to give in to superstition or dogma. In order to answer such questions in an undogmatic or unprejudiced way, Kant suggests, we must first anchor our thinking in reason and rationality and then orient ourselves by means of a subjective distinction—what he calls a "rational belief" (*Vernunftglaube*) regarding the existence of God ("WDO"/*AA* 8:139).[7]

On the other hand, we also need to orient ourselves in certain *theoretical* inquiries—and it is the theoretical inquiry into history that I am interested in here. Disorientation in theoretical inquiries arises only if and when we are asking questions about the unity of and the connection between all our cognitions. When we want to make generalizations either about things that we have not yet encountered or about things which we have no way of encountering, we become disoriented because we must take leave of the objects of our senses ("WDO"/*AA* 8:133). This initial disorientation takes the form of the following questions: Should we posit a purposive unity of nature, or proceed as if there were no such unity? Is the world as a whole purposive, or not? It turns out, then, that we need to orient ourselves somehow, to anchor our thinking in reason and to use a specific compass in order to avoid both dogmatism (positing purposes everywhere) and skepticism (assuming the reign of chance everywhere). In response to these questions, Kant claims that we are allowed to posit what is called a "rational hypothesis" (*Vernunfthypothese*) regarding the existence of God ("WDO"/*AA* 8:139).

The idea of God that allows us to orient our inquiries, then, functions in two ways. For practical questions, we must have rational faith in the unity of our moral efforts and purposes so that is understood as more than an empty or abstract ideal. For theoretical questions, we must posit rational hypotheses about the purposive unity of particulars if and when we want to make generalizing judgments about the interconnectedness of seemingly contingent things ("WDO"/*AA* 8:139). Such a rational hypothesis will serve as a compass for our thinking although it should neither be understood as unconditionally necessary nor should it overdetermine our thinking.

It bears repeating that such purposiveness of the world can never be found in our experience: we may experience a regularity of particular events, for instance, but we will never experience all these events as dispensed and constituted by an intelligent agent in a purposive manner. Be that as it may, Kant claims that we can nevertheless presuppose as a hypothesis that all phenomena in the world come together as a unified and purposive interconnected whole. In this way, we are allowed to view all empirical particularities *as if* they were purposive and originating from one root, imagined original ground, or imaginary focal point. Orienting oneself by means of a rational hypothesis, therefore, functions just like the hypothetical use of reason in the first *Critique*. In both cases, we proceed from diverse particulars to problematic universals, operate in a rational or reasonable space, and are oriented by an overarching idea of a purposive unity. Critical philosophy affords us a subjective and yet legitimate compass for directing our inquiries toward unity and systematicity: the regulative principle or the rational hypothesis of the purposiveness of nature.

Purposiveness as a Compass

In the "Orientation" essay, the subjective compass of our theoretical inquiries, the major rational hypothesis with which all systematic endeavors must begin, is the idea of God, together with its corollary maxim, purposiveness. Kant reminds us once again that we cannot claim to know that God exists; however, we can use the mere idea of God as a rational hypothesis when we ask questions about the systematic unity of nature. Without this hypothesis

> one can provide no satisfactory ground at all for the contingency of the existence of things in the world, let alone for the purposiveness [*Zweckmässigkeit*] and order which is encountered everywhere in such a wondrous degree. Without assuming an intelligent author we cannot give any intelligible ground of it without falling into plain absurdities; and although we cannot prove the impossibility of such a purposiveness apart from an intelligent cause (for then we would have sufficient objective grounds for this assertion and would not need to appeal to subjective ones), given our lack of insight there yet remains a sufficient ground for assuming such a cause in reason's need to presuppose something intelligible in order to explain this given appearance, since nothing with which reason can combine any concept provides a remedy for this need. ("WDO"/*AA* 8:138)

Orienting our thinking about the world as a whole by using the idea of God as a rational hypothesis is nothing more than using our reason hypothetically by means of the subjective principle of purposiveness. We take the idea of God as the origin of the purposive unity of the particulars under investigation, or in other words, we take the concept of purposiveness as the grid of intelligibility in our empirical inquiries aimed at unity and make it our compass for thinking about unity. Kant dubs this endeavor "orientation in thinking."

Orientation in Thinking about History:
Between Skepticism and Dogmatism

Thus far, I have focused on the epistemic and methodological status of the notion of God in Kant's critical philosophy and have shown that a systematic investigation of diverse particulars in the world requires that we use our reason hypothetically, or—what amounts to the same thing—that we orient our thinking by means of a rational hypothesis of God, the regulative principle of purposiveness. The conclusion I draw from this is that the epistemic-metaphysical status of regulative principles is weak and fallible. Next I will explore what this fallibility means for using such principles and procedures in thinking about history and politics. The hypothetical use of reason is what Kant employs in his "Idea for a

A MATTER OF ORIENTATION

Universal History with a Cosmopolitan Aim" in order to argue that—when we properly orient our thinking in history—we can presuppose, but can never know or prove, that history is progressing toward an ideal condition in which we can develop our innate rational capacities.

In the next chapter, I turn to Kant's famous "Idea" essay to provide a concrete example of how these epistemological and metaphysical claims about the hypothetical use of reason and orientation cash out in his claims about history. The same notion of purposiveness provides the guiding thread of this historico-political essay, and thus his arguments concerning the aims and direction of universal history originate out of a specific orientation in thinking about the course of human affairs as a whole. I argue that the hypothetical use of reason is the *method* by which Kant orients his thinking about universal history and it is thanks to this orientation that he is able to generate a narrative of universal history as a cosmopolitan world order. This picture of universal history only later becomes the touchstone of a practical political agenda.

Kant admits that his investigation in this text—regarding whether or not history as a whole has a discernible pattern and a goal toward which it is progressing—can be a disorienting endeavor. We are immediately confronted with two conflicting paths: we can either limit ourselves to observing the contingent realm of historical events and hope that we will *by chance* stumble across some similarities or a unifying pattern, or we can assume that Providence is behind all historical progress and that we can completely subsume all historical occurrences under one determinate universal idea. If we take the former path, we will remain forever skeptical about the aim of history. If we take the latter, we risk becoming dogmatic and making claims that we have no way of justifying. Here Kant offers a third, critical path: he suggests that we begin with the rational hypothesis that there is an overall pattern in history—that is, an order and purposiveness to human interactions as a whole within which we may discover sufficient continuities and affinities. The usefulness of this guiding thread can then be measured by its helpfulness for identifying the direction or aim (*Absicht*) of history.

The way in which Kant poses the question of the meaning of history and then suggests a third, critical path is not unprecedented: it parallels the so-called Copernican revolution of his *Critique of Pure Reason*. As in the former work, which revolutionized metaphysics by placing it in a uniquely human domain neither skeptical of all knowledge claims nor fully confident in the power of pure reason alone, the solution to the question of whether history has an overall aim also operates between the extremes of nihilism and unwarranted optimism. By orienting our thinking about history by means of the rational hypothesis of purposiveness, we are able to generate a universal concept that both adequately describes particular historical events as part of a whole and provides a rule for judging them.

His cosmopolitan political proposal, I will argue, originates out of a specific picture of universal history—a picture constructed by means of a hypothetical and provisional guiding thread—as a matter of orientation that avoids both dogmatism and skepticism. This picture of history, which is concerned with adequately describing the course of history, constitutes a part of what I am calling Kant's nonideal theory of politics. Kant argues that if we can identify the direction of history, even if tentatively and with all the caveats of critical philosophy, we can then bring our actions into alignment with it. In this way, he is able to attribute an aim to history (and justify the hope that accompanies such an attribution), even as he remains pragmatically wary of the possibility of its attainment. One of the most compelling things about Kant's philosophy of history, understood in this way, is that it reminds us of the need to tell a compelling story about the world if we are to propose a convincing and viable political agenda.

2

Historical Patterns, Political Aims

An underappreciated insight of Kant's is that history matters for politics. It is underappreciated for a couple of reasons: first, the teleological language that he employs in talking about history seems outdated or dogmatic; and second, the normative force of Kant's ideal practical philosophy overshadows the significance of his philosophy of history. Some scholars assume that Kant's teleological philosophy of history is precritical or juvenile. Along these lines, Yovel argues that Kant did not have a critical notion of teleology before the *Critique of Judgment*, so all the writings on history that utilize teleology prior to the third *Critique* must be seen as dogmatic; while Ameriks sees Kant's "Idea" essay as an "unfortunate relic, a matter of trying to keep too much in step with the fashions and science of one's youth."[1] My demonstration in the previous chapter of the critical status of the principle of purposiveness in the *Critique of Pure Reason* should put these worries to rest, at least for the moment; other scholars, furthermore—most notably Kleingeld and Riley—agree that a preliminary critical teleology is evident in the first *Critique*.[2]

In this chapter, I trace the hypothetical use of reason in "Idea for a Universal History with a Cosmopolitan Aim" and make visible the link between a specific theoretical orientation toward history and a definite political vision. Having identified the methodological tools we find in Kant's critical philosophy in the previous chapter, here I utilize these tools in my interpretation of the "Idea" essay and show that a cosmopolitan political agenda originates out of a particular historical narrative that, for Kant, is supplied by the hypothetical use of reason (to use the language of the Appendix in the first *Critique*) or by orienting ourselves by means of a rational hypothesis (to use the language of the "Orientation" essay) about historical reality as a whole. These ways of thinking, as I have shown, are hypothetical and subjective. The concept of a cosmopolitan world order as the proposed aim of history and politics therefore has a provisional basis, for it originates out of the hypothetical use of reason which takes purposiveness to be an imaginary focal point of our investigation of reality as a whole.

CHAPTER 2

The predominant interpretations of the "Idea" essay often make a distinction between its theoretical and practical contributions to Kant's philosophy and tend to emphasize either one or the other.[3] I am one of those that is primarily interested in its theoretical role, but I also ask a rather different question about the significance of history for Kant's politics. Although the "Idea" essay integrates theoretical and practical concerns about history, here I emphasize its theoretical background, and specifically the method that Kant employs in articulating the cosmopolitan ideal for universal history. I believe that it behooves us to keep the theoretical and practical utilities of such a history of philosophy separate, since if we subsume the former under the latter we risk misrepresenting the epistemic-metaphysical cautiousness of Kant's overall method.[4] Thus, I do not view Kant's teleological philosophy of history as primarily or exclusively grounded in moral-practical considerations, but rather—in Cohen's terms—as belonging to "a theoretical map-making venture."[5] Highlighting the theoretical contribution of the essay and asking what this picture of history means for Kant's political thought allows me to show that both the "Idea" essay and Kant's larger philosophy of history belong to a nonideal theory of politics.

My focus on the theoretical status of Kant's picture of a universal history with a cosmopolitan aim underscores the dynamic relationship between history and politics. A broader implication of my claim is that, depending on how one orients oneself in thinking about history and on what picture of universal history one works with, the aim of history and therefore that of politics might be construed in different ways—and not exclusively in the exact terms that Kant himself laid out. Here I focus on Kant's version of this picture and pay attention to how he constructs it. I show that, in the end, we do not need to subscribe to his particular picture or narrative, one which is most definitely Eurocentric in its terms and scope. His methodological point, however, which lays out the interconnectedness of history and politics, can still be useful for exploring the relationship between different historical narratives and political agendas. In Kant's formulation, therefore, history matters for politics. That Kant's particular cosmopolitan political agenda has a hypothetical basis is something to be celebrated, for it means that our political aims can vary depending on the specific compasses we use in our descriptions of reality, the diverse historical situations in which we find ourselves, and the multiple narratives that we may have at hand. We gain this advantage, however, only when we distinguish between Kant's ideal and nonideal theories of politics and explore the extent to which the nonideal bears on the ideal.

How to Navigate the Labyrinth of History

Kant's main question in the "Idea" essay has to do with how one navigates the labyrinth of history—it is a question of interpretation. An empirical survey of various historical events taking place independently of each other and seemingly at random shows that the meaning of history is not found directly in our experience of it. The question of whether historical events as a whole have a meaning, however, immediately invokes notions of unity and purpose. To be sure, empirical history, as a series of events occurring in space and time, can be accounted for in terms of causal relationships. We can say that the assassination of Franz Ferdinand *caused* the First World War; the First World War *led to* the dissolution of the Ottoman Empire. When taken *as a whole*, however, no single or overarching concept unites the causes of the war: Did the person who shot Ferdinand intend to start the war? Would the Ottoman Empire have dissolved anyway, even if there had been no war? In what ways were the assassination of Ferdinand or collapse of the Ottoman Empire connected to the rest of the events that contributed to the war? Why was it a *world* war? What was the meaning or purpose of the war? Such questions cannot be answered by empirical research alone: they require a unifying narrative that tells us a coherent story about the war as well as the world.

Similarly, when we ask if the history of the world as a whole has an identifiable trajectory, we cannot simply research every occurrence in the history of the world, put them all side by side, and expect to see a unifying pattern emerge. An empirical historian might be interested in the collection of such facts and the identification of local causal explanations, but this historian cannot give us a unifying, meaningful account of these facts. As Kant sees it, the task of the philosophy of history lies in providing precisely this type of unifying and coherent narrative for the various occurrences in the world. The *method* by means of which a Kantian philosopher of history comes to articulate history's aim is the hypothetical use of reason and requires an orientation in thinking in the ways that I have developed thus far. When we reflect on the question of universal history, we must orient ourselves by means of the guiding thread of purposiveness, and it is thanks to this orientation that we are able to articulate history's aim as a cosmopolitan world order. The aim that we attribute to history, therefore, derives from an imaginary focal point that gathers together all historical events as if they had an overall purpose.

In the "Idea" essay, the imaginary focal point of such a historical narrative is teleological, and the problematic concept that this teleological orientation generates is a political agenda of cosmopolitanism. In other words, Kant advises that we begin by orienting ourselves according to a teleological view of nature and history. With this compass in hand, we turn to the particular occurrences in history and try to construct a universal yet problematic concept that would unite these events. A Kantian account of universal history tells us a specific story about the otherwise meaningless aggregate of historical events, namely, that the aim of history as a whole should be construed as bringing about "a cosmopolitan world-whole [*weltbürgerliches Ganze*]," since such a world order provides the ideal environment in which all our natural predispositions can be fully and completely developed ("IaG"/*AA* 8:22). Rather than giving an exegesis of the entirety of the "Idea" essay, then, here I limit my analysis to the question of unity and meaning in world history in order to show that Kant's notion of a cosmopolitan world order does not get off the ground without a particular type of theoretical orientation. My claim is that, for Kant, history matters for politics: that it is out of a specific yet hypothetically posited picture of universal history that Kant formulates a cosmopolitan political agenda; and that he therefore has a nonideal theory of history which has implications for politics.

The Guiding Thread of Kant's Philosophy of History

Kant begins by admitting that human beings as a whole are neither rational cosmopolitans, who act according to prearranged plans of their own, nor beings like beavers or bees, who act according to natural instinct. In brief, as far as we can tell, history has neither a rational nor a natural plan ("IaG"/*AA* 8:17–18). A philosopher reflecting on history is free to take one of two paths: she can either take the dogmatic path that posits some kind of an invisible hand or a cunning of nature that guides us through the world, or take the skeptical path that denies any final aim or meaning in history and attributes everything to chance. According to these two paths, we are either parts of a historical plan over which we have no control, or we must remain ignorant of whether there is such a plan. The two paths are contradictory in the sense that they seem to cancel each other out. Thinking about history, then, becomes a daunting and disorienting task, for it seems that we do not know what to make of our species or what to think of ourselves ("IaG"/*AA* 8:18).[6]

A third path remains open, however. It would indeed be dogmatic to claim that humankind follows any rational or natural purpose of its own (since such a purpose is not given in experience), but this does not mandate that we give up searching for such a plan altogether and become skeptics claiming that everything we do is purposeless. Historical inquiry, Kant argues, "allows us to *hope* that, if it examines the free exercise of the human will *on a larger scale* [*im Grossen*], it will be able to discover a regular progression among freely willed actions" ("IaG"/*AA* 8:17). Therefore, while there cannot be empirical evidence that history is progressing toward a certain goal, the philosopher of history, if she can reasonably orient herself by means of the purposiveness of nature, can unite these events—though only tentatively or hypothetically—into a coherent whole and draw up a plan. In other words, a Kantian philosophy of history involves telling a story of human actions and events that will form a coherent and developmental narrative when those events are investigated *on a larger scale* or *as a whole*.[7] This story narrates events as if they were made possible by an overall aim, one that is based on an imaginary focal point.

Kant argues that the critical philosopher can attempt to *discover* a plan of history, even when all she has is a collection of facts without a corresponding unifying idea ("IaG"/*AA* 8:18). In order to do this responsibly—that is, without falling into dogmatism or skepticism—she must carefully orient her thinking by means of a rational guiding thread (*Leitfaden*). This guiding thread, which is therefore the guiding thread of Kant's philosophy of history, is the principle of purposiveness that originates out of using the idea of God as a rational hypothesis.

A Kantian critical philosopher of history starts with an empirical collection of particular historical events, even if this collection alone does not yet tell a story. For that, the philosopher needs to orient herself by means of the maxim of purposiveness, the hypothesis that history as a whole has a purpose. From there, she constructs a problematic universal concept that incorporates the empirical collection of events and helps to make sense of the whole; this is the hypothetical use of reason in action, employing the principle of purposiveness as a compass in navigating the labyrinth of history. As I demonstrated in the previous chapter, the hypothetical use of reason starts with the particular (in this case, a collection of our cognitions of particular historical events) for which no universal concept is readily given, and then ascends to a universal concept that must be posited problematically and hypothetically. This universal concept is not assumed dogmatically to be true or constitutive of history. Rather, it is necessitated by our need to unify our empirical cognitions or by our need to orient ourselves with the aid of a subjective maxim. As Kant writes, we are not uncovering nature's plan but *discovering* the plan of history according to our own construction ("IaG"/*AA* 8:18). This is the sense in which the critical philosopher of history *constructs* a story using a unifying umbrella concept.

CHAPTER 2

Teleology in the First Three Propositions of the "Idea" Essay

The "Idea" essay starts with a preamble, then puts forth nine propositions concerning universal history, and then closes with some remarks about the particular historico-political picture that Kant seeks to depict. While in one sense the entirety of the essay can be seen as a contribution to historiography, as Kleingeld notes,[8] here I will focus on the first three propositions of the essay, which explicitly deal with the question of methodology. I will show that these three propositions most directly address the question of what it means to orient our thinking about history by means of the maxim of purposiveness. The rest of the propositions proceed from these methodological points, demonstrating how such ideas can be tested and thus proven useful.

The guiding thread of history in this essay—"Nature does nothing in vain" (*Die Natur thut nichts überflüssig*) ("IaG"/AA 8:19)—is an explicitly teleological maxim. In three propositions, Kant argues that that we must orient our thinking about history by means of this maxim in order to be able to discern an *aim* of universal history—if we do not use this maxim, our thinking about history becomes disoriented. First, the highest purpose (*Zweck*) of history for Kant is the development of all the rational and innate predispositions (*Anlagen*) of human beings. He claims that without the maxim of the purposiveness of nature, we would discern only a random nature governed by the "dismal reign of chance" ("IaG"/AA 8:18). In short, nature as a whole must be presumed to have a purpose or our thinking about the entirety of nature and history will become disoriented. Secondly, Kant claims that the idea of purposiveness must apply to the human species as a whole and not to a single individual. We do not observe any significant development in our natural capacities during an individual lifetime, and so if we did not look to the species as a whole for such purposive development we would be forced to conclude that our natural capacities are accidental and wasted ("IaG"/AA 8:18–19). In short, Kant posits that the activities and capacities of the species as a whole, not those of an individual, must have a purpose. Thirdly, he states that nature has given human beings reason and freedom of the will for them to be able to produce everything entirely out of themselves. We must understand this in terms of the development of our innate capacities through continuous external struggle, for otherwise we cannot explain why earlier generations had to endure such hardship and suffering ("IaG"/AA 8:19). In short, the capacities unique to human species, rationality and freedom, must have a purpose.

As Kleingeld also points out,[9] the idea that as a species we have innate capacities that develop purposively over time is an outdated notion and so I need not defend it here. All I want to claim here is that Kant suggests in these three preliminary propositions that we must orient our inquiries about world history by means of a teleological maxim. Otherwise our thinking becomes disoriented, as we cannot account for why we have certain capacities, why we do not observe a significant development in one individual's lifetime, why earlier generations endured hardship, or why we have rationality and freedom. Together these three propositions serve as a compass for thinking about history on a large scale: unless we orient our philosophy of history by means of the maxim of purposiveness and use these three presuppositions about nature and human beings as a whole as our compass, we cannot have a unified and coherent narrative of the efforts of the human species. That we do come up with such a narrative of universal history, however, is essential for being able to posit a definite political aim for humanity.

Universal History with a Cosmopolitan Aim

In the following five propositions of the "Idea" essay Kant builds upon the idea that nature as a whole is purposive and that its purpose is our development as a species. Here he shows the way in which human species *must* develop in history, or what the final goal of a universal history of human beings *should* look like *if* we were to fulfill the highest purpose of nature. The fourth proposition claims that one of our innate predispositions, *antagonism*, must also be put to the service of the highest purpose of nature ("IaG"/*AA* 8:20). This means that we will hone our innate skills through antagonism and conflict and therefore that social antagonism has a role to play in our development as a species.[10] The fifth proposition holds that the goal of the development of our capacities can be fulfilled only in society and only by establishing a perfectly just "civil constitution [*bürgerliche Gesellschaft*]." The sixth proposition points out the difficulty of such a task and reminds us that this task remains an *idea* which should be *approximated*. While the seventh addresses the problem of relations among states and the idea of a federation of peoples with a united will and power,[11] the eighth proposition tells us, finally, what happens if we fulfill the purported aim of nature, the culmination of the highest and fullest purposive development of all human capacities. Such culmination, according to Kant, must be construed as *the aim of universal history*, "a universal cosmopolitan existence [*ein allgemeiner weltbürgerlicher Zustand*]" ("IaG"/*AA* 8:21 and 28).

Before I turn to the ninth and final proposition, let me note that in these five propositions here Kant's methodology of the hypothetical use of reason and orientation in thinking have come full circle. We have investigated the final aim of history in order to make sense of human actions in the world as an interconnected whole. We oriented our construction of universal history by means of a teleological guiding thread or compass, and hypothesized that nature as a whole, as well as the capacities of human beings as species, are purposeful. This hypothesis allowed us to articulate the highest purpose of nature as the full and complete development of our capacities. We then concluded that the most suitable condition for our full and complete development would be the aim of history, and that this aim of history can be narrated in terms of a progress toward a cosmopolitan world order. A story working toward building a cosmopolitan world order, then, is the story that we must tell about universal history, for it allows us to view our actions as a whole as a systematic and purposive unity with a definite aim or direction (*Absicht*). In other words, the idea of a cosmopolitan world order is a universal concept that retrospectively makes sense of an otherwise meaningless collection of historical occurrences in the world.

This conclusion, however, has an important methodological caveat built into it. Kant does not posit the idea of a universal history with a cosmopolitan aim as a transcendental condition of our experience of world history; that is, the cosmopolitan aim is not the condition for the possibility of the actual unfolding of history ("IaG"/*AA* 8:30). It is merely a *problematic yet universal concept* that can generate an understanding of history as a whole—past, present, and future. This aim, as I have shown, is posited thanks to the imaginary focal point of universal history, the principle of purposiveness, by means of which we make sense of seemingly random historical events by incorporating them in a coherent story.

Let me put this in terms of the methodological tools that I developed in the previous chapter. In trying to discern the aim of history, we have before us a collection of empirical data concerning historical events, but not a single determinate and universal concept under which this collection can be subsumed. That is, we operate in a theoretical rational space where we do not have all the required elements of cognition, and as a result, we need to orient ourselves by means of a guiding thread. Orienting our thinking about history by means of the maxim of purposiveness allows us see history as a whole in an interconnected way, and to posit a plan, aim, or direction. Following Kant, the question of universal history can be formulated thus: "What should the aim of history be, such that all the natural capacities of humankind can be completely developed?" The aim turns out to be the construction of a cosmopolitan world order, because this is the most suitable condition in which we can become fully developed human beings.

A teleological guiding thread in interpreting universal history is useful, therefore, to the extent that it generates a specific plan or aim. When we reflect on history as a whole from a teleological perspective, we are relying on an imaginary focal point, and we judge its aim, its *Absicht*, to be cosmopolitanism. Kant himself acknowledges in the closing remarks of the "Idea" essay that it is a strange endeavor to write a plan of history according to how world events must develop; it is almost as if one is writing a novel (*Roman*) ("IaG"/*AA* 8:29). And yet, he argues that—if it may be assumed that nature has a plan, even for seemingly contingent human actions—this narrative is *useful* in that it may "serve as a guide to us in representing an otherwise planless *aggregate* of human actions as conforming, at least when considered as a whole, to a *system*" ("IaG"/*AA* 8:29).

It seems that Kant has written a particular type of a *Bildungsroman* that has captivated the imagination of political thinkers for the past two centuries, perhaps because his cosmopolitan novel—or better yet, his cosmopolitan script—becomes uniquely convincing when we put it to the test. That is, if we take Kant's script to provide a rule for judging history as a whole—past, present, and future—it proves both theoretically and practically useful.

Testing the Cosmopolitan Narrative: Past, Present, and Future

In the ninth and final proposition of the "Idea" essay, Kant goes on to *test* his plan for history, to determine whether his cosmopolitan narrative is a useful one and to what extent it can help us make sense of history as a whole. On the one hand, Kant writes, when we reflect on historical events as a whole, we do not *directly* perceive a purpose of nature to bring about a determinate end such as a rational cosmopolitan existence ("IaG"/*AA* 8:27). On the other hand, he claims, we can utilize the idea of a cosmopolitan world order to see if and how the past, the present, and the future unfold according to this script. Thus, we can test whether the concept in fact adequately captures what it purports to capture.

First, he argues that we can retrospectively judge past civilizations according to whether and how they contributed to the cosmopolitan plan. He writes,

> For if we start from Greek history as that in which all other earlier or contemporary histories are preserved or at least authenticated, if we next trace the influence of the Greeks upon the shaping and mis-shaping of the

CHAPTER 2

> body politic of Rome, which engulfed the Greek state, and follow down to our own times the influence of Rome upon the Barbarians who in turn destroyed it, and if we finally add the political history of other peoples episodically, insofar as knowledge of them has gradually come down to us through these enlightened nations, we shall discover a regular process of improvement in the political constitutions of our continent (which will probably legislate eventually for all other continents). ("IaG"/*AA* 8:29–30)

It is clear that the Greeks and Romans did not actually take themselves to be contributing to the cosmopolitan plan of history; however, *ex post facto* and armed with this narrative of cosmopolitanism, Kant is now able to claim that there has been political improvement throughout "the continent" over the course of the past two millennia.[12] His cosmopolitan script, while not directly referring to the actual unfolding of historical events of the past, serves as a concept by means of which we are able to tell a coherent narrative in which the past and the present are continuous with each other.

Second, when Kant looks at the present socio-political conditions through the lens of purposiveness and assumes that the aim of history is cosmopolitanism, he claims to observe *a gradual increase of freedom and enlightenment* that points to a future with a happy ending: "It seems as if a feeling is beginning to stir in all its [possible] members [of a cosmopolitical world order], each of which has an interest in maintaining the whole,"[13] which gives one hope that "the highest purpose of nature, a universal *cosmopolitan existence*, will at last be realized as the matrix within which all the original capacities of the human race may develop" ("IaG"/*AA* 8:28). He is able to interpret the gradual increase of freedom and the ideals of enlightenment that he observes in his time as *a sign* that proves we are progressively emancipating ourselves—both from the rule of nature and the despotic reign of political and judicial institutions—and approaching a condition in which we will be able to develop our capacities further (if we can assume that this is what nature intends us to do).

Third, a cosmopolitan plan "opens up the comforting prospect of a future in which we are shown from afar how the human race eventually works its way upward to a situation in which all the germs implanted by nature can be developed fully, and in which man's destiny can be fulfilled here on earth" ("IaG"/*AA* 8:30). Here, Kant reminds us that this standpoint further provides our remote descendants with a way to cope with "the burden of history [*die Last von Geschichte*]": he claims, for instance, that with this plan in mind future generations can judge their past "only from the point of view of what interests them, i.e., the positive and negative achievements of nations and governments in relation to the cosmopolitan goal" ("IaG"/*AA* 8:31).

Cosmopolitanism as a Historical Narrative and a Political Goal

I have shown that a teleological interpretation of history is not constitutive of the empirical-historical occurrences themselves. Indeed, Kant reminds us repeatedly that the cosmopolitan script is not a sure thing. His narrative is a useful interpretation, and as such, it is not meant to be a substitute for or supersede the task of the empirical historian. It is just an idea that a critical philosopher of history can provide from another standpoint (*Standpunkt*) ("IaG"/*AA* 8:30). It follows from the special status of the maxim of purposiveness—which I analyzed in the Appendix to the *Critique of Pure Reason* and in the "Orientation" essay—that the relationship between a universal concept of history and the empirical composition of historical events must be articulated as a matter of orientation. The teleological philosophy of history in the "Idea" essay presents a narrative of empirical history *only for the purpose of our making better sense of it*; the narrative does *not* explain how these events themselves are constituted. As Kant himself admits, it only provides a useful perspective. The principle of purposiveness applied to history is not *objectively* justified, for it does not establish that empirical history has a determinate purpose. It is justified only on *subjective* or *indirectly objective* grounds (*KrV*, A665–66/B693–94), to enable us to treat history *as if* it unfolded purposively and tell ourselves a coherent story.

If the justifying ground of Kant's teleological philosophy of history is orientational, hypothetical, and subjective, one must conclude that cosmopolitanism is a political goal that arises out of the imaginary focal point of Kant's critical philosophy. It is a story we tell ourselves so that we can navigate our way in the labyrinth of history. The only way to account for the relationship between empirical history and a teleological philosophy of history in a way that does not violate Kant's distinctions is to keep in mind that the latter rests solely on a theoretical guiding principle or a principle of orientation, which is necessitated by the limits of our understanding. Kant's specific claim is that we do not *experience* history as a unified coherent whole progressing toward a cosmopolitan existence but only *project* such a unity on to historical events.

Such a projected unity operates on the basis of a rational hypothesis that orients our thinking about history.[14] The purposiveness of nature is not the transcendental condition for the possibility of universal history, but neither is it an empirically observable event or a sensible intuition. It provides a guiding thread that leads us to a narrative with which we navigate the labyrinth of history and orient our political thinking in the midst of ever-changing realities. The teleological unity presupposed by means of an imaginary focal point directs us toward a certain aim—in this case, toward a cosmopolitan existence—but this claim about the overall direction of world history is valid *a priori* only *indirectly* for universal history. This seems to be what Kant has in mind when he says that history follows "*a certain kind* of *a priori* rule" in the "Idea" essay ("IaG"/*AA* 8:30). It is a certain kind of *a priori* rule because it is not based on experience; however, it is not *a priori* in the sense that the categories are, because unlike the categories the idea for a universal history does not determine the actual experience of history—it is only *indirectly valid* for historical events considered as a whole.

Philosophy of History as a Part of Kant's Nonideal Theory of Politics

Kleingeld argues that the question of whether history as a whole shows a pattern is a useful one for the philosophy of history.[15] I would add that the search for a historical narrative and the resulting philosophy of history are also useful and important for political thought. The "Idea" essay is first and foremost an essay on the philosophy of history, where Kant grapples with the question of how we can configure historical narratives in a space of political disorientation. In the end, his vision of history has a political character and this shows that he understands history to inform or at the very least to matter a great deal to politics. A philosophy of history that offers a cosmopolitan script, then, is an important part of Kant's political thought. Kant articulates and solidifies a political vision by means of a specific historical narrative in the "Idea" essay; to that extent, Kant's philosophy of history must be understood as a part of a nonideal theory of politics.

Since Kant in this essay begins with particular realities and ascends from those to a hypothetical universal concept about political history, his methodology exemplifies what Charles Mills calls nonideal theory.[16] Thus, the underlying methodological or metatheoretical point that the "Idea" essay makes is that a particular view of history is crucial for developing a political agenda. What Kant is doing here is a nonideal theory of politics that aims at an adequate description of our current circumstances, that develops a theoretical map of history, and that is grounded on hypothetical and tentative grounds. That history matters to politics is a point that is still valid and useful for contemporary political thought. We only uncover this important methodological point about a nonideal theory in Kant's work, however, if we turn our attention to the ways in which he justifies his particular claims about history and politics in light of his larger epistemology and metaphysics, that is, to the complex technical principles of his critical philosophy, and most importantly, to teleology.

Focusing on the complex technical principles of Kant's critical philosophy and their role in the formulation of a cosmopolitan world order shows us that, at least in the "Idea" essay itself, Kant's notion of cosmopolitanism does *not* originate out of his moral theory. That is, the "cosmopolitan world order" does not refer to a normative transhistorical and transcultural political ideal. Rather, it is a concept tied to a particular orientation toward history and thus is a concept that belongs to his philosophy of history. If my interpretation of the relationship between history and politics in Kant's thought is valid, then Kant's political philosophy has a partial footing and investment in an adequate description of the nonideal context in which he finds himself. Thus, we see that Kant's philosophy of history and its concept of a cosmopolitan world order must be taken as part of his nonideal theory. Uncovering Kant's nonideal theory of politics and separating it from his ideal theory, especially in the context of the relationship between history and political goals, will in the first instance allow us to acknowledge the fallible nature of our descriptions of the world and the tentativeness that is required in theoretical map-making ventures. Acknowledging this, in turn, will inform how we can honestly address and deal with the Eurocentrism of Kant's cosmopolitan idea.

The Problem of Eurocentrism in Kant's Picture of Universal History

Kant's idea of a universal history is not as "universal" as it purports to be. In the "Idea" essay, he puts forth at least three different yet related claims that make his formulation regarding the cosmopolitan aim of universal history a Eurocentric one. These claims mean that his concept of universal history falls short of universality, as I will detail in what follows. Furthermore, I will argue that understanding his philosophy of history as part of his nonideal theory allows us to acknowledge this problem more honestly and productively.

First, when Kant offers a way to retrospectively judge historical civilizations according to whether and how they contributed to the cosmopolitan aim, his genealogy is exclusively that of Europe, starting with the Greek states and continuing through the Roman empire to the Barbarians ("IaG"/*AA* 8:29). More importantly, he writes that the political history of other, i.e., non-European peoples, are to be incorporated into this genealogy "only episodically" and "as told by these enlightened [i.e., European or Western] nations" ("IaG"/*AA* 8:29). Here, he identifies world history with European history and the world with Europe. He furthermore allows non-European histories to enter into the picture peripherally and episodically, that is, only as they are told from the perspective of Europe and only insofar as they fit in with the European vision and narratives of history. Thus, Kant's own notion of a cosmopolitan world order as the aim of universal history is tied to a particular type of narrative, one that is Eurocentric in its insistence that all other histories be corroborated by Western or European sources.

Second, where Kant is concerned with discovering a regular process of improvement in the political constitutions of "our continent" (i.e., Europe), he famously writes that Europe "will probably eventually legislate for or give law to [*Gesetze geben*] all other continents" ("IaG"/*AA* 8:29–30). Here he puts the European model of civil society and political institutions at the center of his understanding of development at best, and at worst he embraces a paternalistic or colonial project whereby Europe leads all other continents.[17] In either case, however, his view of cultural and political development remains Eurocentric, for his cosmopolitan vision takes Europe as the leading force of "universal" history.

Third, as Kant sees it, the main reason why the cosmopolitan aim of history is useful for politics has to do with the fact that a cosmopolitan world order facilitates the complete development of our innate rational capacities. In reflecting on what the future of the world will look like, he writes that a cosmopolitan plan allows us to hope that "the human race eventually works its way upward to a situation in which all the germs implanted by nature can be developed fully, and in which man's destiny can be fulfilled here on earth" ("IaG"/*AA* 8:30) As has been pointed out by a variety of scholars, most notably and recently by Kleingeld, here Kant limits the idea of human development to the development of white male citizens of western Europe and thus "excludes women and non-whites from much of what the historical development consists in."[18] Kant identifies human development with the development of European white men, which makes his idea for a universal history Eurocentric, as well as racist and sexist, and ties it to a particular, hierarchical notion of humanity.

The last two points about Kant's notions of the world and of humanity have been well established in the scholarship, and I will not elaborate on them further;[19] instead, I will limit my remarks to the first point about the supposed universal character of his notion of world history. It is a fact rarely acknowledged by mainstream Kant scholars that Kant's idea of universal history does not include histories of non-European or nonwestern peoples.[20] He is, nonetheless, quite explicit about what he means when he says "universal" history—it is one that is told and corroborated by Europe. Put directly, Kant's idea of the "world-whole" in the "Idea" essay does not seem to be as holistic or all-encompassing as we often imagine it to be. It includes a specific and not an actual whole in that it is made up of western European men narrating the political histories of the rest of the world and leading the way toward enlightened progress.

One way to respond to Kant's Eurocentrism and to correct it has been to treat the problem merely as a conceptual one. If cosmopolitanism is at bottom a transhistorical and transcultural universal ideal, all we need to do to avoid such bias in Kantian political thought today would be to enlarge our current concept of the "world" or "humanity." We can say that we now know better than Kant and we know better than to include only Europe in world history: we could add our knowledge of non-European and nonwestern histories to the mix and make the ideal truly cosmopolitan. We could say that the problem is that Kant misunderstood the scope of his ideal theory of cosmopolitanism but that our contemporary ideal theories need not repeat this conceptual mistake.[21]

This response, however, would not much differ from adding the histories of non-European peoples episodically or as told by European nations, since it still does not take into account the particularly different conceptions of history that may exist outside of Europe. Insofar as we are bound by the same European paradigm of progress and proceed from supposedly unchanging ideals (in this case, a cosmopolitan world order) to changing particulars (in this case, particular histories), we will be unable to rethink or problematize the very construction of this supposedly universal ideal of cosmopolitanism. Precisely because such a "universal" history with a cosmopolitan aim is not and never has been in fact universal, it will not necessarily be the type of story that people in other parts of the planet would tell themselves or about themselves. In other words, a simple conceptual extension of the notion of "universal history" from Europe to the rest of the world does not undo the Eurocentrism embedded in the Kantian philosophy of history that culminates in idea of a cosmopolitan world order.

As Serequeberhan puts it, in Kant's own view of a cosmopolitan world order "the lived situatedness and cultural-historical particularity of the thinker is negated and elevated to the status of universality and the other side of this is the necessary dehumanization and thus negation of the non-European."[22] In this sense, then, Eurocentrism is not just a conceptual problem; it is a problem about the choice of model that is then imposed upon the rest of the world. Kant's choice of Europe as model—his Eurocentrism—is partly a result of mistaking particularity for universality and partly a result of his denigration of the importance of non-European and nonmale people's contributions to historical and cultural development.[23] Kant's philosophy of history argues that a cosmopolitan world order consists of European peoples, institutions, and cultural development *at the expense of non-Europeans*. His Eurocentrism does not only prioritize a certain conceptual model, then, but does so at the expense of declaring non-European and nonmale people peripheral to universal history.

On the other hand, informed by the distinction between ideal and nonideal theories of politics in Kant's work and by the fact that the latter bears on the former, we can give a more honest and productive response to the problem of Eurocentrism in Kant's philosophy of history. According to this distinction, Kant's Eurocentrism in the "Idea essay" is not merely a conceptual problem but an empirical one; furthermore, in my interpretation its solution requires a different methodological orientation toward the relationship between history and politics. When we allocate Kant's universal history with a cosmopolitan aim to a nonideal theory of politics, we will also be able to recognize and acknowledge that his idea of a cosmopolitan world order originates out of the methodology of orienting his political goals by means of a particular notion of history. If we make room for nonideal theory in his political philosophy, we can posit a completely different understanding of history—not just one with non-European notions relegated to the periphery or appended afterthoughts. There could be multiple narratives of history, and from these orientations we could arrive at a plurality of political agendas. This would require not just a conceptual extension of the notion of universal history but a different orientation toward it.

When I called cosmopolitanism a story or a *Bildungsroman* limited to a particular space and time, it may have seemed as if I minimized or rejected its significance for developing an understanding of history. On the contrary, I meant to emphasize its particularity and its provinciality as a theoretical strength. What I reject, therefore, is not the significance of history for politics, but Kant's limited understanding of the terms "world history" and "universality" in this context. According to Kantian methodology if not to Kant, I would wager that there can be other useful concepts that allow us to bring together disparate historical realities, including nonwestern and non-European ones. This is why it is crucial to acknowledge that Kant's own Eurocentric version of world history has important limitations when it comes to the global aspirations of cosmopolitanism. Therefore, I am suggesting that another more productive response to the problem of Eurocentrism in Kant's thought would be to admit that a nonideal theory of politics implicitly or explicitly undergirds his ideal theory, and thus that his thought is wrought with a Eurocentric view of the world.

Addressing the problem of Eurocentrism in Kant's thought would then require that we actually pay attention to other historical narratives and views of history, as well as to how those narratives and views might shape and inform our politics. If we do not distinguish between the two or if we take Kantian cosmopolitanism to be untouched by the nonideal theory of history that has undergirded it for centuries, we are prone to making the same error and to claim that it is in fact universal. Simple conceptual correction or extension will not do; we need to understand the problem as an empirical one, and this requires a more nuanced approach to the underlying theories of the nonideal circumstances of politics—in this case, to the underlying theory of history and historiography.

I contend that Kant's methodology, due to its subjective and hypothetical orientation, allows room to acknowledge the limitations of a Eurocentric picture of a supposedly universal history, even if Kant himself did not do so. He did not propose teleology as the transcendental condition for the possibility of world history as such, as I have shown, but neither did he see any problem with positing Europe as equivalent to the "world." Here he seems to have forgotten his own precautions regarding the epistemic limits of the cosmopolitan vision that the hypothetical use of reason produces. By acknowledging that Kant's own vision of world history is a Eurocentric and thus a limited one, then, I intend to free up the sphere of politics to different narratives of the world that may shape different political visions. Pointing out the limits of Kant's philosophy of history paves the way for construing different narratives, ones with potentially different political agendas. We come to discover the possibility of diverse and multiple narratives informing different political visions, however, only when we separate Kant's ideal theory from his nonideal theory in the way that I have described here.

In sum, while from his actual construction of the cosmopolitan ideal we can *logically infer* a non-Eurocentric and truly global cosmopolitanism, this logical or conceptual inference does not mean that we can also easily, actually bring about actual global justice. Eurocentrism, like global injustice, is not just a conceptual problem but an empirical one. As Mills puts it, in the context of addressing the sexist nature of many normative theories, the use of gender-neutral pronouns in ethical and political theory does not automatically undo systemic gender injustice;[24] such undoing requires an actual rethinking of what kinds of principles and institutions we would need in order to ensure women are treated equally and fairly in every aspect of their lives. Similarly, undoing global injustice will require a rethinking and reimagining of a cosmopolitan world order in the context of our neocolonial world, one in which we may need a different story or stories about world history. To achieve justice in the real world we require "empirical input and awareness of how the real-life nonideal world actually works."[25] My point is that in Kant's attention to history and in his methodology for constructing a historical narrative, we find a way to organize empirical input around the regulative principle of teleology. Since this methodology has tentative grounds, we should be open to the possibility that there may be better empirical concepts that more adequately describe historical phenomena, broadly and teleologically considered, or the possibility that we no longer need a world history but local histories.[26]

Politics out of History?

When we admit and take responsibility for the narrowly Eurocentric formulation of cosmopolitanism in Kant's text while also insisting on its central insight that history matters for politics, the legacy of Kantian political thought is not merely an ideal theory of a mostly Eurocentric western cosmopolitanism that can be revised for our needs today but rather becomes an insistence on the interconnectedness between a particular view of history and a specific political program, between history and politics. This is revealed only when we focus on Kant's method and the systematic points underlying his political ideals, and this is why it has proven helpful to carefully develop Kant's nonideal theory and its major principle, teleology.

I have shown that Kant's critical method requires an orientation toward history out of which we can posit a particular political goal. Once we alter our orientation, guiding threads, and focal points, our political goals may change as well. In addition to the geographical and historical limitations of Kant's own cosmopolitanism, therefore, I also want to emphasize that in following the methodological insight of his nonideal theory we can develop a politics out of a history. A different orientation toward history may generate new political directions, but we do not yet know what other political agendas might look like because we have not yet considered, let alone explored, these possibilities.

The subjective basis of Kant's historico-political thought that I have recovered in this chapter is, in my view, something to be celebrated for opening up new avenues for political thought. First, Kant's notion of subjectivity is not one of relativism, but rather a robust notion that cautions us to be aware of the finitude of the structures, concepts, and capabilities of our mind. If a particular political goal such as cosmopolitanism is grounded on a subjective hypothesis in this robust sense, then this means that different hypotheses are possible; what is more, different hypotheses may ground different narratives, which in turn may point to different political goals. The key Kantian insight that I want to salvage here is that a particular construction of history grounds particular political goals and that we must be cautious about the limitations of any political agenda, remembering that we can construct and reconstruct history in a way that is better suited for our purposes. While Kant's own narrative is Eurocentric, as I have shown, it may be possible to utilize Kant's method and nonideal theory to come up with other narratives that will generate other political aims or at least sharpen and deepen existing ones.

The aim of history and politics in Kant's account are closely intertwined and cannot be easily separated. This means that not only is his account of universal history in the "Idea" essay fallibilistic, as Kleingeld and others have suggested, but also that the particular political aim or direction that supports such a universal history must also be subject to revision and reconsideration. It should be possible, on Kantian grounds, to adopt a different orientation toward history, to come up with a different narrative and as a result to articulate a different political agenda. This holistic and methodologically-informed interpretation offers us a startlingly new and possibly pluralistic picture of Kantian political thought that we miss when we focus too narrowly on his stated goals. Focusing on the method and his use of teleology rather than the particular products and aims of Kant's political philosophy frees up a space for political thought and specifically for a nonideal theory of politics that we have yet to explore.

I have shown that the status of teleology in the first *Critique* as well as in the "Orientation" essay remains that of a subjective principle originating out of the hypothetical use of reason, specifically the idea of God employed as a hypothesis for orienting ourselves in thinking. I pointed out that this is exactly the procedure at stake in the "Idea" essay, where Kant provides a historical orientation for the general direction of the world and articulates a political telos for humanity based on this orientation. Thus, the regulative principle of teleology, which allows us to presuppose a hypothetical lawfulness of contingent particulars, must be understood as part and parcel of his nonideal theory approach to politics. As is well known, Kant further develops the concept teleology in the *Critique of Judgment*, and that is what I will look at in the next two chapters. I show first that he gives us a richer language to talk about the epistemic and metaphysical status of teleology and second that he once again employs teleological principles and arguments in putting forth a culturally-specific theory of human development in relation to our political goals. Next, therefore, I argue that anthropology matters for politics in the Kantian system.

Part II

Nature, Culture, and Politics
Political Anthropology and Cosmopolitanism

I have shown that for Kant history matters for politics; his nonideal political theory in the form of a philosophy of history gives an account of seemingly contingent historical events and thus shows us the importance of telling ourselves a compelling narrative about them. Regulative teleology, then, promises to be the systematic entry point into Kant's nonideal political theory. Here, I will show that it plays a second and related role in Kant's political thought: a teleological perspective offers complex and realistic descriptions of human beings as natural phenomena and allows Kant to produce a developmental view of political progress as a part of his nonideal theory of politics. I argue that the regulative principle of purposiveness that is rehabilitated in the *Critique of Judgment* provides us with a fruitful analogy between ideal bodies politic and organisms, and that one methodologically and systematically important upshot of Kant's use of organic language in political philosophy is that this language allows us to view human beings as earth-bound creatures as opposed to merely idealized, rational, political agents. For this reason, I locate the systematic significance of the principle of purposiveness, what Kant in the *Critique of Judgment* calls "the lawfulness of the contingent," in the fact that it brings Kant's politics down to earth. His organic-teleological language therefore authorizes a natural and anthropological approach to politics, allowing those less-than-ideal features of human beings and their interactions to enter into the picture. This more realistic picture is part of what I call Kant's nonideal political theory in that it provides a bottom-up approach to cultural and political formation as opposed to the top-down approach exemplified in ideal theory's picture of human beings as idealized agents with idealized capacities. Once again, we uncover Kant's nonideal theory only when we attend to the way in which he employs teleological language and arguments in political discourse. In the next two chapters I will develop what I call a notion of "political *Zweckmässigkeit*" to tease out

PART II

the implications of the link between organisms, teleology, and politics in Kant's political thought and to show that in addition to a political history, teleology allows Kant to articulate a preliminary political anthropology.

Kant resorts to an organism analogy in describing an ideal state in the *Critique of Judgment*, and this analogy is my interpretive clue for exploring three related points about Kant's political thought overall and his nonideal theory in particular. First, we are reminded that any political formation, as he points out in the "Enlightenment" essay, must be seen as a living, breathing whole, as an organism and not just as a mere machine. Second, as he argues in *The Doctrine of Right*, we are reminded that—in order to be realistic and long-lasting—political change must work with the grain and to that extent should be seen as a natural-cultural formation. Third, as he claims in his description of cultural development from a state of nature to freedom in §§82–84 of the Critique of Teleological Judgment, a body politic must be understood as comprising actual, living, not-yet-fully-rational human beings. Here, "a cosmopolitan world-whole" is not an ideal moral whole, but the name that Kant gives to the culmination of our natural-cultural-civil development, a preparatory civil-cultural-political stage. This last stage or aim of politics arises in his argument not as a moral consideration but primarily as an anthropological one.

To be sure, states are not self-organizing beings like organisms and do not exhibit a self-propagating, formative power (*eine sich fortpflanzende bildende Kraft*) like organisms do (*KU/AA* 5:374). However, Kant's argument is that the regulative principle of purposiveness provides a model for and a rule of reflection on an ideal state in two related ways and thus there are two similarities between organisms and bodies-politic. First, it enables us to see that the movement of *the parts* or *the members* of a state can be judged mechanically; and second, that *the whole* must be judged teleologically, or in other words, in terms of a causality of purposes. I show in chapter 3 that—in both the "Enlightenment" essay and *The Doctrine of Right*—we are reminded, through the use of teleological language and organism analogies, that human beings and their interactions must be understood as embedded in nature. In the "Enlightenment" essay, the first similarity is prefigured in Kant's discussion of the *mechanism* of the private use of reason, which can be limited without deterring the overall purpose of humanity, whereas the second similarity constitutes the backdrop of his insistence on the unconditional freedom that must be granted to the public use of reason. Furthermore, in *The Doctrine of Right*, we find that genuine political change does not occur through a fresh and abrupt start, as if one were creating an entirely new organism. Rather, ideal political change must be understood as the gradual development of the organism toward a better overall condition.

As far as we can comprehend, according to Kant, there is no necessity to the way in which organic nature behaves; at first sight, organisms seem quite contingent in their constitution and movements. We are equipped with some universal laws applicable to nature in general to render it legible, but such laws do not help us when it comes to organisms, which seem to act in terms of an overall internal purpose or with some kind of teleological necessity rather than according to a mere mechanistic one. This is why, Kant concludes, we must judge the contingencies of organisms according to a regulative principle of purposiveness, as if they behaved in a lawful manner according to an intention of their own. For instance, even if we did not know with certainty that the hollowness of the bones or the placement of the wings in a bird served the purpose of flight, judging them to be purposive for such movement helps us gain a deeper understanding of the organism than merely presupposing that birds can fly as a matter of chance (*KU/AA* 5:360). Kant then extends this hermeneutic principle to certain other objects of theoretical inquiry, such as cultural development, both to emphasize a similarity between organic and social wholes and to remind us that the theoretical field of cultural anthropology deals with freely acting purposeful human beings situated in nature and not with mechanistically determined agents. Accordingly, Kant claims that—to obtain a more useful theory of human cultural development than if we were merely to suppose it entirely accidental—we must judge the collective lives of human beings as a whole, not by means of mechanical laws and not by means of freedom, either, but as if our lives and actions all together constituted teleological or purposeful wholes.

It is through teleological language or the principle of political *Zweckmässigkeit* that Kant brings into play the natural elements of politics: human nature and our natural habitat, or in other words, nature within and outside us. This is further articulated in §§82–84 of the *Critique of Judgment*, which I analyze at length in chapter 4. Because Kant's writings here feature a notion of the human being located at the intersection of nature and freedom—not a mere machine but not yet a rational moral agent—his political philosophy is neither like pure physics nor a pure metaphysics of morals. In the Kantian system, a teleological way of thinking (*Denkungsart*) brings together a deterministic account of nature with freely willed human actions, and so the principle of *Zweckmässigkeit* allows him to articulate what lies between the two: his particular conception of cultural development from nature to freedom. The account of the transition from the less-than-ideal circumstances to ideal ones that we find in these sections of the third *Critique* is part of what I am calling Kant's nonideal theory of politics—namely, a theory of the human condition and of cultural development, or, a political anthropology.

PART II

Kant calls this particular transition—from a natural state to a state of freedom—a "culture of skill" (*Geschicklichkeit*), which culminates in a cosmopolitan world order. I will show that what allows him to incorporate into his political philosophy a particular cultural construction as a transitory stage is a teleological language, and that by means of this language he gives us a nonideal theory of culture and development. Thanks to the regulative principle of purposiveness, Kant is able both to produce a concept descriptive of our cultural activities in the world and to identify how these activities pertain to our political goals. It is important to remember, therefore, that the idea of a cosmopolitan order here is not primarily a moral goal produced by an ideal ethical theory, but a name for the intermediary phase of our cultural activities, a preparatory stage that is most appropriate for further moral development.

Lastly, I will show that Kant's own articulation of the natural-cultural development of human beings prioritizes a certain European or Western way of life above others, especially when we consider his emphasis on a culture of skill over other kinds of cultural activities. Nevertheless, because the underlying method constructed by his regulative teleology at least speculatively allows for different conceptualizations, we need not buy into his particular understanding of culture or development. Rather, we can hold on to teleology as the basic principle of organization of our activities in this world while explicitly critiquing Kant's particular, Eurocentric version of such political anthropology. Thus, what remains most relevant to political theory in my interpretation here is his insight about the importance of theorizing the nonideal conditions of our lives in terms of a political anthropology. The use of teleological language that we find in his political writings therefore signals something deeper about his very conception of politics. It reminds us that political formations or goals are not simply about the ideal principles of justice or right; they must work with the very nature of human beings and so require a theorization of our less-than-ideal natural and cultural circumstances. Kant's overall methodological point, which demonstrates a connection between culture and politics, is still useful for exploring the relationship between different notions of cultural activities and political goals. If Kant's ideal theory of politics prescribes the path toward political improvement in terms directed by the *a priori* ideal of the pure republic, then, his nonideal theory describes its actual unfolding here and now in terms of our natural and cultural transformations. For Kant, in other words, anthropology matters to politics.

3

Organisms, Bodies Politic, and Progress

Kant often resorts to organic metaphors while describing what an ideal body politic or ideal political progress should look like. I will argue that these are not just random metaphors that he happened to have on hand; rather, his use of teleological language here reveals something significant about the nature and the epistemic-metaphysical commitments of his political thought, especially his nonideal theory of our cultural and moral development. If there are similarities between the way we must judge an organism and an ideal state or political progress, this is because both mechanistic language and moral explanations remain somehow insufficient for talking about the organization of our collective lives and therefore benefit from resorting to the regulative principle of purposiveness. In other words, for Kant, neither a mechanistic-physicalist determinism nor a language of moral freedom will exactly capture what is unique about our collective lives or political organizations. This uniqueness can be understood as the underlying developmental idea of human beings as creatures on earth attempting to lead themselves from a state of nature to a civil state, and from there toward a moral existence. Consequently, we will see that Kant's political philosophy must heavily borrow from teleological language, because Kant conceives of politics as closely related to and having a stake in natural bodies and processes. This means that a complete political theory for him consists of neither a physical-biological determinism nor a morality of freedom—that is, its methodology will not be satisfied with mathematical explanations or a metaphysics of morals. Furthermore, by means of such a teleological perspective of human beings, one that conceptualizes them as more than machines but less than fully rational agents, Kant is able to supply his political theory with a view of how we can *transition* from our current conditions to a better civil state by means of natural-cultural activities and ends. This view is an important part of what I name, throughout this book, Kant's nonideal theory of politics.

In a curious footnote, in the context of his definition of organisms and their unique features in §65 of the *Critique of Judgment*, Kant claims that we can accurately describe an ideal state by means of an analogy with

CHAPTER 3

an organism (*KU/AA* 5:375). Earlier, in §59 he suggests that we can symbolize a just state with the idea of body with a soul, while a despotic state can be likened to a hand mill, a mere machine (*KU/AA* 5:352). In what follows, I analyze the use of these analogies in order to uncover the significance of organic language for Kant's political philosophy. I begin with an exegetical account of the principle of purposiveness, or "the lawfulness of the contingent," as Kant develops it in the *Critique of Judgment*, and then I articulate the similarities between an ideal body politic and an organism as Kant sees them in both §59 and §65 of the third *Critique*. The analogy is not between a state and an organism but in the rule for reflecting on or judging each: this analogy recasts the distinction between the private and public uses of reason in "What Is Enlightenment?" in a new light. Both an organism and an ideal state must be judged by means of the regulative principle of purposiveness, that is, with reference to the purpose of the whole and not just the parts. Keeping Kant's analogy between an organism and an ideal state in mind, we can see in the "Enlightenment" essay that both an ideal state and the progress toward an ideal political condition are best conceptualized in terms of a causality of purposes, namely, in terms of a causality akin to that of an organism. The difference is that the purpose of an organism is self-propagation, while the purpose of an ideal body politic is the progress of the entirety of humankind.

The use of teleological principles in reference to bodies politic and progress provides an important point of entry into what I name Kant's principle of political *Zweckmässigkeit*. After the "Enlightenment" essay, I turn to his use of another organic metaphor in political philosophy: his argument in *The Doctrine of Right* that political progress must be likened not to palingenesis but metamorphosis. This argument again uses a teleological and organic language to describe a political formation. While this formulation may have something to do with Kant's interest in the life sciences of his time, I will argue that it accomplishes a more substantial theoretical point. His analogy between revolution and metamorphosis continues his organic way of thinking about an ideal state and confirms that for him political thought must work with a conceptualization of the human being as less than ideal and must include a nonideal theory of our natural and cultural development. Both the organism–body politic and the metamorphosis–political reform analogies provide us with prime examples of how teleology enhances political discourse by bringing in a nonideal and quasi-natural picture of human beings. Thus, Kant conceives of political thought not only as an ideal theory that begins with the *a priori* ideals of justice or a pure republic, but also as a nonideal theory that begins with natural circumstances and rises from them to the cultural and the political development of our collective lives.

Paying attention to the organic-teleological language in both "What Is Enlightenment?" and §52 of *The Doctrine of Right* therefore reminds us of two things: Kant's political philosophy operates with the notion that the human being is neither subject simply to the mechanism of nature nor yet a free moral agent, and that a body politic must be conceived neither simply as a machine nor yet as a moral whole. Political theory provides reflections on the organization of our collective lives, and as such it deals with not just the natural-biological or the free-moral but also the cultural formation and development of human beings and their institutions. This is the unique notion of the human being that is at stake in Kant's nonideal political philosophy; the significance of this notion for Kant's political philosophy will become clearer in §§82–84 of the *Critique of Judgment*, to which I turn in chapter 4.

"The Lawfulness of the Contingent" in the Critique of Teleological Judgment

In the First Introduction to the *Critique of Judgment* (this introduction is hereafter cited as EEKU), Kant defines *Zweckmässigkeit* as an assumption pertaining to the subject's capacity for judging in general, not as a feature of the judged object itself (EEKU/AA 20:202). The second book of the third *Critique*, the Critique of the Teleological Judgment, is concerned with "objective purposiveness" that nonetheless signifies a subjective commitment of our capacity to judge.[1] Kant distinguishes between two types of material-objective purposiveness in §63: namely, between the principle of internal (*innere*) purposiveness, which judges organisms immediately as natural ends, and the principle of external (*äusser*) or relative (*relativ*) purposiveness, which judges the advantageousness or usefulness of a natural end for other natural beings' purposes (KU/AA 5:367). Regardless of whether we refer to the inner structure of an organism or judge the external relationship between two natural things, however, the principle of objective *Zweckmässigkeit* is a critical regulative principle, one that the judging subject must bring to bear on the object at hand in order to make better sense of it. In brief, when we say that nature or an organism is purposive, we are referring to the relationship between that object and our faculty of cognition rather than declaring that nature itself is constituted purposively. The principle of purposiveness is a subjective principle, with all the caveats of the term "subjective" that we find in the Kantian system.

Kant further defines the purposiveness (*Zweckmässigkeit*) of nature in the First Introduction to the *Critique of Judgment* as "an objectively

CHAPTER 3

contingent [*Zufälligen*] but subjectively (for our faculty of cognition) necessary *lawfulness* [*Gesetzmässigkeit*]" (EEKU/AA 20:243, emphases added), and again in §76 as "the lawfulness of the contingent as such [*Gesetzlichkeit des Zufälligen*]" (*KU/AA* 5:404). Once again, we see that the purposiveness of nature is assumed in the subject's capacity for judging in general and not in the object. When we say, for instance, that "nature does nothing in vain," and employ this principle in our judgment of organisms or of nature as a whole, we have not issued a blanket denial of all contingency in nature. Rather, we have merely asserted that, as a special principle of reflection, *the lawfulness of the contingent as such* in nature must be presupposed, even though such lawfulness remains contingent upon the peculiar constitution of our faculties of judgment and cognition (EEKU/AA 20:209; *KU/AA* 5:397–98). In other words, Kant's argument here is that this principle does not and cannot constitute the objective *a priori* conditions for the possibility of the object to which it applies, be it an organism or nature as a whole, but serves only as a *subjective* condition for its being judged and reflected upon.

We are allowed to see certain contingencies in nature as lawful from the perspective of the reflecting judgment, that is, hypothetically. While it may seem paradoxical at first to interpret nature as a whole as *both* lawful *and* contingent, once we better articulate the underlying assumptions of the Kantian critical and regulative principle of *Zweckmässigkeit*, this paradox is removed. Kant argues that nature as a whole can be judged reflectively to be both contingent and lawful as long as we also keep in mind that we can neither discover all of these purposes and laws nor claim that purposiveness is the necessary constitutive condition of nature in itself.

Here I do not wish to settle the debate over the systematic continuities between the *Critique of Pure Reason* and the *Critique of Judgment* with regard to the concept of purposiveness.[2] My view is that in the Appendix to the Transcendental Dialectic in the first *Critique*, Kant has already accepted the possibility that teleology and its principle of *Zweckmässigkeit* can be applied to nature as a whole on regulative grounds, due to its theoretical and practical usefulness and as a supplement to mechanistic investigation (*KrV*, A619/B647). In the *Critique of Judgment*, Kant further develops the idea that this regulative principle can be used without harm to the mechanism of nature, for it makes it possible to view nature, as an experiment, as a purposive whole for the purposes of our investigation.[3] Our cognition of the entirety of nature will always remain contingent since such a totality is never given to us as an object of experience. Nevertheless, we attempt to represent nature as a whole to ourselves as necessary and lawful in order to understand its laws better as a system and to extend our research beyond mere mechanistic principles. In line with his position in the "Idea" essay—that we need a guiding thread to view history as a whole—in the third *Critique* Kant tells us that any time we attempt to reflect on the entirety of nature we must use the critical and regulative principle of purposiveness to orient ourselves, and that it is this principle that allows us to hypothesize that all natural occurrences originate from one single source or purpose.

These remarks should suffice as brief points unpacking the critical and regulative basis of the *Zweckmässigkeit* of nature in general and the reason why *Zweckmässigkeit* is "a principle of the lawfulness of the contingent as such" in the third *Critique*. Here Kant uses a richer language to describe the epistemological stakes and the methodological status of teleology than what he had provided in either the first *Critique* or the "Orientation" essay; nevertheless, this account is continuous with and builds on those earlier conceptions in that the principle of teleology is still subjective, regulative, and hypothetical. In what follows, I delve into Kant's definition of organisms and, more importantly, into his analogy between organisms and ideal bodies politic to show how Kant uses these ideas as an entryway into thinking about human beings and their union under laws in less-than-ideal circumstances. That is to say that the analogy between organisms and bodies politic provides us with a clue as to how both organic and political development benefit from a teleological conceptualization.

What Organisms and Ideal Political States Have in Common

While he is enumerating the differences between a machine and an organism in §65 of the third *Critique*, Kant claims in a footnote that an ideal state can be likened to the latter; he writes:

> One can illuminate a certain association, *though one that is encountered more in the idea than in reality,* by means of an analogy with the immediate ends of nature [organisms] that have been mentioned. Thus, in the case of a recently undertaken fundamental transformation of a great people into a state, the word "organization" has frequently been quite appropriately used for the institution of the magistracies, etc., and even of the entire body politic. For in such a whole, each member should certainly be not merely a means but at the same time also an end, and, insofar as it contributes to the possibility of the whole, its position and function should also be determined by the idea of the whole. (*KU/AA* 5:375, emphasis added)[4]

This is a curious claim, because states are not self-organizing beings: a body politic is not a natural but a *social* formation. How must we understand, then, what this analogy aims to convey with regard to a body politic? While Kant does not elaborate on the details, I will reconstruct his argument and point out two similarities between *the way we must judge* an organism and an ideal state. We will see that Kant's ideal state must be viewed as more than a machine, as exhibiting a purposive alignment between the parts and whole—a position prefigured in his views on political progress in "What Is Enlightenment?"

First, Kant's definition of an organism in §65 of the *Critique of Judgment* primarily revolves around how we must conceive of its parts-whole relationship. He claims that each part of an organism must be seen as if it exists only through and for the sake of all the others—on account of the whole (*KU/AA* 5:373–74). When we make judgments concerning machines and their parts, we are satisfied with mere mechanistic principles that posit a cause-effect relationship. When it comes to organisms, however, mechanistic principles fail to fully capture their inner workings: in the case of judging organisms, we need the principle of purposiveness to provide a rule for reflecting on the interrelatedness of the parts and the whole. Because organisms differ significantly from machines in this regard (namely, in terms of their parts-whole relationship), we must judge organisms as if they are possible through a causality of purposes (*KU/AA* 5:375–76).[5]

Second, Kant further explains that the *parts* of an organism—the skin, hair, and bones of an animal, for instance, as well as its physical movement—can be understood in terms of the mechanistic principles of cause and effect; however, the development of the animal *as a whole* cannot be explained by means of this causality and must be judged with the purpose of the whole in mind (*KU/AA* 5:377, 5:249). This means that in judging organisms the principle of mechanism must be subordinated to that of teleology: parts of an organism and their individual movements may be judged mechanistically, but their relationship to the organism as a whole must be judged in terms of the purpose of the organism. There is no contradiction between a mechanistic conceptualization of the parts of an organism and a teleological picture of the relationship between the parts of the organism and the whole.

In sum, Kant defines a natural end or an organism as a being in which each part is possible only through its relation to the whole; in other words, each part of an organism is reciprocally the cause and the effect of the whole (*KU/AA* 5:373). Here we can see that organisms are already *more than machines* in the sense that they require not just efficient causality but something like final causality. Kant goes on to argue in the footnote that it is apt to refer to an ideal body politic as an "organization": in such a body—just as in an organism—each member should not be merely a means but also an end for the whole, and, reciprocally, the idea of the whole should determine the position and function of each of the members.

Before proceeding, however, let me clarify that we must maintain this as an analogy specifically in the manner of judging. What Kant proposes here is not, strictly speaking, an analogy between *states and organisms*, but an analogy *between the ways in which we must judge them*. If we make no distinction between the natural teleology of organisms and the use of teleology in describing ideal bodies politic, we risk concluding that for Kant political thought is equivalent to biology and that political bodies and actions are just like organisms. Equating states with organisms, however, contradicts Kant's formulation of the principle of *Zweckmässigkeit* in the third *Critique* and elsewhere as a critical and regulative principle of judgment, pertaining to the subject's capacity to judge.[6] We must utilize the principle of *Zweckmässigkeit* in judging organisms not because this principle represents an *a priori* condition for the possibility of such beings but because our intellect cannot understand organisms by means of mechanistic principles alone. In other words, this principle does not yield a determining judgment but remains regulative, yielding only reflective judgments (*KU/AA* 5:378–79). While the organism analogy is helpful for a better understanding of Kant's theory of an ideal state, we must also remember not to take this analogy so far as to claim, as Hegel did, that a state is and ought to be understood as an organic unity.

In sum, while I agree with Sedgwick that Kant's theory of purposiveness in nature, together with the analogy between an ideal body politic and an organism, prefigures Hegel's organic theory of the state in his *Philosophy of Right*,[7] I insist that here it must be read in the Kantian terms that I have developed thus far: not as an organic theory of the state but as a reflective judgment about an ideal state likened to an organic whole in its parts-whole relationship. The notion of reflective teleological judgment is in line with what Kant earlier called the hypothetical use of reason, by means of which we are allowed to employ the idea of God as a hypothesis when we reflect on the entirety of nature.[8] What I suggest here, then, is not a concrete interpretation of this analogy in which a state *is* an organic unity, but rather the idea that the reflection on and theorization of each necessitates a teleological consideration of the regulative kind. That is, in both states and organisms the parts must coordinate with one another in order to advance the purposes of the whole. Kant makes a similar point about the ideal state being more than a machine in §59 of the *Critique of Judgment*: in both cases, the idea that our judgment of bodies politic benefits from an analogy with the judgments of organisms signals that politics deals with more than machines and that political thought needs more than mechanistic principles.

CHAPTER 3

How the State Functions: A Hand Mill versus A Body with a Soul

Another analogy in the *Critique of Judgment* confirms my interpretation of the role of Kant's organic language in his conceptualization of politics. In §59 Kant writes that symbolically "a monarchical state is represented by a body with a soul if it is ruled in accordance with laws internal to the people, but by a mere machine (like a hand mill) if it is ruled by a single absolute will" (*KU/AA* 5:352). The point that a machine-like state is far from ideal further suggests that a mechanistic worldview is insufficient either for talking about organisms or about ideal political bodies.[9] We judge organisms as natural ends not because we know that an organism *is* a natural end independent of our judging it so, but because it remains contingent with respect to the already-known mechanical laws as to why it ought to be organized exactly the way it is. Similarly, an ideal state cannot be like a mere machine, because a mechanistic view of the body politic cannot by itself justify how the parts (citizens), all of which act freely, ought to come and act together in concert in a commonwealth. Metaphorically speaking, such a state does not let its citizens grow or breathe freely. If their ruling principle is mechanistic causality, then it is as if the will of the ruler is the sole organizing principle of the individual wills of the citizens. Because we cannot give a full account of an ideal state in terms of a well-oiled machine, or, to put it differently, because an ideal state cannot be just a mechanical whole comprising human beings as its parts, we must resort to an analogy with an organic whole. We must symbolize such a state as a combination of a body—acting according to mechanistic rules, and compulsorily so—and a soul acting according to freedom.

The insight that this analogy provides is this: human beings and their union in any ideal political body must be judged as "more than a machine." If the state is a mere machine, it may guarantee public order through the subordination of every person's will, but it cannot promote growth or progress; through this kind of subjugation the state risks becoming just like a hand mill. An ideal state must allow its members to move about freely while also maintaining their commitments to the whole; for Kant, as we will see, this is the only way in which a body politic, local or global, can become a facilitator of progress toward an ideal political condition, enlightenment. An ideal political condition, then, must be judged in teleological terms, as one would judge an organism, in which each member is judged to be connected to the purpose of the whole. If a body politic is a mechanistic whole determined solely by the will of the monarch, it is a despotic state, propelled merely by the force of the ruler's will. If, on the other hand, a body politic is ruled in accordance with laws internal to the people, it can be understood as a body with a soul, an organism animated by the purpose of the whole. It is the latter that Kant prefers in the "Enlightenment" essay, where individuals ought to be not only cogs in a machine, compelled to act in accordance with the will of the ruler, but end-setting agents who act together in accordance with the purposes of the entirety of humankind. In making progress toward an ideal global condition, individuals will eventually come to rely only on themselves—and this will happen only if they develop their innate vocation to think freely.

Machines and Organisms in "What Is Enlightenment?"

As I indicated above, the similarity between judging an organism and judging an ideal state has two main features for Kant. First, in such a unified whole "each member should be not only a means but also an end"; and second, "insofar as each member contributes to the possibility of the whole, its position and function should be determined by the idea of the whole" (*KU/AA* 5:373). In both an ideal state and an organism, the parts-whole relationship must be judged in terms of the purposes of the whole, while the movement of the parts without relation to the whole can be judged mechanistically. I now turn to Kant's famous essay, "What Is Enlightenment?," and argue that these two criteria are in the background of the distinction between private and public uses of reason. It turns out that these two features of organisms must figure in our judgment regarding an ideal state and political progress.[10] While commentators agree that the "Enlightenment" essay makes important contributions to Kant's political theory and to his views on progress toward an ideal state, they largely downplay or overlook the language of mechanism and purposiveness. Ellis and Honneth, for example, both argue against bringing purposiveness into our interpretation of the "Enlightenment" essay; Ellis interprets teleology as a determinative principle and denies its significance for freely willed human actions, whereas Honneth argues that in this essay Kant substitutes freedom of the public use of reason for his archaic notion of purposiveness.[11] Both commentators frame this essay in terms of its proposals for the freedom of thought; while I generally agree with this framework, here I show that attending to the organism analogy in the essay in fact provides a richer account of political formation and progress. This analogy allows Kant to describe how to move from the nonideal circumstances to ideal ones and therefore to produce a theory of transition for beginning to achieve our political goals here and now.

In the "Enlightenment" essay Kant makes a famous distinction between the private and public uses of reason. A person in the realm of the private use of reason, that is, in her role as an officer of the state, is considered to be a "part of the machine [*teil der Machine*]" ("WA"/*AA* 8:37).[12] Because individuals in this role merely move the bureaucratic machinery, they are not considered to be political agents in the proper sense. Here, we are members or limbs (*Glieder*) of the state and are required to behave passively to promote the ends of our particular commonwealth, or are at the very least required "to be prevented from destroying such ends" ("WA"/*AA* 8:37). Thus, Kant argues, the private use of reason must be restricted: here, one must not argue or think (*räsonieren*) but obey ("WA"/*AA* 8:37).

Scholars explain the private use of reason by pointing out that it is already an incomplete, insufficient, or merely instrumental use of reason and that therefore restrictions to it need not bother one's conscience.[13] While I agree with this characterization, it proves illuminating here to pay attention to the language of machines and organisms. Consider the first similarity between an organism and an ideal state that I developed earlier, that the parts must be viewed not only as means but also as ends in themselves. We can then conclude that the private use of reason in any given state cannot actively contribute to an ideal political condition, because as parts of a mechanistic whole (as cogs or limbs) we are conceived of as merely means to an end for our commonwealth. We are not viewed as ends but only as means for the machinery of the state, subordinated to the overall end of a given commonwealth: public safety and order (*öffentliche Ruhe*). Thus, because the private use of reason cannot and does not contribute to the telos of the whole of humankind (i.e., progress toward an ideal political condition), it is acceptable to explain the movement of the state bureaucracy in mechanistic terms and therefore restrict the private use of reason to such machine-like obedience.

In contrast to the private use of reason, the public use of reason considers the individual as a member of a larger community in the role of a scholar ("WA"/*AA* 8:37). In this role, we are considered parts of a cosmopolis and not just our own particular commonwealth. Thus we are not merely cogs in the machine or means to an end: our purpose as public scholars is intimately linked with the purpose of the entirety of humankind. We must freely contest the principles governing our lives as a whole, and for Kant, the propensity for such freedom of thought is found in our nature. More importantly, the topic of scholarly argument may include the principles of the existing government. Kant argues that if, as a result of free scholarly discussion, the public reaches the conclusion that the existing principles no longer serve them, they should be left free to put these laws before public appraisal, to criticize the inappropriateness or even injustice of these laws, and to make suggestions for a better arrangement of the existing institutions ("WA" 8:37–38).[14] The public use of reason must be unlimited so that we can criticize and eventually revise even the fundamental principles of the machinery of the state and so that we can progress toward a more ideal social and political condition by developing our natural propensity for free thought.[15] This use of reason serves the ends of all of humanity, understood as an organism, and not just a given particular commonwealth or machinery.

Scholars explain the significance of the public use of reason in terms of Kant's fondness for a free exchange of ideas, his insistence that publicity will be the touchstone of truth, and his need to reassure Frederick the Great that free and rational public debate will not threaten the status quo. While these considerations may have played a role in his formulation, utilizing the analogy between an ideal state and an organism once again proves instructive. That the freedom of the public use of reason can and should influence the rules and principles of the government has been well established by all commentators, but the reasons why this can and should happen are not indicated by all.[16] Paying attention to the organic language provides an interpretive key here. In the freedom of the public use of reason, our purposes are intertwined with the purposes of the whole of humankind, as in an organism where the purposes of the parts are intertwined with the purpose of the whole. With regard to the second similarity, that in both organisms and ideal states the position and function of each part must be determined in relation to the whole, we see that it is only in the public use of reason that the individual can be viewed as a citizen of the world as a whole, with their purposes aligned with that of the whole. Because our purposes or ends ought to be the same as the purposes of the whole, as in an organism, the use of reason that allows for this alignment must be unlimited. This is why Kant claims that the freedom of the public use of reason alone can bring about enlightenment among human beings ("WA"/*AA* 8:37). At stake in the public use of reason is nothing less than the overall growth of humanity conceived of as an organism and as a species toward what it ought to be. The organism analogy gives Kant a global and species-level perspective from which he is able to articulate his preferred means for the development of humanity: the freedom of the pen. While we may want to criticize the means that he chooses as elitist or historically contingent, what I would underscore here is that Kant describes the transition of humanity from a self-incurred immaturity to a self-directed maturity by means of an organic language and in terms of the growth and well-being of the entire human kind.

The Purpose of a Commonwealth versus The Purpose of Humanity

In this essay Kant further defines the "original vocation [*ursprüngliche Bestimmung*]" of humankind as progress and claims that the seed (*Keim*) for progress is found in humankind's "propensity and calling to think freely" ("WA"/*AA* 8:41).[17] If we want to develop this seed and thereby achieve our original vocation or telos, he argues that we distinguish our role in an existing commonwealth from that in a cosmopolis. This distinction gives rise to what he calls the paradox of enlightenment: "Argue as much as you will, and about what you will, but obey!" ("WA"/*AA* 8:41). Viewing an ideal body politic as an organism helps us to make sense of this paradox, since it allows us to judge each use of reason by means of the principle of purposiveness and discern whether and how each aids our original vocation, to make progress. The ends of any given particular commonwealth can never be prescribed as the telos of humankind; any action serving this particular end should be restricted through a machine-like obedience. In order to achieve our collective end, the end of humanity, however, we need unlimited freedom. The criterion of the principle of purposiveness allows Kant to conclude that the private use of reason can be machine-like and therefore limited, for it does not contribute to the purpose of humankind as a whole, whereas the public use of reason must be permitted to grow, since it alone will help us to develop our propensity to think freely.

When we bring the principle of purposiveness to bear on our reflection upon our political condition, we see that in the "Enlightenment" essay the private use of reason corresponds to a mechanical movement of individuals, while the public use of reason corresponds to the *virtually organic interconnectedness* of the citizens of the world. From the perspective of the purpose of the whole of humankind (i.e., progress), we can see that the private use of reason is irrelevant on two accounts: it treats human beings merely as cogs in the machine, and it conceives of the existing commonwealth as a mechanistic whole. In other words, the deeds of a person in her role as an officer of the state can be restricted without hindrance to the overall goal of enlightenment because a mechanistic obedience in the realm of the private use of reason does not contribute to the progress of the humankind as a whole—even if such obedience serves the purpose of a particular commonwealth in that it *moves* its bureaucracy. In an organism, likewise, mechanistic principles have their place, but in the final analysis they must be subordinated to teleological principles (*KU*/*AA* 5:414–16).[18] In terms of judging our progress toward an ideal body politic, this means that the mechanism of any given particular state must be subordinated to the purpose of the whole of humankind.

This view allows us to see why freedom of the public use of reason must be unlimited: Kant's point is that only in this way will we prioritize the ends of humanity over the ends of our particular states and finally be able to influence the laws of the government and make progress toward a better condition overall ("WA"/*AA* 8:41–42).

The analogy between judging an organism and judging an ideal state proves instructive for interpreting the "Enlightenment" essay. We know that we must interpret an organism as a specific sort of unity, one in which each part works mechanistically but as part of a larger whole works toward the purpose of the whole. By analogy, an ideal body politic must be a unified whole in which the individuals and their movement in relation to other individuals may be understood mechanistically, but their relation to the whole must be judged teleologically, with the purpose of the entire body politic, the cosmopolis, in mind. Just as we must conceive of an organism not only as governed by mechanical laws but also by purposiveness (in the service of the telos of the whole), we must conceive of an ideal body politic as governed not only by mechanical laws that aim to maintain a well-oiled bureaucracy in a particular state, but also by the telos of the whole, the progress of humankind. A mechanical obedience or civil compulsion has its place in a body politic.[19] However, an ideal state ought to be conceived of as a global condition, as an organic unity in which its members are not only like parts of a machine—not merely means to an end—but also work collectively toward a common goal as end-setting agents, where their ends coincide with the ends of the whole. This requires that we judge our progress toward an ideal state from the perspective of the whole of humanity by means of the regulative principle of purposiveness. An ideal political condition is more than a well-oiled machine; it is akin to organic growth.

Palingenesis and Metamorphosis in *The Doctrine of Right*

In *The Doctrine of Right*, a work that is generally taken to belong to his formal theory of rights or his ideal theory of politics,[20] Kant uses yet another organic metaphor, likening slow political reform to metamorphosis and revolution to palingenesis. We have already seen that an analogy between bodies politic and organisms is useful for Kant, not because the former is a natural product, but because there seems to be a similarity in the manner of judging each from the perspective of the whole. Here in *The Doctrine of Right*, he further asserts that—because revolutions do not bring about actual change but only the dissolution of the rule of law—revolution can be likened to palingenesis (MS/AA 6:340). This organic analogy once again helps Kant to judge political change from the perspective of the life of the entire organism. I will show that the metamorphosis-palingenesis metaphors must be interpreted along the lines of the broader argument that I have developed thus far—namely, that Kant's political theory benefits from organic metaphors and teleological language—because a consideration of human beings and bodies politic as less than perfect, as more than machines but not yet rational agents or wholes, requires reflective teleological judgments. In other words, Kant's teleological language here is not just heuristically useful, but is in fact required by the very nature of the phenomena that he addresses in these passages. His teleological view of political change here presents a nonideal theory of transition, since it considers human beings as embedded in nature, describing how our collective life *transitions* from where it is to where it ought to be.

It is well established that—when it comes to political change—Kant favors slow, gradual reforms over sudden revolutions: he gives various arguments to support this view and argue against the legitimacy of revolution throughout his historico-political writings.[21] For instance, as we have seen in the "Enlightenment" essay, his defense of the unlimited freedom of the public use of reason is supposed to justify just such slow reforms. One of his arguments against revolutions is that they are disruptive and, as a result, often fail to be long-lasting. Absolute freedom of the public use of reason allows us to question and criticize the rules governing our lives and to replace them with better ones; we will reach enlightenment not all at once but slowly, and slow reforms will ensure that the mindsets of citizens are changing alongside the principles of society—and thus that change will be lasting. As he puts it in that essay, "Thus a public can achieve enlightenment only slowly. A revolution may well bring about a falling off of a personal despotism and avaricious or tyrannical oppression, but never a true reform in one's way of thinking" ("WA"/AA 8:36).

In the passage from *The Doctrine of Right* in which Kant compares political reform to the metamorphosis of an organism, he is similarly concerned with changing existing customs in addition to the formal laws of a given society; he writes,

> The different forms of states are only the *letter* (*littera*) of the original legislation in the civil state, and they may therefore remain as long as they are taken, by old and long-standing custom (and so only subjectively), to belong necessarily to the machinery of the constitution. But the *spirit* of the original contract (*anima pacti originarii*) involves an obligation on the part of the constituting authority to make the *kind of government* suited

> to the idea of the original contract. Accordingly, even if this cannot be done all at once, it is under obligation to change the kind of government gradually and continually so that it harmonizes *in its effect* with the only constitution that accords with right, that of a pure republic in such a way that [the old forms] ... are replaced by the original (rational) form, the only form which makes *freedom* the principle and indeed the condition for any exercise of *coercion*, as is required by a rightful constitution of a state in the strict sense of the word. Only it will finally lead to what is literally a state. (*MS/AA* 6:340–41, emphases in original)

Here, we see that for Kant all existing states operate mechanistically and by means of the coercion of customs built into the letter of their constitution. This means that any existing body politic, even with the machinery of its constitution, is not yet a rightful state in which freedom and coercion are in tandem with each other. The spirit of the original contract, the idea of a pure republic, is what should be guiding the slow, gradual amendment of the existing machinery of the constitution, and it is this slow metamorphosis-like change that Kant prefers over sudden or violent palingenesis-like revolution. Thus, we have to start with the less-than-ideal machinery that we have and make slow amendments to it that gradually approximate the ideal of a pure republic.

Consistent with his preference for political reform over revolution or rebellion, then, the point of the reform-metamorphosis analogy in *The Doctrine of Right* seems to be the following: just as an organism can better improve its health and well-being through metamorphosis than through palingenesis, a political state can change for the better only through gradual metamorphosis-like reforms and not through sudden, palingenesis-like revolutions. Palingenesis disrupts the life-cycle of an organism in a kind of rebirth that does away with earlier forms; this is the way in which palingenesis is akin to revolutions, which completely destroy the previous institutions of a body politic. By contrast, metamorphosis ensures that we are still dealing with the same organism, only now in a better condition and fulfilling its main purpose. In the case of a body politic, this main purpose is balancing freedom and coercion in the organization of our collective lives. Such a change, for Kant, is akin to the slow and gradual reforms that work with and through the existing political structures rather than by simply overthrowing them.

Interestingly, not many scholars comment on the use of organic language in *The Doctrine of Right*; two exceptions to this are Susan Meld Shell and Howard Williams. Susan Meld Shell offers a reading of the passage I quoted above regarding the gap between the ideal and the real state and points out that, since the state is like a living organism,

CHAPTER 3

> to suspend this process [of life of the organism or the state] 'even for an instant' (that is, by violent revolution) is as deadly as that dreamless sleep, which ... would sever the vital connection in a living animal between mind and viscera. Hope of perpetual progress toward a perfect constitution is a permissible and, indeed, necessary dream that facilitates the state's *ongoing metamorphosis* toward a condition in which the spiritual and empirical forms (of ideal state) finally converge."[22]

For Meld Shell, Kant understands political change to be an ongoing metamorphosis toward the ideal state. Along similar lines, Williams notes that the analogy between metamorphosis and political reform is useful for us today in the need to understand political change as requiring patience and gradualism.[23] He further argues that Kant resorts to an analogy between metamorphosis and political change in order to preserve a link with nature: "In favoring the analogy with metamorphosis Kant retains a connection between the understanding of a natural transition and the understanding of a social transition. Social transitions for Kant should be seen as having a natural element to them."[24] This rings especially true, as Williams reminds us, when we consider the natural constraints to our condition, namely, the facts that we are finite, fallible, and affected by emotion and our environment; all of these factors imply that we are embedded in nature and that "we still have a foot in the animal world."[25] The virtue of resorting to a natural (organism) metaphor in talking about political change, then, in both Meld Shell's and Williams's view, is to underscore this natural element in politics.[26]

We must be careful, however, not to take this analogy too far or we risk denying the role of the *a priori* ideas of right and justice for Kant's political thought. At first sight, *The Doctrine of Right* might imply a concrete interpretation of the organism analogy and we might be tempted to conclude, wrongly, that we are just another part of nature's causal chain and that therefore our behavior is also naturally determined. Williams cautions us not to overemphasize the significance of this analogy because such overemphasis introduces a strong biological determinism to politics.[27] He argues that we must resist such an interpretation, especially when we consider human beings from the practical standpoint or at the intelligible level, where they are regarded as noumena.[28] According to this standpoint, no political change will be a natural one and must take the direction implied by the *a priori* ideals of right and justice.[29]

I will explain what it means to consider human beings as noumena in moral and political discourse more fully in the next chapter. My point here is that we can read this organism analogy in a broader way, however, without downplaying or erasing the role of the *a priori* ideals of right and justice. Kant's political philosophy does not (only) consider human beings in their idealized capacities, but also as natural organisms, as beings in the world. In resorting to an organic metaphor here, we must see Kant as answering a different question than that of which *a priori* principles ought to govern our collective lives:he is answering the question of how, as naturally embedded beings, we can aim to move toward a better civil condition.

In brief, Kant uses an organic metaphor here because of what teleological language affords his political thought—namely, a theory of transition. He is showing us that the natural aspect of humanity is quite relevant to politics, and he is therefore putting forth a second political standpoint according to which we are able to envision political change in terms of our natural-cultural formation. A civil constitution for Kant is not only prescribed by *a priori* ideals of right and justice, but also represents "the highest degree of artificial improvement of the human species's good predispositions to the final end [*Zweck*] of its destiny" (*Anth/AA* 7:327). In this latter sense, a theory of our full development will have to work with how we are doing here and now, since "nature within the human being strives to lead him from culture to morality, and not (as reason prescribes) beginning with morality and its law, to lead him to a culture designed to be appropriate to morality" (*Anth/AA* 7:327–28). Thus, in a nonideal world, we have to start with where we are, first trying to describe its current state as accurately as possible, and then attempt to build a civil constitution from there. This civil constitution for Kant represents a second-best to our final end, morality.

While I generally agree with Williams that the metamorphosis analogy reminds us of the natural element in politics, I urge us to consider this analogy not only in the limited context of what it may mean for Kant's views on political change, but in broader terms. Informed by the benefits of teleological language for Kant's political philosophy, we can see that what is at stake here is also a nonideal theory concerning a *transition* to a better civil condition. In Williams's account, Kant's use of teleology cannot be taken too seriously and its role must be confined to heuristics; he writes that "both analogies [palingenesis or metamorphosis] refer to a kind of teleology that might be said to be at work in human society and history. We cannot take it for granted that such teleology is actually at work. Kant thinks *we can only impute teleology to human society for heuristic and moral purposes.*"[30] In my view, Kant's organism metaphors must be read as a part of his use of teleological language in politics and as such must be taken as rooted in the larger epistemic-metaphysical commitments of his political philosophy. Much more than being a heuristic, teleological language here helps Kant to develop a nonideal theory of human development, from a natural condition to a cultural-civil one. This language reminds us of an important aspect of political philosophy, namely, that it is neither a pure metaphysics of morals nor a deterministic physical or biological inquiry. A richer interpretation of the organism metaphors in Kant's political writings offers a developmental picture of human beings as biologically determined, emotional, fallible, and finite beings. As we are not yet perfectly rational beings, our development and activities in this very nonideal world—what we make out of nature within and outside us—matter to politics. A theorization of these contingencies by means of the principle of purposiveness constitutes a part of Kant's nonideal theory of politics.

In brief, Williams is right to point out that the language of metamorphosis and palingenesis cannot be more than analogy; otherwise Kant would become Herder or even Hegel. But I disagree with Williams's interpretation of the significance that this analogy and of the significance that teleological language hold for Kant's political thought overall. Williams eventually sides with an ideal theory of politics, emphasizing Kant's *a priori* ideals of justice and demoting teleology to a heuristic device, while I read this organic analogy, understood in connection to Kant's other teleological arguments, as part of Kant's nonideal theory. Systematically speaking, then, these analogies are not just figures that Kant happened to have on hand due to his interest in the life sciences. The teleological language at work in Kant's conceptions of social and cultural formations reminds us that political theory is not merely about the prescription of rights and institutions that best accord with *a priori* ideals of justice, but also about accurately describing current human conditions and activities, taking human beings as situated in this less-than-ideal world.

Furthermore, since "a teleological judgment compares the concept of a product of nature as it is with one of what it ought to be is" (EEKU/AA 20:240), we can see that in describing, by means of teleological language, how we may transition from a mechanistic state to a better civil condition, Kant is answering one of the questions of a nonideal theory of politics: how we can judge where we are now with respect to where we ought to be. The conception of the human being at stake in this view of political transition—one that is somewhere between a purely natural condition determined by physico-mechanistic causality and a purely rational one of autonomy in the kingdom of ends—is best captured by reflective teleological judgments. Thus, there is a deeper philosophical reason behind Kant's use of teleological language and principles in politics.

Next, I will take a closer look at the systematic reasons why Kant favors an organic, natural view of social and political formation and why he uses teleological language in describing human development from an actual natural condition to an ideal sociopolitical one. That teleology, for Kant, maintains a deeper systematic connection to political thought in general will be especially clear when we look at how he articulates, in §§82–84 of the Critique of Teleological Judgment, a cosmopolitan world order in terms of a cultural and civil formation that is our ultimate end in this world as opposed to a moral goal in and of itself. Here, we will begin to see the two pictures of political progress in the Kantian system more clearly: an ideal picture painted by the *a priori* principle of *Recht* (this is the perspective in Kant's legacy with which we are most familiar) and a nonideal picture painted by the regulative principle of *Zweckmässigkeit*, a teleological perspective that takes into account the natural embeddedness of human beings and their interactions. The former gives us the rational ideas and principles that we ought to have in mind for assessing political states and constitutions, while the latter gives us a developmental view of how we can achieve, through our own natural and cultural activities and as if by an ongoing metamorphosis, a better global civil condition. Thus, in addition to the picture of a pure republic provided by the *a priori* principles of justice (i.e., Kant's ideal theory), we will have a complementary and developmental picture of a natural-cultural formation provided by the principle of purposiveness. This second picture constitutes Kant's nonideal theory, which works with our natural embeddedness and describes how we may approach a state of freedom by means of an ongoing evolution, by taking a cultural path to political change, from a state of nature to a cosmopolitan state. I will name this use of the principle of purposiveness in Kant's political writings "political *Zweckmässigkeit*" and develop its role in his nonideal theory of politics further in the next chapters.

4

Political *Zweckmässigkeit*, or From Nature to Culture

Kant resorts to teleological judgments to underscore the role of our cultural development in achieving our political goals: this account of development is a nonideal theory of politics concerning our *transition* from where we are to where we ought to be. I have shown that Kant's analogy between organisms and ideal bodies politic in the third *Critique* provides us with an interpretive clue for how the language of teleology enriches Kant's political thought, and specifically his view of political progress and change. This quasi-organic notion of an ideal state and of its development, I have argued, also had an important role to play in the "Enlightenment" essay and in understanding Kant's preference for political reform over revolution in *The Doctrine of Right*. In this chapter, I take a closer look at the three distinct yet related roles that teleology plays in Kant's political thought, especially in §§82–84 of the third *Critique*, of the Methodology of the Critique of Teleological Judgment, where Kant rehashes some of the themes from the "Idea" essay. First, the hypothesis that nature is purposive establishes a baseline for politics by allowing us to conceptualize our freely formulated goals as *feasible*. Second, a regulatively teleological way of thinking provides us with a nonideal view of human beings, as situated between nature's mechanism and moral autonomy, as well as with a nonideal view of their transition from a state of nature to a civil society. Third, the use of teleology in these sections of the third *Critique* reminds us that our ultimate end in this world must be conceived as the highest artificial (i.e., cultural and political) construct—namely, a cosmopolitan world-whole. Thus, paying closer attention to the teleological language in Kant's formulation of a cosmopolitan world order reveals that cosmopolitanism here is a specifically cultural and political goal rather than a final moral end. I will show that the systematic significance and place of what I call Kant's principle of "political *Zweckmässigkeit*" is that it produces a nonideal theory of politics, an articulation of our cultural and civil development. A regulatively teleological view of nature allows Kant to develop a preliminary political anthropology of how we can work toward a cosmopolitan world order.

In the Critique of Teleological Judgment Kant argues that, once we use the language of teleology and find it reliable in the case of organisms, it might make sense to attempt to extend it to nature as a whole, *at least as an experiment*, to see if we can discover more than would be possible by means of merely mechanistic principles (*KU/AA* 5:398). In other words, the regulative principle of internal purposiveness, which we use for judging organisms' inner structure, further provides us with an occasion to use teleological language as a test in our investigation of nature as a whole. Here, through my analysis of Kant's experiments in the third *Critique* with the usefulness of teleology for politics, I will show that in this work he articulates a robust notion of "political *Zweckmässigkeit*," a principle of political philosophy that is ultimately grounded in the principle of *external* or *relative purposiveness*, a hypothetical and pragmatic extension of internal purposiveness that we use in the case of judging organisms.

In §§82–84 of the *Critique of Judgment* Kant discusses civil society and theorizes human beings as phenomena, natural organisms endowed with the capacity of reason or as animals endowed with rationality—and not primarily as noumena or as ideal rational agents. Thus, starting with the hypothetical or regulative teleological assertion that nature as a whole is purposive for our goals, Kant develops a theory of human nature as well as an account of how we transition from the state of nature to that of culture and civil society. As a result, we see that Kant's political philosophy acknowledges the important role of a theory of human nature and development, of cultural anthropology, for articulating plausible political ideals and how we can achieve them. This, I will show, is a preliminary political anthropology and must be construed as a part of his nonideal theory of politics.

Furthermore, the term "cosmopolitan world order" as it comes up in this text must be understood as the name of the intermediate state of cultural development or as the name of the political condition that Kant thinks is most conducive to moral progress. Such a peculiar, culturally-coded condition will *prepare* us for morality and is the empirical staging ground for moral development, but it is not, in the way that Kant conceptualizes it here by means a teleological view of nature, an egalitarian-moral goal in itself and not a direct consequence or derivative of Kant's moral principles. This means that to think that a cosmopolitan world order is primarily a moral ideal is a mistaken assumption stemming from our contemporary sensibilities: especially in the third *Critique*, a cosmopolitan world-whole is posited as a cultural-political goal that names our transition from a state of nature to a civil society and is primarily a goal about developing our innate skills and dispositions in a certain way. Furthermore, our development from a natural condition toward an eventual cosmopolitan one both requires inequalities among peoples and proposes industry to be that development's leading force. Kant's conceptualization of the cosmopolitan civil condition here prioritizes and is modelled after a certain European way of life, one that takes only particular kinds of cultural activities (e.g., labor and industry) as suitable for inclusion in a cosmopolitan world-whole while excluding others. The view of cultural and civil development that Kant presents here is Eurocentric and thus limited.

In brief, my account of the role that teleology plays in these political sections of the third *Critique* further shows that, systematically speaking, Kant's political thought consists not only of his ideal moral and legal theory but also requires a nonideal theory, one that provides descriptions of ourselves and our activities here and now *from a pragmatic point of view*. What I call Kant's nonideal theory of political anthropology is similar to what Zöller calls the geo-anthropological basis of Kant's political thought.[1] However, while Zöller exclusively locates this basis in his writings on history and anthropology, or what he calls "the natural history of reason in Kant as opposed to the critical theory of reason,"[2] I find just such a geo-anthropological discourse in the third *Critique*—a work that is part of Kant's central critical project. While Kant's own political anthropology turns out to be Eurocentric, the Kantian insight that anthropology matters to politics is an important one that broadens our understanding of political philosophy. It is only when we are reminded of this important insight that we can move on to incorporate diverse and multiple nonideal theories or anthropologies into our political visions.

From Organisms to Nature as a Whole: External and Political *Zweckmässigkeit*

Patrick Riley argues that Kant's political philosophy must be integrated into his critical system via a theory of ends, or by means of what he calls "a radically teleological reading of all of Kant."[3] In this systematic account, while Riley correctly distinguishes internal ("strong") from external ("weak") purposiveness and shows that Kant's political thought makes use of the latter, he does not adequately address how the purposiveness of an organism or of nature differs from purposiveness in politics.[4] This leads Elisabeth Ellis to question the utility of even a weak teleological language in politics, for she takes this language to dogmatically imply "a working assumption of nature's lawfulness" at best or a strong language of nature's purposes at worst.[5] In a related vein, Howard Williams claims that Kant uses teleology for moral and heuristic purposes only and that if we take his teleological language too seriously we risk reducing politics to biology.[6]

CHAPTER 4

It is far from my aim here to reduce politics to biology or to claim that natural or teleological considerations have primacy over others in Kant's politics. I will, however, respond to these authors' stated ambiguities about the specific benefits of teleology for Kant's political thought by offering a systematic reconstruction of political *Zweckmässigkeit* as developed and used in the Critique of the Teleological Judgment. This reconstruction will demonstrate that one real benefit of this principle for politics is that it allows us to judge nature as a whole to be externally purposive for our free goals and purposes. To put this in stronger terms: we cannot have political discourse in Kant's critical philosophy without the baseline assumption that nature is not just a mechanism but is at least receptive to our freely designed social and cultural goals. This type of purposiveness must be understood as a "weak" one, but it is neither used solely as a heuristic for moral purposes nor does it reduce Kant's politics to biology.

In the second half of the third *Critique*, in the Critique of Teleological Judgment, Kant argues that organisms provide natural science with *the basis for a critical teleology of nature*, that is, a hypothetical indication of the purposiveness of nature as a whole (*KU/AA* 5:380). Because we are justified in making reflective teleological judgments about organisms and because we have gained so much from teleological language in our study of such beings, we can take the inner purposiveness of organisms as a *clue* or *guideline* (*Leitfaden*) for inquiring whether or not nature as a whole is also organized in a purposive manner. This extension of teleological inquiry into the broader realm of nature as a whole is experimental, or a test (*Versuch*) at best (*KU/AA* 5:379) because it is a hypothetical and pragmatic extension. The principle of reflective judgments of nature as a whole is not the internal but rather the *external* or *relative* principle of purposiveness.

External, or relative, purposiveness indicates a relationship of *usefulness* between human beings and other natural objects or a relationship of *advantageousness* among other organisms (*KU/AA* 5:367). Kant's examples of relative-external purposiveness in §63 include the relationship between a natural end and a natural object: rivers carrying nutrients for plants and thus increasing the *usefulness* of land for human beings; and the *advantageousness* of sandy soil for pine trees; of grass for cattle, sheep, and horses; of saltwort for camels; and of these and other herbivorous animals for wolves, tigers, and lions (*KU/AA* 5:368).[7]

Before I proceed, it is necessary to relate a few important axioms about the epistemic status and utility of the principle of external purposiveness. First, the fact that we may use teleological language when referring to nature as a whole does not mean that nature is a giant organism. The extended use of purposiveness does not refer to the inner organization of nature as a whole, but rather to whether or not nature is suitable for our goals. Therefore, it is not the case that we have concluded or proven that nature as a whole *is* purposive or sets purposes for us. This principle is not constitutive of nature as a whole *a priori*—it is not the transcendental condition of its possibility. As I showed in the previous chapter, it involves a subjective commitment to judging nature. Second, as Kant explains in §75, the ground of the distinction between the internal principle of objective purposiveness and the external or relative principle of objective *Zweckmässigkeit* is that the latter may be used as a guideline for the study of nature as a whole, but only if it proves *useful* for the inquiry at hand, not because it is an absolutely necessary or indispensable principle. (*KU/AA* 5:398). This is what it means for this principle to be a regulative one.

The external principle of purposiveness gives us a guideline or a hypothetical indication of purposes (*KU/AA* 5:379) and reminds us of the contingency of the arrangement of nature for our intellect (*KU/AA* 5:406). Just as it was useful to resort to an organisms analogy in talking about an ideal body politic or about political change, it might prove useful to envision nature as a whole as purposive in talking about our political goals. For these reasons, we must understand the extended use of teleology in the "weak" sense as it is contrasted with the "strong" sense of the internal purposiveness of organisms. Contrary to Ellis's claim, furthermore, this use of teleology does not amount to a strong or deterministic view of human actions. Rather, it offers the baseline assumption that nature is more than a mechanism and that there is a correspondence between our goals and nature.

Kant claims that the guiding principle of a teleological world-whole is useful for positing a unity or a system of nature (*KU/AA* 5:417–19). In other words, a teleological conceptualization of the world-whole provided by the extended use of the principle of purposiveness, is useful for research in natural science in that it promises us something more than a mere mechanistic view of nature: a system (*KU/AA* 5:417–19). Likewise, an external purposiveness between nature and our goals provides a useful regulative maxim for political philosophy for it at least allows us to see human beings and bodies politic as more than mere machines, as similar to organic wholes or systems. It is not immediately clear, however, what other kinds of specific benefits political philosophy acquires from making use of a teleological guiding principle. The point that remains to be made, then, is that political discourse does indeed benefit from a teleological and therefore a developmental view of nature.

CHAPTER 4

The Usefulness of Political *Zweckmässigkeit* in §§82–84 of the Third *Critique*

Kant's reliance on teleology in history and politics in the "Idea" essay as well as in §83 of the third *Critique* makes the claim that human progress has two stages. In both texts Kant describes human history as moving naturally toward a cultural maturation first—a transition from nature to culture, as it were. We see this stage demonstrated in the "Idea" essay in his claim that the "human being is an animal, which, when it lives among others of its species, has need of a master" ("IaG"/*AA* 8:23) and in his insistence that it is nature's aim, not ours, that culminates in a cosmopolitan condition, for such a condition is basically a state of equilibrium that brings our unsociable sociability temporarily to a halt ("IaG"/*AA* 8:26–28).[8] While this may at first seem to make a cosmopolitan world order a dogmatic goal, brought about not by our freely willed actions but by a cunning of nature, I have already shown in chapter 2 that we must read this claim as a part of Kant's nonideal theory of political history, that is, as providing a compelling narrative that will help us to orient ourselves in the midst of contingent historical events so that we can articulate our collective political goals. Next, in the second stage of human history, culture becomes the vehicle through which we can further develop as rational and moral agents: here, the supposed transition from culture to freedom is still teleological, but it takes the form of an ongoing approximation from a given cultural condition to an ideal moral one ("IaG"/*AA* 8:21 and 26). Allen Wood aptly dubs these two stages of human development the "epoch of nature" and the "epoch of freedom": the former refers to the culmination of natural mechanisms promoting cultural progress toward a cosmopolitan union; the latter is characterized by the moral progress brought about by human freedom.[9]

In §§82–84 of the third *Critique* Kant rehashes his two-stage account of human development and also demonstrates the epistemic and practical utility of the principle of *Zweckmässigkeit* by providing a transitional theory regarding our political lives.[10] He relies on the use of teleology to articulate how best to construct a cultural and civil condition together, given that we are earthbound creatures with less-than-noble natural inclinations. That is, insofar as the transition from the epoch of nature to the epoch of freedom is an important issue that political philosophy must address, teleological language is necessary to give an account of such a transition in Kantian terms. Kant shows that the view provided by the principle of purposiveness is in fact quite useful for politics in answering fundamental political questions about how we may work toward our collective goals here and now. In sum, the systematic significance of the principle of *Zweckmässigkeit* for Kant's political thought lies in helping him to theorize about precisely this transition.

In the Methodology of the Teleological Judgment, Kant provides examples of various applications of teleological judgment, and these applications include a case study in the principle of political *Zweckmässigkeit*. Specifically, §§82–84 show that the success of the application of this principle must be according to two criteria: first, on the basis of whether or not an externally purposive conceptualization of nature answers more questions for politics than a mechanistic conceptualization does; and second, on the extent to which the view afforded by this principle is capable of producing feasible political goals for real-world circumstances. Teleological judgments are reflective judgments which ascend from particulars to universals, and Kant here starts with the particular natural, cultural, social, and historical conditions in which we find ourselves. As a result, Kant produces a more realistic description of human nature, or a theory that takes into consideration the material contingencies of human nature and development. This account of our transition from nature to freedom is part of Kant's nonideal theory of politics.

In Ellis's view, §§82–84 of the third *Critique* are incompatible with the rest of Kant's political theory due to their strong teleological language.[11] Although in Kant's assessment we need an assumption that nature is on our side, Ellis claims that this is unnecessary, for it is sufficient to assert that, if one aims to be a rationally acting being, one must pursue goals determined by reason.[12] The political question at stake in these sections of the third *Critique*, however, is not whether or not we must pursue goals determined by reason; Kant is clear that we must do so, for nature cannot set any goals for us. The political question here is whether, in pursuing our rational goals, we can count on being able to bring them about even when our experience is inconclusive on this matter. This is the question that a teleological worldview, adduced by the principle of political *Zweckmässigkeit*, answers more sufficiently than a merely mechanistic view. A mechanistic view requires mathematical formulas about human interactions and a hard determinism, as it were, with respect to the choices of quasi-rational agents such as ourselves. Such a view is neither appropriate nor useful for political philosophy and Kant acknowledges it; this is why he resorts to a teleological language in describing an ideal political condition in the "Enlightenment" essay as well as earlier in the third *Critique*, as I have argued in chapter 3.

The main issue here seems to be that both Ellis and Williams take a teleological-historical account of political progress to be incompatible with an account of freely willed human action as a causal force in history, for they seem to take teleology to imply a natural determinism.[13] This would be true if the principle of purposiveness for Kant were a constitutive principle of nature and teleological judgments determinate ones. The dichotomy in Kant's critical philosophy, however, is located not between teleology and free will but between the mechanism of nature and the freedom of human beings, and the use of teleology as a regulative principle is one way to consider these two as coherent. Indeed, Kant resorts to the teleological perspective in order to bring together nature and freedom in a "way of thinking" (*Denkungsart*) (*KU/AA* 5:176).[14] My point here is that rather than posing problems for free agency or establishing a dogmatic view of nature, teleology is in fact invoked to solve many problems raised by Kant's political philosophy, specifically those pertaining to issues of transition to a better political condition, as I show in what follows.

For What Purpose Does the Human Being Exist? The Ultimate End of Nature and Political *Zweckmässigkeit*

In §82, Kant asks whether or not there is an ultimate end (*letzte Zweck*) of nature, a natural end or an organism for which everything else would be a means (*KU/AA* 5:425). Seen from the perspective of a mechanistic nature or based only on our experience, he contends that we cannot answer this question (*KU/AA* 5:426). Experience clearly shows that when it comes to human beings "nature has not made the least exception to its generative as well as destructive powers, but has rather subjected them to its mechanism without any end" (*KU/AA* 5:427). Figuring out the ultimate end of nature, then, is not possible based solely on experience, and to claim that the human being exists as the ultimate end of nature would therefore be dogmatic. Human beings are organisms, and as such are internally purposive, but it is far from being the case that nature as a whole is purposive *for them* (*KU/AA* 5:427).

If a mechanistic conceptualization of nature is all we have for answering the question of the ultimate end of our lives, then there is no way to propose a plan or a purpose for the coexistence of human beings: there will be no passageway to a civil state, let alone to freedom or morality. On this view, we have no reason to think that nature did us a favor. In fact, we have in front of us "every appearance of the products of wild, all-powerful forces of a nature working in a chaotic state" (*KU/AA* 5:427). A mechanistic conceptualization of nature does not allow us to envision a society in which human beings can coexist peacefully under their own laws—such a conceptualization is more appropriate for a monarchy ruled by a despot, as we saw in the case of Kant's hand mill analogy earlier. Without a different perspective on nature and our place within it, it seems as if we are destined to live under the capricious and destructive reign of a chaotic nature or an authoritarian despot. In other words, if a mechanistic conception of nature and politics is all that we have, it seems as if we are forever doomed to a despotic regime at best or a state of nature at worst, with no possible way to imagine why or how we should leave these conditions behind. If we can give a satisfactory answer to the question of the ultimate end of nature, however, we might be able to conceptualize an alternative way in which we ourselves become responsible for working ourselves out of such undesirable circumstances. The question regarding the ultimate end of nature, therefore, has political significance.

Furthermore, the important political question of how to organize our collective lives in relation to one another in the Kantian system does not even make sense in the terms of a mechanistic view of the relationship between nature and human beings—until we presuppose, hypothetically, that nature as a whole is purposive for our goals and that we are at the top of the chain of nature. While from a mechanistic point of view it would be dogmatic to claim that the human being is the ultimate end of nature, we are allowed this claim from a regulatively purposive view of nature. According to this latter perspective, we are qualified to be the ultimate ends, or as Kant puts it, "the titular lords of nature" (*KU/AA* 5:431), because we are the only natural organisms capable of setting ends and organizing these ends into a system.

Note, however, that this view construes human beings as a part of nature, not as idealized rational agents of a moral order, and here nature is understood to be more than a mere machine. Thanks to political *Zweckmässigkeit*, then, we can start with the hypothesis that nature as a whole is purposive for us, judge the relationship between human beings and nature to be purposive for each other, and assert that the chain of natural ends in this world stops at the human being. This view—one that allows us to claim that human beings are the only natural creatures qualified to have anything to do with the ultimate end of nature (*KU/AA* 5:429)—is preferable for its usefulness in articulating answers to the political question, "For what purpose does the human being exist?" By taking the human being to be a part of nature but more than a machine, the principle of political *Zweckmässigkeit* lays the groundwork for articulating answers about our collective ends in this world.

Whatever our ultimate goals ought to be, they cannot come from nature; they must be given by our own end-setting capacities and must take into account our natural situatedness. Ellis is right to point out that "a naturally given set of necessary ends toward which human action unconsciously and inexorably moves" cannot have any place in politics[15]—but this is not Kant's claim. Rather, his claim is that unless we view nature as a whole and our place in it teleologically, we do not have a conceptualization of ourselves as end-setting beings whose goals are supported by nature. Political theory, to be successful at all, must minimally presuppose this as a starting point and it must do so by reference to human beings understood as earthbound creatures with goals.

Human beings are organisms considered from the point of view of nature; however, from another perspective they are also "final ends" or rational agents that are ends in themselves, i.e., noumena. Furthermore, workings of politics include questions of the lawful organization of the relationships among *freely acting human beings insofar as they are also part of nature*. The fact that Kant's politics deals with human beings not only as free agents but also as naturally situated beings already anticipates and undermines Ellis's and others' critiques of teleology. Ellis argues that, for Kant, freely-willed human action has been the motor of progress throughout history.[16] However, as my earlier reading of the "Idea" and the "Enlightenment" essays shows, nature within and outside us is the responsible force at work in historical and cultural progress, at least until we reach a point in our cultural condition in which we can also develop as rational and moral agents. In other words, Ellis provides an ideal theory perspective, starting with an ideal condition in which we are already rational agents simply trying to implement our ideals in our civil life. A teleological consideration of politics, by contrast, provides a nonideal theory perspective, which starts with the natural, historical, and cultural conditions in which we actually find ourselves.

The Human Being between Nature and Freedom in §§82–84 of the *Critique of Judgment*

In the Introduction to the *Critique of Judgment*, Kant casts the problem of the gap between nature and freedom in terms of a great chasm between mechanistic causality, which we must presuppose for the advancement of the natural sciences, and freedom, which we must presuppose for the advancement of morality. He writes,

> The concept of freedom determines nothing in regard to the theoretical cognition of nature; the concept of nature likewise determines nothing in regard to the practical laws of freedom: *it is to this extent not possible to throw a bridge from one domain to the other* [es ist insofern nicht möglich, eine Brücke

von einem Gebiete zu dem andern hinüberzuschlagen] (*KU/AA* 5:195, emphases added).

Following this assertion, however, Kant goes on to claim that if we were able to find a being in nature which embodied the concept of *causality through freedom* (*Causalität durch Freiheit*), that is, a being whose actions could be construed both from the perspective of freedom and from the perspective of natural causality, then we would be able to throw a bridge from one domain to the other (*KU/AA* 5:195–96).[17]

While practical reason postulates that the human being is a final end (i.e., an autonomous subject), theoretical reason insists that we are subordinated to the mechanistic laws of nature just like any other being. Thus, while from the perspective of morality the human being is a free person with rights and duties, from the perspective of knowledge we are just like any other natural object. The *Critique of Judgment* shows that these two perspectives, which refer to one and the same subject, can only be unified in a regulatively teleological conceptualization of the world together with our place in it. This way of thinking (*Denkungsart*) about the world, therefore, proves that it is *possible* to throw a bridge, albeit a tentative one, from the domain of freedom to the domain of nature, and that this bridge can be articulated in terms of the efforts of human beings in this world as natural and not yet fully moral beings (*KU/AA* 5:176).

We already know that freedom and mechanism are not incompatible in Kant's critical system. The idea that every action of human beings is completely determined by mechanistic causality corresponds to the Antithesis of the Third Antinomy in the *Critique of Pure Reason* (see esp. *KrV* A445–51/B473–79). In the resolution of this antinomy, Kant shows that legislation through freedom and legislation through causality within one and the same domain are *logically compatible*.[18] It is in the third *Critique*, especially in the notion of the human being as acting according to a *causality through freedom*, that we find out exactly how this logical compatibility or possibility plays out in the real world. The perspective afforded to us by the principle of purposiveness reveals the coexistence of freedom and causality in the human being. While there is no experiential basis for referring to human beings as purposive (*zweckmässig*), Kant argues that viewing human beings and their place in nature *in a regulatively teleological way* would help us to gain the ground to talk about an ultimate end, and would allow us to further conjecture that the purposes of human beings are supported by nature. In other words, by adding purposiveness to our conceptualization of mechanistic nature, we can now answer the question of why human beings, as the kinds of organisms they are, *ought* to exist, the question that Kant investigates in §84.

Between Ultimate and Final Ends of Nature: *Geschicklichkeit*

When we consider the human being as noumenon or as an ideal rational agent in the language of Kant's moral philosophy or ideal theory, we cannot even ask for what end or purpose she ought to exist. It is immediately clear that her existence contains the highest end in herself, due to the fact that she can, as a free agent of morality, subordinate the whole of nature teleologically to her free will and law-giving (*KU/AA* 5:435). This is to say that human beings ought to be understood as ends in themselves. In this view, we are the final end (*Endzweck*), or as Kant puts it in §84, "that end which needs no other as the condition of its possibility" (*KU/AA* 5:434). The question then becomes: If we are both the ultimate and the final ends of nature, what must we do with our lives, here and now? What is the highest good on earth that we ought to accomplish? In other words, "As the particular kind of organisms that the human beings are, for what purpose ought they to exist?"

These are, once again, political questions, and what is more, they cannot be fully answered by merely stating that we are the final ends of nature or that we are, as noumena, also intelligible beings. The "ought" in the question, "For what purpose ought the human being to exist?," seeks a more specific answer than what morality is capable of giving, in that it asks us to give a goal that we can pursue in this world, here and now. Our collective purposes should reflect our duality in this world, where we exist both as end-setting organisms and free agents. Our ultimate end furthermore must be something that would bring us closer to being final ends. As such, Kant states that this goal must fulfill two conditions: it must be a goal to which we ourselves can contribute, and a goal that a teleological nature can support (*KU/AA* 5:430).

Kant here considers happiness (*Glückseligkeit*) as a possibility for a goal that specifies what we ought to do given our dual nature and immediately rejects it. Happiness, understood as the complete satisfaction of all our desires, cannot be the ultimate end (*letzte Zweck*) since this is clearly neither a purpose to which we ourselves can contribute—given the empirical insatiability of human beings and the destructive effects of nature itself—nor an end that can be pursued by rational and free agents. According to Kant, happiness is a state of fulfilling certain ends that change rapidly from one moment to another and is better attained by instincts and inclinations (*KU/AA* 5:430). If we presume that nature had a purpose in giving us a rational capacity, our end cannot be the pursuit of happiness, for instinct would do a better job of securing this purpose, making reason counter-purposive.[19]

Setting aside happiness, Kant describes the ultimate goal of our lives as "the formal, subjective condition, namely the aptitude for setting himself ends at all and [. . .] using nature as a means appropriate to the maxims of his free ends in general" (*KU/AA* 5:431). This is called "culture" (*Kultur*). Kant writes,

> The production of the aptitude of a rational being for any ends in general (thus those of his freedom) is culture. Thus only culture can be the ultimate end that one has cause to ascribe to nature in regard to the human species (not its own earthly happiness or even merely being the foremost instrument for establishing order and consensus in irrational nature outside him). (*KU/AA* 5:431)

Culture has two components: a culture of discipline (*Kultur der Zucht [Disziplin]*) and a culture of skill (*Geschicklichkeit*). The former type of culture is one of training and refers to the activities by means of which we can overcome our innate unsociability and cultivate practices that liberate our will from the despotism of our desires, from "being a slave to the passions." This type of training would include developing a good taste for the arts and forming good habits of conduct. This is in a sense a preparation of our sensible nature for rationality and as Kant himself acknowledges it is a necessary but insufficient step toward morality (*KU AA*, 5:431–33 and 299–300).[20] The latter type of culture, the culture of skill, is a social-cultural set of activities by means of which we can develop our rational end-setting capacities to their fullest extent in order to come closer to being final ends of nature (*KU/AA* 5:431). By "culture," then, Kant does not only mean what we would today understand by it, incorporating things that pertain to the arts, letters, or manners; rather, it should be taken in a more general sense as the process by means of which human beings leave their mark in the world, as their ways of life.

Geschicklichkeit is a broader term that functions as the condition for the possibility of further moral development.[21] Rather than being a mechanism of nature's purposes that precludes any meaningful voluntary action, as Ellis claims,[22] *Geschicklichkeit* is the name of the aptitude through which human beings may use nature as a means to their ends in order to make something out of it, that is, in order to shape their surroundings under the direction of goals that they themselves posit. The idea of a "culture of skill," therefore, is the specific goal that brings together our duality: it is generated by the principle of political *Zweckmässigkeit*, which posits that nature is purposive for human freedom, and thus encapsulates a possible reciprocity between our free actions and nature.

In other words, the only end that merits being considered the ultimate end of both nature and human beings is "what nature is capable of doing in order to prepare [*vorzubereiten*] human beings for what they themselves must do in order to be a final end [*Endzweck*]" (*KU/AA* 5:431). This means that human beings are the ultimate end of nature *if and only if* they are also a final end of freedom. The idea that we are both the ultimate end of nature and the final end of freedom, an idea based on the regulative use of the principle of purposiveness, leads Kant to conclude that the ultimate goal of a purposive nature would coincide with the final goal of humanity in a cultural condition in which human beings are able to actualize their own free ends. To establish such a cultural condition, we have to develop our culture of skill (*Geschicklichkeit*). The activities of a culture of skill amount to working in and through nature by means of freedom, and therefore, to an alignment between nature and freedom in the actions of human beings: the arena of this alignment is what Kant calls *Kultur*.

Here I agree with Riley that *Kultur* is the bridge between nature and freedom;[23] however, I would state this claim a bit more cautiously and tentatively. Riley's argument is that a teleological reading of Kant's critical system as a whole solves various interpretive problems in his political thought, whereas my claim is that Kant's principle of political *Zweckmässigkeit* allows him to produce a largely nonideal theory of politics in §§82–84 of the third *Critique*—in this instance, a theory of cultural development. In my account, this principle allows us to posit a minimal sense of correspondence between our free actions and a deterministic nature, and furthermore to articulate a specific cultural goal that will help to support our political ideals. We are in the domain of Kant's nonideal theory here, because he is *describing* traits and activities by means of which we can develop our skills as beings situated between nature and freedom, not *prescribing* ideals toward which we should work.

In sum, working with a notion of human beings as situated between a state of nature determined by mechanistic causality and a state of freedom in which they act freely, Kant brings in a reflective teleological judgment to articulate what ultimate and final ends we can propose for the organization of our collective lives. While the form of this judgment is teleological, the content of it is a specific kind of cultural-civil condition, a lawful civil society in a cosmopolitan world order. In other words, in this text we only arrive at Kant's idea of a cosmopolitan world order by first positing a regulatively teleological view of human nature and culture. Furthermore, this is not a purely moral ideal; cosmopolitanism comes up here as a stopgap measure for ongoing wars and necessary inequalities in the world, as I show next.

The Role of War and Inequality in Kant's Account of Cultural Development

In §83 of the third *Critique*, Kant assigns war and social inequality important roles in his account of cultural development,[24] and the fact that cultural or political progress necessitates conflict for him suggests that a civil society, together with the requirement for a cosmopolitan world order, are not in his terms primarily moral ideals. He proposes that cultural advancement requires a certain type of bifurcation in society between a majority and a minority; as he writes, "skill cannot be very well developed in the human race except by means of inequality among people" (*KU/AA* 5:432). In Kant's model of this two-class society, people in the majority produce the necessary elements of culture, science, and art, and oppress the minority. Such social antagonisms and bifurcations originate from our unsociable sociability, and this type of social conflict, while it may not lead to an all-out war, causes friction between the two classes in terms of their goals. Thus, in the first instance it is out of necessity and not out of moral considerations that we will have to leave this state behind.

Kant writes that, after a while, problems start to develop on both sides and such a bitter existence becomes unsustainable. Those in the majority grow dissatisfied with themselves, and those who are maintained in a state of oppression, bitter work, and little enjoyment, start to get tired of the violence imposed on them by the majority (*KU/AA* 5:432-34). This miserable condition is seen by Kant as the *facilitator* by means of which we can develop our skills to their fullest extent and eventually accomplish the ultimate end of nature. As unpleasant and miserable as this condition might be, it is to be celebrated, because it is

> bound up with the development of the natural predispositions [*Naturanlagen*] in the human race, and the end of nature itself, even if it is not our end, is hereby attained. The formal condition under which alone nature can attain this its final aim is that constitution in the relations of human beings with one another in which the abuse of reciprocally conflicting freedom is opposed by lawful power in a whole [*gesetzmässige Gewalt in einem Ganzen*], which is called civil society [*bürgerliche Gesellschaft*]; for only in this can the greatest development of the natural predispositions [*Naturanlagen*] occur. (*KU/AA* 5:432-33)

Human beings will work themselves out of these miserable conditions of inequality and war by developing their skills and will reach a lawful civil order, which should be constituted such that the freedoms of each person

CHAPTER 4

and of the state are guaranteed. For nature to attain this ultimate end of making sure that we develop our skills fully, we need to enter into a civil society, which in turn necessitates a cosmopolitan world order.

Kant here goes on to say that war "is a deeply hidden but perhaps intentional effort of supreme wisdom if not to establish then at least to prepare the way for the lawfulness together with the freedom of the states" (*KU/AA* 5:433). This view may strike us as odd; indeed, Ellis describes the section of the third *Critique* that glorifies war and inequality as "especially distasteful" since here Kant seems to be precluding any meaningful voluntary action and glorifying war as a necessary preparation for an international lawful condition.[25] However, when we interpret this passage in terms of the regulative guiding principle of politics that nature is purposive for our goals, we can see that all that Kant is claiming here is that aspects of our current nonideal circumstances (such as ongoing wars) will eventually motivate us to do what we ought to do, not that we ought to do what nature sets for us as a goal. Remember that Kant is describing where we find ourselves here and now—in Wood's terms, in the "epoch of nature," and giving an account of our pathological-natural tendencies.

While our unsociably sociable inclinations will lead us to endless wars, it is by means of the same selfish and yet natural inclinations that we will also eventually come to realize that wars are too costly and counterproductive for our purposes, and as a result we will start working toward establishing peace, first through a civil society, and then through a "cosmopolitan world-whole [*weltbürgerliches Ganze*]" (*KU/AA* 5:432–33).[26] These phases of civil society and then a cosmopolitan world order are the result of the full development of our capacities and nature's end, if not immediately our own. That is, if we look at the present conditions of social conflicts and antagonisms in which we find ourselves, we come to realize that it is not in our interest to continue these wars and that we should put an end to them and unite around a civil order.

It should be clear from the above analysis that the requirement of a lawful constitution of states for Kant does *not* arise out of moral considerations; rather, such a civil society can be conceived as the end of cultural development only when we judge nature as a whole and judge the relationships between human beings in teleological terms. The requirement of a cosmopolitan world order comes along with the critical-regulative teleological presupposition that the ultimate end of nature is the complete development of all of the innate capacities of human beings. This teleological presupposition, we should remember, is based on the principle of external purposiveness. Thus, "a cosmopolitan world order" is not an egalitarian moral goal dictated by Kant's ideal theory, but only the step toward morality, a step that describes a specific cultural and civil condition as the culmination of our natural development through inequality and conflict. In other words, by means of a nonideal theory approach Kant claims that we will indeed work toward establishing the ideal conditions of right and justice, not primarily through moral incentives but through natural-pathological incentives.[27]

For Kant, culture by itself does not make us moral beings: it *prepares* us to be moral agents by means of providing opportunities to discipline our sensibility by means of arts and letters as well as to develop our skills by means of inequality and conflict.[28] In the end, only by means of a culture of skill (*Geschicklichkeit*) can we hope to create a cultural backdrop in which we can also eventually develop as moral agents, and perhaps at a later time the mere cultural and civil condition of cosmopolitanism will give rise to a moral one. At this point, however, Kant is articulating the cultural background of cosmopolitanism not as a moral egalitarian ideal, but mainly as a stopgap measure for the social inequalities that are supposed to foster the full development of our skills. Thus, the culture that Kant favors in §83 of the third *Critique*, a lawful civil society in a cosmopolitan world order, should be conceived of as the medium in which we transition from the epoch of nature to the epoch of freedom, a medium that, while providing the basis for an eventual moral community, does not in itself arise out of moral considerations.

Kant's proposed cosmopolitan cultural condition favors the development of skills in a climate characterized by activity (rather than passivity) and inequality (rather than equality); and furthermore, in both cases, he positions the ultimate end of human existence against happiness. Next, I will show that the vision for a cosmopolitan world order that leads him to reject happiness here implicitly presupposes a particular understanding of what counts as the right kind of culture. Kant's vision does not support or even propose a diversity of cultural models or ways of life, but only one specific culture of skill (*Geschicklichkeit*) combined with a culture of discipline, and his model has a distinctly European bent. Thus, the cultural anthropology that he articulates here by means of his regulatively teleological notion of human cultural development and as a part of his nonideal theory of politics is embedded in a Eurocentric view of culture.

Culture and Happiness: Kant's Eurocentric Political Anthropology

In Kant's terms, "not every kind of culture is adequate for the ultimate end of nature"; what's more, I will show that what he calls a culture of skill

CHAPTER 4

(*Geschicklichkeit*), the form of culture that he deems to be the most adequate and appropriate one for building a cosmopolitan world order, refers to a particular kind of activity that has to do with the full development of our abilities and talents. This presumes a way of life that Kant contrasts with and prioritizes over others that prize passivity or mere happiness. In his regulatively teleological construction of cultural development, then, Kant inserts into his nonideal theory a certain idea of what counts as a set of desirable cultural and civil aptitudes, those which enable a specific kind of transition from a state of nature to a civil state. Kant's own view of cultural development is thus far from neutral: it prioritizes activity over passivity because it is modelled after a Western and European way of life. In other words, it is on the basis of a European model that Kant excludes happiness and enjoyment from being meaningful cultural goals, and in this way he also excludes any way of life or culture that prioritizes happiness from the cosmopolitan world order.

Kant's rejection of happiness as a moral goal is well known from the *Groundwork of the Metaphysics of Morals*, in which he puts forth a philosophical basis for a pure and ideal theory of morals by abstracting away from the worldly and natural concerns of morality (*GMS/AA* 4:388–90). Happiness seems to be too worldly; it may be a natural end goal in that all organisms try to attain their welfare, but it is best left to instinct (*GMS/AA* 4:395). Since Kant is interested in founding a morality on pure practical reason, a natural goal belonging to instinct will have no place in it. Pure practical reason must be aimed at producing an unconditionally good will to motivate action, which ought to be moral regardless of whether or not it results in happiness. (*GMS/AA* 4:395–97). Thus, from the perspective of an ideal theory of ethics, which many scholars agree that the *Groundwork* provides,[29] it makes sense for Kant to exclude happiness from being a relevant goal for morality, understood here as a system of practical reason.

His reasons for rejecting happiness in the political anthropology sections of the third *Critique* that I have highlighted are different. We find him rejecting happiness this time as a cultural goal; and here, his rejection has to do not with the proper task of practical reason but with his endorsement of a particular kind of cultural activity and development. He is not providing an account of our moral development from the transcendental perspective as he did in the *Groundwork* but from an anthropological perspective, and in this account, he assigns happiness or enjoyment less than zero value. He writes,

> It is easy to decide what sort of value life has for us it if is assessed merely by what one enjoys (the natural end of the sum of all inclinations,

happiness). Less than zero: for who would start life anew under the same conditions, or even according to a new and self-designed plan (but one still in accord with the course of nature), which would, however, still be aimed merely at enjoyment? (*KU/AA* 5:434n)

Here, he states explicitly that life spent on mere enjoyment is a waste of our capacities because, even if it is our own plan or decision to spend our time aiming at happiness, this form of existence is exactly what nature wants of us and therefore has less than zero value.

Kant dismisses those forms of life prioritizing enjoyment in various places in the third *Critique*, but especially during an important discussion of why it is necessary that human beings exist in §67. Prefiguring his discussion of the ultimate and final ends of nature, here Kant expresses a concern about being able to identify a final end of nature. Similar to his claim in §84, he argues that we cannot really locate a final, unconditioned end *in* nature: everything in nature must be explained by means of physico-mechanistic laws, and these laws give us only conditioned ends. While we can ask and answer, albeit regulatively, for what purpose a plant or an animal exists, we cannot do the same for human beings as natural beings. Kant continues, "Yet one does not see why it is necessary that human beings exist (a question which, if one thinks about the New Hollanders or the Fuegians, might not be so easy to answer)" (*KU/AA* 5:378). The question of why humans ought to exist is not answerable from a physico-mechanistic point of view, according to which we are just cogs in the mechanism of nature. The simple point here is that the final, unconditioned end of human existence cannot be found in nature. However, Kant for some reason adds here that the question of the final purpose of our existence is even harder to ponder when we consider the activities of human beings like the New Hollanders (an eighteenth-century name for the indigenous peoples of Australia), and the Fuegians (referring to the indigenous inhabitants of Tierra del Fuego in Argentina)—in other words, peoples outside of European culture or civilization.

The implication here is that these non-European peoples' existence does not seem to contribute to any cultural or moral end, as far as Kant can see, for they do not seem to engage in a culture of skill and, presumably, their way of life prioritizes happiness or mere enjoyment. At the very least, the underlying presupposition in Kant's specific remarks about the "New Hollanders" and "Fuegians" is that there is such a radical difference between the cultural contributions of these non-European peoples and the Europeans that Kant feels the need to specify that the question of our final end is especially hard to answer when we think of those non-European aboriginal peoples' existence.[30] It is not only the case that

CHAPTER 4

human existence has no purpose; there is something about indigenous forms of living that makes it harder for Kant to conceive or ponder what purpose existence might have.

Culture for Kant is an unavoidable dimension of our collective moral education and yet, as Inder Marwah puts it, "problematically, not all forms of collective life stand equally capable of moving us toward our moral improvement; non-European societies appear incapable of fulfilling this critical moral-developmental function."[31] In the same vein as his doubts regarding especially the final purpose of the "New Hollanders" or the "Fuegians," note that in his "Review of J. G. Herder's *Ideas for the Philosophy of the History of Humanity*" Kant questions the value of the lifestyles of "the happy inhabitants of Tahiti," who would have existed "for thousands of centuries in their tranquil indolence if they had not been visited by more cultured nations"; he follows this remark with the claim that Tahiti without European contact would have been no different than an island populated by happy sheep and cattle ("RezHerder," AA 8:56). In the "Idea" essay, likewise, Kant describes a "pastoral existence of perfect concord, self-sufficiency, and mutual love" to be only as valuable as the existence of an animal, and he does not consider people in this state to be the legislators of their own goals ("IaG"/AA 8:21). Lastly, in the *Groundwork*, we are told that the South Sea Islanders, who "let their talents rust and are concerned with devoting their lives merely to idleness, amusement, procreation—in a word, enjoyment," are more or less going against the purpose of nature by not developing their talents through industry and labor and giving themselves over to passivity (GMS/AA 4:423).

On the one hand, Kant's rejection of happiness follows from his idea that a culture of skill is the most appropriate way of developing our capacities: the value of life will have to be assessed by what we ourselves do, independently of nature, according to the purposes that we actively set (KU/AA 5:434n). These cannot be the purposes that are set by nature, such as happiness or enjoyment, since those are, in his view, passive goals. On the other hand, however, the activity-passivity distinction that Kant makes in assessing different forms of life and in rejecting happiness does not seem so neutral, especially when we look at how this dichotomy plays out in his anthropology and politics. As Zöller puts it,

> The philosophical point behind Kant's anti-eudaemonistic anthropological vision is the exclusive linkage of the human vocation with activity, spontaneity, or work [*Arbeit*] rather than passivity, receptivity, or "enjoyment" [*Genuss*] . . . A politically sensitive consequence [of this rejection of happiness as an end of human existence] is *the exclusion of modes of human life that he considers to be merely "passive" and oriented solely to sensory*

gratification ("ease" [*Gemächlichkeit*], "good living" [*Wohlleben*], "happiness" [*Glückseligkeit*]).[32]

This point rings especially true when we look at Kant's remarks about "savages," or peoples without a civil condition, who he claims aim at mere enjoyment. As I have shown above, given his own criteria, the value of those non-European peoples' lives or cultural ways of being is "less than zero."

Kant's cosmopolitan vision, considered to be the cornerstone of his theory of politics, is thus embedded in and dependent upon a Eurocentric nonideal theory of human development and capabilities. This means that non-European forms of culture or cultural development do not aid us in forming a cosmopolitan whole, because they cannot be considered "cultures" in the true sense of the term as Kant uses it. Other cultures not oriented toward a *Geschicklichkeit* are at best irrelevant to the ultimate end of our existence, a global peaceful constitution. A closer look at the notion of *Geschicklichkeit* and the kind of activities that it includes therefore helps us to see that it does not tolerate just any type of cultural practice; it is not the happy multicultural mosaic that we may today imagine it to be.

I agree with Inder Marwah that the kind of cultural development Kant has in mind here does not refer to a plurality of skills, ways of life, or diverse abilities, as, for instance, Sankar Muthu has interpreted it.[33] The cosmopolitan world-whole, as the matrix in which a culture of skill will fully develop, seems especially open to and suitable for the development of European culture and talent—and definitely not those of the "New Hollander," "Fuegian," Tahitian, or South Sea Islander. As Marwah puts it, "Culture, for Kant, concerns the development of our basic capacity to exercise reason and to set ends, which is inexorably connected to our social existence. *Civilized* culture, then, refers to a *particular* form of social life that enables the development of particular skills and aptitudes."[34]

To reiterate, a truly cosmopolitan existence in Kant's view cannot come about without *Geschicklichkeit*, a culture of skill and industry. A culture of skill, however, refers to quite a specific set of practices and activities modeled after a specifically western European conception of culture; it excludes non- or preindustrial ways of life that focus on enjoyment or happiness. By excluding those ways of living and being from *Geschicklichkeit*, Kant excludes them from a cosmopolitan community. Thus, Kant's characterization in the third *Critique* of the kind of cultural development which constitutes the ultimate end of human existence remains a Eurocentric one. This characterization favors the particular kinds of activities exemplified by European cultures and takes them as the only genuine elements of development and civilization, excluding and rejecting others characterized by mere passivity, enjoyment, or happiness (*Glückseligkeit*). In Pagden's terms, because Kant's vision of a cosmopolitan world order is clearly dependent on a notion of culture, "it is equally clear that a condition of true culture, and thus the truly 'cosmopolitan existence,' cannot come about in a world in which *Geschicklichkeit* is wholly absent."[35]

My point here is that Kant's cosmopolitan ideal is not, as we often imagine today, a world in which a plurality of cultures coexist peacefully and respect each other as equal contributors of human civilization. On the contrary, seen from the perspective of the nonideal theory that provides a regulatively teleological view of culture, Kant's idea of a cosmopolitan world-whole is clearly a construction that safeguards the full development of certain skills and talents through inequality and war, and furthermore is predicated upon a particular view of European civilization. According to Kant's nonideal theory here, the development of our skills and aptitudes must not be oriented toward passivity or the mere enjoyment of life, but must only incorporate activities that will cultivate the faculties and dispositions as European civilizations would have them. Thus, Kant's nonideal theory of human development and of the transition from nature to freedom proposes a teleology of European or Western cultural and social life.

Cultural Anthropology as Part of Kant's Nonideal Theory of Politics

In the third *Critique*, we have seen Kant giving us a nonideal theory of human nature or what I called a political anthropology. Just as his story of a universal history was limited to a European genealogy, as I showed in my analysis of the "Idea" essay, his account of cultural development and activities in these sections of the third *Critique* also favors the European way of life.[36] The underlying idea in his construction of a cosmopolitan condition is Eurocentric in that it prioritizes a European way of living and cultural development.

The larger or systematic point, however, is that Kant shows an awareness of the natural-cultural embeddedness of politics. With his organic metaphors for political change and progress in the "Enlightenment" essay and *The Doctrine of Right*, then, Kant incorporates, although not always in a satisfactory manner, a theory of human natural and cultural development into his political philosophy of cosmopolitanism. Thus, a regulatively teleological view of nature, together with the emphasis on the place of human beings in such a framework, constitutes cultural or political anthropology as a part of Kant's nonideal theory of politics. Even as I admit

Pagden's point that the genealogy of cosmopolitanism seems particularly European and difficult to untangle from the civilizing mission of the colonial projects of the West,[37] an understanding of cultural habits and development is necessary for politics, and this idea is still an important insight of Kant's political philosophy of cosmopolitanism. Thus, I take a crucial insight of his to be that an account of cultural production matters for setting and pursuing collective political agendas.

I have articulated the systematic place of anthropology in Kant's and Kantian political thought by developing the notion of purposiveness as he uses it in his political writings. I have shown that his use of teleology in politics does not indicate a dogmatic view of the relationship between our goals and nature as a whole. Rather, a teleological language proves useful for political philosophy especially because political thought initially requires a nonmechanistic worldview and a working assumption that our goals are achievable in this world. In the first instance, Kant's analogy between judging an ideal body politic and an organism in §65 demonstrates that we cannot even have a properly political discourse using only mechanistic principles or based only on a mechanistic worldview. Articulating an ideal body politic requires that we view the state as well as the human being as more than a machine, as an organism. The fact that Kant resorts to natural and organic metaphors again in describing the proper form of political change as metamorphosis in *The Doctrine of Right* gives us a further clue that teleological language is not incidental his political thought. The inadequacy of a mechanistic view for politics is the reason why Kant draws an analogy between an ideal state and organism in the first place. Taking these analogies as my interpretive clues for further investigating the role of teleology, finally I have assessed the status of Kant's application, in §§82–84 of the Critique of Teleological Judgment, of the principle of external or relative purposiveness, or what I have come to call "political *Zweckmässigkeit*." These sections of the third *Critique* show that Kant's political philosophy does indeed benefit from employing a teleological language, and in two related ways: the teleological view of the world provided by the principle of *Zweckmässigkeit* establishes as a baseline for politics that nature is purposive for our goals, and furthermore brings together the two aspects of our existence as both natural organisms and free agents. Thus, the principle of political *Zweckmässigkeit* is useful in that it gives specific answers, by way of a nonideal theory of anthropology, to fundamental political questions that a mere mechanistic or idealized moral view cannot hope to address. In §83 of the third *Critique* Kant articulates the idea of a cosmopolitan world-whole as a realistic cultural and political goal primarily from a regulatively teleological perspective of the human being as a natural organism, for whom nature as a whole is purposive. In acknowledging that we are a product of nature as ultimate ends, Kant is able to describe how we can achieve our purposes in this world. The specific answer that the principle of purposiveness gives to the question of how we should work toward a peaceful coexistence in the third *Critique* therefore allows Kant to produce a nonideal theory of cultural development–or in other words, a political anthropology.

Günter Zöller has recently made a convincing case for what he calls the anthropological foundations of Kant's political thought or "Kant's Political Anthropology."[38] Political anthropology is not a term that Kant himself uses, but Zöller helpfully suggests that we use this term to describe his anthropological project and its pertinence to politics: while Kant's critical project offers a top-down account of reason and rationality, his anthropological project, one that he pursues throughout his career in short essays and lectures, gives us a bottom-up account of human reason, tracing its development in nature and culture.[39] Zöller argues therefore that "Kant's work in anthropology counterbalances the intentionally narrow methodological and systematical orientation of the critique of reason, geared at a critical theory of *a priori* principles with a broadly conceived, empirically informed and practically geared account of the human condition."[40] Here, Zöller takes Kant's work on anthropology to include his writings on culture as well as history and geography in which Kant gives a natural history of reason regarding the origin, development, and actualization of the potential for rationality in the human species.[41]

Where Zöller makes the distinction between two accounts of reason in Kant's oeuvre, I make a distinction between Kant's two accounts of politics, one grounded in *a priori* principles of practical reason and another grounded in the regulative principle of purposiveness. Thus, in parallel with Zöller's account of two mutually supplementary theories of reason, I am suggesting here that Kant has two complementary theories or accounts of politics. One is the more familiar picture of his ideal theory, which offers a top-down account of ideal political institutions and laws, and the other is his nonideal theory, which offers a historical, anthropological, and geographical picture of human development over space and time. In my account, then, we get a broader conception of politics in Kant than we would from a theory led principally by his practical-moral principles. Furthermore, we are able to pinpoint the exact use of teleological principles as the other normative principle at stake in his political thought, the normative principle of his nonideal theory.

Kant's view of nature in the third *Critique* is not a deterministic one that is set up against freely willed rational human action. Instead, in this work he reenchants nature, so to speak, by means of conceptualizing it teleologically—that is, as harmonious with and amenable to human action. In Kant's system, teleology is already a hybrid of freedom and nature; this is why he writes that a teleological way of thinking (*Denkungsart*) bridges the gap between nature and freedom (*KU/AA* 5:176). By employing a regulatively teleological language in politics, Kant shows an awareness that political theory is like neither physics (a natural hard science organized by determinism) nor morals (an ideal theory organized by freedom). Rather, human interactions on a large scale are rich and complex, and the material conditions of politics are contingent and ever-changing. We need a theory that conceptualizes such contingent conditions surrounding our interactions with nature and each other, and the main guiding principle of such a nonideal theory in the Kantian framework is that of regulative teleology.

Without taking into consideration that we are embedded in nature, pure principles of justice and right—because such principles do not offer developmental accounts—will not get us anywhere. Only the regulative principle of teleology gives us this developmental view, a nonideal theory of cultural and political formations in the actual world. Kant puts forth just such a view of human culture and development in §§82–84 of the *Critique of Judgment*, as I have shown in this chapter. This complementary view is his nonideal theory of politics that works with the regulative principle of purposiveness. In short, political theory as Kant understands it also requires a consideration of natural and cultural activities of human beings: it requires anthropology. Thus, in Zöller's terms, we can say that there is an anthropological foundation for Kant's political though, although my contention is that this foundation is not only worked out in his popular philosophical writings on history, anthropology, and geography, as Zöller argues,[42] but also in the third *Critique*, a critical work.

The principle of purposiveness is the material principle of Kant's political philosophy that gives us culturally specific political ends to pursue. I will call this approach to politics an ends- or *Zweck*-based approach. It is an ends-based approach not only in the sense that it focuses on our collective ideal ends, but that it articulates our civil and political ends in the ways I have developed throughout this chapter: political ends are construed from the bottom up, starting with nature within and outside us, going from there to articulating a specific cultural end. This means that the cultural-civil end of our existence as Kant sees it—namely, a cosmopolitan world order—is not, as is often argued, a transhistorical, transracial, or transcultural ideal, at least not in these writings that I have analyzed. Instead, it is the logical conclusion and end of Kant's teleological view of history, human nature, and culture. Thus, in the third *Critique* a cosmopolitan condition is not, as we might assume, an ideal or morally egalitarian goal; it is first and foremost a cultural or civil goal adduced by the principle of political *Zweckmässigkeit*, the guiding principle of Kant's nonideal theory of politics. Kant's cosmopolitan vision here is embedded in a particular notion of culture, and as a result, a cosmopolitan world-whole in his terms becomes a global condition in which all ways of life or different cultural contributions are *not* valued equally.

A mechanistic conceptualization of nature and human beings, by itself, does not even allow us to formulate political questions, as I have shown. A purely moral and idealized consideration of human beings goes further in that it posits that we are the final ends of nature because of our freedom; however, this consideration does not specifically address or answer the question of how we, as natural beings existing in this world, *will* put our capacities to use in order to shape nature according to our own purposes, but only that we *ought to* do so. In §83 of the Critique of Teleological Judgment, Kant answers exactly this important political question by arguing that human beings will attempt to create, through a *Geschicklichkeit*, the kind of a civil society that will bring them closer to being the final ends of nature. This is sufficient to establish the principle of purposiveness as a principle of Kant's political thought in its own right, for it reminds us that political discourse also deals with empirical, natural human beings (i.e., organisms) and not only with rational human beings with idealized capacities. The major formal principle of Kant's political philosophy, namely, the principle of *Recht*, can articulate an answer along the lines of what we *ought to* establish and accordingly can lay out the ideal laws and institutions of justice—and such theorization definitely takes place in Kant's more explicitly political writings, namely, "Toward Perpetual Peace" and *The Doctrine of Right*. To provide a fuller comparison between the roles that *Recht* and *Zweckmässigkeit* play in Kant's political thought, I turn to these works next.

Part III

Nature and Politics
Political Geography and the Cosmopolitan Right

If we consider Kant a major political thinker today, this is mainly on account of two later works: the essay "Toward Perpetual Peace: A Philosophical Sketch" (1795) and *The Doctrine of Right* (1797). In the former, he proposes a league of nations as well as a universal right of hospitality, whereas in the latter juridico-political treatise, he develops detailed expositions of private and public rights (*Recht*), or justice, further specifying the stakes of accomplishing peace on earth. These two later works, which crown Kant a political thinker in his own right, are normatively grounded on the formal and universal principle of *Recht*, namely, the idea that "any action is *right* [*Recht*] if it can coexist with everyone's freedom in accordance with a universal law, or if on its maxim the freedom of choice of each can coexist with everyone's freedom in accordance with a universal law" (*MS/AA* 6:230). While "Toward Perpetual Peace" and *The Doctrine of Right* are undoubtedly contributions to Kant's ideal theory of politics—and they have been rightly taken up as such by numerous political thinkers[1]—I will also locate in these texts a nonideal theory of feasibility that consists of arguments regarding geography and geopolitics, especially in Kant's formulations regarding the guarantee of nature and the cosmopolitan right of universal hospitality. Finally, I will argue that, while the geographic knowledge of the world that undergirds Kant's formulation of the cosmopolitan right is somewhat limited, following his insight that geography matters to politics makes producing multiple views of the world, and thus multiple nonideal theories, possible.

I will show that if *Recht* is the formal principle of Kant's ideal political theory, then the principle of political *Zweckmässigkeit* is the material principle that orients his other, nonideal theory of politics. As such, it is an important supplement to the formal principle of *Recht* in that it provides a physical and political geography of the nonideal circumstances of the world. Such a physical-political geography, which I will show plays a role both in "Toward Perpetual Peace" and *The Doctrine of Right*, serves two theoretical purposes: first, a reflection on the natural and geographical conditions in which we find ourselves helps to render our ideal political goals feasible; and second, a political geography provided by the principle of political *Zweckmässigkeit* will afford the dictums of *Recht* further specificity. It is in this way that the two principles of Kant's political theory, namely, political *Zweckmässigkeit* and *Recht*, complement each other.

In chapter 5 I focus on "Toward Perpetual Peace" and argue that the specific benefit of regulative teleology for politics in this essay first lies in providing us with a bottom-up approach to political questions and the nondogmatic judgment that we can achieve our rational aims because we can count on a correspondence between our goals and nature. This is what a teleological language accomplishes in the definitive articles of the essay regarding the feasibility of a republican constitution, a federation of free states, and the cosmopolitan right of universal hospitality. Second, rather than being merely an interpretive tool, a spiritual comfort, or a relic of Kant's philosophy of nature, I argue that political *Zweckmässigkeit* is a principle that yields a nonideal theory of politics, one that begins with the material and contingent conditions of politics including—nature outside and within us—and from there ascends to a lawful construction of political ends. Such a preliminary political geography, I will show, is the task and accomplishment of especially the First Supplement in the "Perpetual Peace" essay, where Kant enigmatically claims that nature guarantees perpetual peace.

My emphasis on the uses of teleology in Kant's politics aims to go beyond the basic sense of the ends-means formulations necessary in any political discourse in order to open up a new and underdeveloped dimension of his political thought. Paul Formosa argues for the basic significance of Kant's political teleology "for showing us the political *ends* toward which we should work and the *means* by which we should pursue them."[2] Here, Formosa's approach remains committed to a view that understands political ends in idealized terms.[3] By contrast, what I term an ends-based approach to politics would in the first instance bring politics down to earth, so to speak, by showing us that our ideal ends must be compatible with the natural and cultural ends that we ourselves can identify and pursue. Thus, an ends-based approach to politics in the sense that I develop grants Kant the conjecture that, while our current material conditions are far from the ideal of perpetual peace, war (considered in long term) is ultimately against our individual and collective inclinations. As a result, Kant shows us the *feasibility* of peace: peace is not only a theoretical hypothesis, but is in fact feasible, especially if we pay attention to and theorize nature within and outside us. In order for the goals of a

Recht-based political theory to be feasible in actual world, then, we need a lower-level abstraction by means of which we are able to offer an account of the natural conditions in which we find ourselves, and this lower-level abstraction comes from a regulatively teleological consideration of nature within and outside us in the First Supplement. I identify this "feasibility concern" as part of Kant's nonideal political theory; more specifically, it constitutes the basic question of his theory of political geography as oriented by the principle of political *Zweckmässigkeit*.

In chapter 6, I turn to *The Doctrine of Right* and offer an interpretation of Kant's cosmopolitan right of universal hospitality from a nonideal theory perspective. I first establish, with the help of various interpreters of Kantian political thought, that Kant's theory of rights is not a simple extension of his ethics or of the Categorical Imperative. *Recht*, in the way Kant defines it, already incorporates a view of spatial relations between embodied beings. Accordingly, I show that his formulation of the cosmopolitan right is about figuring out the just way of navigating an enclosed space, which we all originally possess in common. By taking spatial considerations seriously, Kant first argues that, because we all eventually have to come into contact with one another due to the spherical shape of the earth, we must implement a cosmopolitan right (*Weltbürgerrecht*) regulating our movements around the globe. The principle of *Recht* still does not tell us the specific form that our global interactions must take in such a space or what the cosmopolitan right regulating our interactions should look like. Such further specificity, I will argue, comes from Kant's teleological perspective on his own geopolitical conditions, namely, the growing intensity of commercial relations and colonial injustices. When Kant reflects on these circumstances, he proposes that the cosmopolitan right must take the shape of universal hospitality, not as an unlimited right to visit but as a circumscribed right of peaceful commerce. The right of hospitality, as far as he sees it, will mitigate the injustices that he observes around him and bring us closer to our goal of achieving peace on earth. This cosmopolitan right, then, arises out of a theorization of the less-than-ideal conditions in which Kant finds himself, out of a nonideal theory of politics that employs the principle of political *Zweckmässigkeit*, and in this case, produces a preliminary political geography about commerce and colonialism.

In Kant's own terms, the domain of politics is circumscribed to that of *Recht*. For this reason, it may seem as if the principle of *Recht* is the exclusive principle of Kantian political philosophy—although my point is that his writings point us to a broader conception of politics. I will show that Kant cared about the feasibility and empirical conditions of his proposed political ideals more than is immediately evident. One way to articulate the systematic place of the care that Kant showed about the feasibility and the empirical in politics is to focus on what a political *Zweckmässigkeit* achieves in these writings. In "Toward Perpetual Peace," this principle helps Kant to address feasibility concerns regarding his ideal theory; in *The Doctrine of Right*, it allows him to make his political proposals more responsive to the concrete geopolitical circumstances around him. I am not suggesting here that the material principle of *Zweckmässigkeit* has priority or precedence over the formal principle of *Recht* or that it possesses any independent normative force for Kant's political thought. We will see, however, that Kantian political philosophy is much broader in its scope and questions than matters exclusively dealing with rights. Lastly, when we uncover the nonideal theory undergirding the formulation of some of Kant's better known political precepts, such as the cosmopolitan right of universal hospitality, we may be able to articulate different nonideal theories that will require us to work with better, closer maps of the reality in which we live today.

5

Teleology and Peace on Earth

Kant's "Toward Perpetual Peace" employs a regulatively teleological view, not only in the puzzling language of the First Supplement asserting that "nature guarantees peace," ("ZeF"/AA 8:360) but also in the definitive articles regarding his proposals for a republican constitution, a federation of free states, and universal hospitality. In this chapter, I will show that— far from being a dogmatic or unnecessary appendage to the project of perpetual peace, as Ellis claims[1]—the teleological language in "Toward Perpetual Peace" must be interpreted along the lines of the principle of political *Zweckmässigkeit*. Teleological language here plays two important and interrelated roles: first, by orienting Kant's reflections on his own nonideal circumstances, it addresses the question of whether and how peace can be made feasible here and now; and second, by providing a nondogmatic perspective on natural and climatic conditions, it allows Kant to develop a preliminary political geography. In both cases, political *Zweckmässigkeit* produces a nonideal theory of politics, a theory that addresses feasibility concerns and provides an important view of the geographical conditions that are relevant to our efforts to establish peace through institutions of law. Thus, Kant uses a regulative teleology in order to account for the gap between ideal and real political circumstances as well as to investigate, nondogmatically and pragmatically, "what nature makes of the human being" with a view to "what they ought to make of themselves."[2] He provides a pragmatic knowledge of the world that is relevant and important for politics.

In what are called the definitive articles of "Toward Perpetual Peace," Kant puts forth three concrete political proposals and explains why they are the necessary (if not the sufficient) conditions of establishing lasting peace on earth. These proposals start at the national level and proceed to the international and then global levels. Kant requires that the constitution of each state government be republican, that the relations among states be regulated by a federation or a league of nations, and that all nations of the globe institute a limited condition of universal hospitality. These three political proposals mirror what he would later develop in the Public Right section of *The Doctrine of Right*. If "peace" is the highest order ideal of Kantian political philosophy, what he calls "the highest political good" at the end of *The Doctrine of Right*, then the principle of *Recht* is the normative basis upon which Kant makes concrete proposals regarding national and international governance. In this essay, Kant locates the *a priori* origin of these proposals in the principle of *Recht*, but also gives additional teleological arguments as to why these three requirements are indeed capable of bringing about the desired result, peace on earth. I will show that these additional arguments, which at first seem like random empirical considerations, are part of a nonideal theory employing the principle of political *Zweckmässigkeit* in order to tease out the feasibility of Kant's proposals.

A closer look at how these definitive articles are formulated and justified reveals that the requirements of a universal hospitality, a federation of free states, and a republican constitution are also teleologically justified with a view to achieving peace on earth. Thus, Kant here resorts to a regulatively teleological view of the current sociopolitical conditions in which he finds himself in order to address the concern of whether or not peace is *feasible* here and now. That is, by means of his teleological principles, he is able to orient his thinking about his present situation and about the actions of the European states, and this reflection leads him to conclude that, if we are to achieve everlasting peace, we should make sure to minimize the existing causes of conflict. Among the chief causes of conflict, as he sees them, are the arbitrariness of the decision-making processes of nonrepublican governments, the lack of a judge to arbitrate international disagreements, and hostility toward foreigners. As a result, he concludes that it benefits us pragmatically—and thus makes peace more feasible—to ensure that every human being is granted the right to universal hospitality, that a global institution of all free states is put in place, and that the rule of each state is made republican. These three proposals are not only unconditional ideal requirements but also realistic ones, which shows us that Kant is concerned about the feasibility of peace. Kant's teleological view of his own historico-political context provides him with further assurance that these three articles make it more likely that perpetual peace will eventually be achieved, as I show below.

Political *Zweckmässigkeit* in the Definitive Articles of "Toward Perpetual Peace"

The first definitive article of perpetual peace holds that the constitution of every state must be republican. Republicanism, to Kant, means a civil union in which the principles of freedom, interdependence, and equality are established as fundamental conditions ("ZeF"/*AA* 8:349–50). A republican constitution, "having arisen from the pure source of the concept of right,"("ZeF"/*AA* 8:350) is pure in its origin. Additionally, here Kant goes on to investigate whether or not this is *empirically* the only type of constitution that can lead us to perpetual peace. Thus, the question here is one of the suitability of political means for certain ends: whether, considered from a teleological view of the less-than-ideal circumstances of the world, republicanism is the best political means to achieve peace at the state level.

In this teleological consideration, Kant arrives at the conclusion that republicanism indeed "offers the prospect of the result wished for, namely perpetual peace" ("ZeF"/*AA* 8:350). The argument here is that a republican constitution will give the citizens a say in whether or not a state should declare war, and citizens will choose to avoid war due to the potentially disastrous effects that they themselves will experience. He conjectures that a greedy monarch in a nonrepublican constitution would more easily declare war, because he would not be the one enduring its hardships—risking his life, paying for the war, and suffering the destruction of his belongings ("ZeF"/*AA* 8:350). As Kant writes,

> Under a constitution in which subjects are not citizens of the state, which is therefore not republican, [deciding upon war] is the easiest thing in the world; because the head of state is not a member of the state but its proprietor and gives up nothing at all of his feasts, hunts, pleasure palaces, court festivals, and so forth, he can decide upon war, as upon a kind of pleasure party, for insignificant cause. ("ZeF"/*AA* 8:350)

Wars are more likely to continue under nonrepublican constitutions at the whim of a ruler; a necessary condition of achieving peace, therefore, is to have a republican constitution in place. Kant arrives at this conclusion by means of a teleological consideration of his present circumstances. It is an empirical fact that wars cause hardship, suffering, and debt, and as long as declaring war becomes the right of those who will endure these hardships, wars will become less likely—citizens in republican states will avoid war in order to avoid its undesirable consequences. We can already see here that Kant is working with a very nonidealized view of humans, nations, and institutions to supplement his dictum of republicanism, which has its pure origin in the *a priori* principle *Recht*.

The second definitive article proposes that the rights of nations must be based on a federation of free states ("ZeF"/*AA* 8:354). This can be seen as instituting a kind of a republican union on an international level so as to further decrease the chances of states warring against each other.

CHAPTER 5

In the first instance, the right of states mirrors the right of a state and is thus similarly ideal in its origin. Additionally, just as it is in the interest of human beings to leave a lawless condition behind and enter into a civil union governed by laws, Kant argues that it is in the interest of free states to enter into a global union governed by international laws that regulate relations and arbitrate potential conflicts. He writes,

> In accordance with reason there is only one way that states in relation with one another can leave the lawless condition, which involves nothing but war; it is that, like individual human beings, they give up their savage (lawless) freedom, accommodate themselves to public coercive laws, and so form an (always growing) state of nations (*civitas gentium*) that would finally encompass all the nations of the earth. ("ZeF"/*AA* 8:357)

For peace to remain a realistic goal on an international level, we need to find ways to make sure that states will not have reasons to declare war against one another at will and to resolve conflicts among them before they escalate into war. The principle of right tells us that, because peace is a direct duty, "there must be a league of a special kind . . . [that] seeks to end *all war* forever" ("ZeF"/*AA* 8:356). One way to institute peace is to ensure that the constitution of each state is republican, as I have shown above. This is not by itself sufficient, since it is still possible that citizens of one republican state will decide to go to war against another. In order to avoid this, Kant takes a step back, reflects on the states as parts of a larger whole, and concludes that a federation of free states must be in place so that any conflict between states can be arbitrated before a political body resorts to war.

What Kant is proposing here is not a world republic to rule the world;[3] however, he does not rule out a scenario in which an enlightened nation would lead the way toward a federation. The reasonableness of this ideal of a federalism, he argues, can be shown as follows:

> For if good fortune should ordain that a powerful and enlightened people can form itself into a republic (which by its nature must be inclined to perpetual peace), this would provide a focal point of federative union for other states, to attach themselves to it and so to secure a condition of freedom of states conformably with the idea of the right of nations; and by further alliances of this kind, it would gradually extend further and further. ("ZeF"/*AA* 8:356)

This additional argument about the feasibility of a federation of free states is grounded in an argument from consequences, and it is based on a teleological view of human nature and current political affairs. Kant conjectures that under the leadership of an enlightened republican nation other states would "form an (always growing) state of nations (*civitas gentium*) that would encompass all the nations of the earth" ("ZeF"/*AA* 8:357). What is most conducive to peace, pragmatically speaking, is not a world republic, but an ever-growing federation of free states conceived as a "*negative* surrogate of a *league* that averts war, endures, and always expands can hold back the stream of hostile inclination that shies away from right, though with constant danger of its breaking out" ("ZeF"/*AA* 8:357). Kant seems to conceive of this "negative surrogate" as a foil to a world republic; rather than having power over a multitude of states like an all-powerful world republic, a league of nations would only get involved in cases of conflict, thus holding something like a veto power for possible wars. In any case, the international condition of everlasting peace, therefore, a league of nations who will work together to eliminate reasons for war, can be established by an enlightened nation leading the way. This idea is justified from a nonidealized and pragmatic point of view by means of a consideration of the current (nonideal) interactions of states as a whole.

In the third and final definitive article, we see that a cosmopolitan right of universal hospitality should supplement a republican constitution and a federation of free states. Since hostility toward foreigners can continue to provide reasons for conflict and war, even under the conditions of republicanism and a league of nations, Kant proposes that a limited cosmopolitan right of universal hospitality should be formally instituted. This is a right to visit a foreign country for a limited amount of time for the purposes of possible commerce (*commercium*) ("ZeF"/*AA* 8:358). In the first instance, this right to visit is justified by the principle of *Recht*. Kant states that such a right "belongs to all human beings by virtue of the right of possession in common of the earth's surface on which, as a sphere, they cannot disperse infinitely but must finally put up with being near one another" ("ZeF"/*AA* 8:358). In other words, the principle of *Recht*, together with the actual limits of the shape of the earth, necessitates that the earth's surface belongs in common to the human race for possible commerce or interaction ("ZeF"/*AA* 8:358).[4] In addition, I will show that a cosmopolitan right of universal hospitality and its suitability for peace are further supported by means of Kant's teleological reflections on his present geopolitical conditions: the colonial abuses that he observes around him. Because they address the question of how exactly universal hospitality can bring about peace under less-than-ideal circumstances, these teleological reflections constitute a part of Kant's nonideal theory of politics.

CHAPTER 5

In his investigation of the question of feasibility and suitability, Kant turns to and reflects on the empirical realities of his own sociohistorical circumstances. He looks at the inhospitable conduct of the civilized states of Europe of his time and concludes that their conduct results in a whole litany of evils that can afflict the entire human race ("ZeF"/*AA* 8:358). Because we would like to avoid these evils as well as their major cause (i.e., the inhospitable behavior of states), we should aim at instituting the right of universal hospitality as a cosmopolitan right. This is not an unachievable or impractical idea, but a necessary global policy that should supplement the rights of each nation and those of nations in general. In other words, a right of universal hospitality is necessary for all the people from distant parts of the world to be able to enter into peaceable relations with one another ("ZeF"/*AA* 8:357). Such hospitality then is a universal right of humanity, so much so that only under the condition of universal hospitality "can we flatter ourselves that we are continually *advancing toward* a perpetual peace" ("ZeF"/*AA* 8:360, emphasis added).

The right of universal hospitality, as well as the other specific proposals put forth in "Toward Perpetual Peace," still have relevance for our current sociopolitical conditions.[5] I want to point out here, however, that the necessity of implementing this right of universal hospitality on a global scale is further justified in the text by Kant's appeal to a regulative teleological consideration of the actual and possible *consequences* of the current state of inhospitality in Europe as Kant sees it. In thinking about the relationship between universal hospitality and peace on earth, we also find his famous critique and condemnation of colonial violence. He considers what happens if a state treats foreigners in a hostile way, sees that such treatment will result in more wars between states, and therefore concludes that states or peoples must be universally hospitable to foreigners seeking commerce. On the violence perpetrated by commercial states in their colonies, he writes:

> The worst of this [violence] (or, considered from the standpoint of a moral judge, the best) is that the commercial states do not even profit from this violence, that the Sugar Islands, that place of the cruelest and most calculated slavery, yield no true profit but serve only a mediate and indeed not very laudable purpose, namely, training sailors for warships and so, in turn, carrying on wars in Europe. ("ZeF"/*AA* 8:359)

A moral point of view condemns colonial violence, period; it does not need to take into account the actual or possible consequences of the violence of colonialism or posit an additional duty to mitigate its effects. A pragmatic point of view such as the one Kant provides here is different, in that it takes into consideration the results of this violence and concludes that this kind of hostile behavior in the Caribbean regions is unacceptable because it results in the perpetuation and incentivization of wars. These undesirable results of the inhospitable behavior of the commercial states are pragmatic justifications of the idea that we must institute a cosmopolitan right to universal hospitality—if we do not, there will be more wars, more people trained for war, and we will slip further and further away from the goal of achieving global peace. Thus, the right to universal hospitality constitutes a necessary condition of the feasibility of peace. Kant's reflections on the ongoing colonial violence here are partly provided by means of his regulative teleological commitments that orient his observations about the *consequences* of both the present and the prior inhospitable conduct of European states. In sum, the right to universal hospitality here has an additional pragmatic justification, granted by a consequentialist way of thinking about the past and present violent conduct of the states. This consequentialist perspective *requires* us to posit a specific duty of right, a political duty of limited universal hospitality.

Overall in "Perpetual Peace," republicanism, the federation of states, and universal hospitality are required by the principle of *Recht* and are also sound from a pragmatic and nonidealizing perspective. Thus, thanks to his regulative teleological orientation to reality, Kant is here able to reflect on his present sociopolitical circumstances and recognize both the actual and the potential consequences of certain constraints, such as the hostile conduct of states as well as a number of self-serving tendencies in human nature. From there, he can conclude with sufficient certainty (though not theoretically prove) that he, as a political theorist, can recommend the kinds of policies, rights, and institutions that are suitable for bringing about peace on earth. These teleological considerations show that the three requirements outlined in the definite articles are indeed the necessary means for lasting peace on earth. Demonstrating that the proposed means here are suitable as the necessary if not the sufficient conditions of peace is the task of political *Zweckmässigkeit* in this context.

The significance of the principle of political *Zweckmässigkeit* as well as the place of a nonideal theory of politics provided by means of this principle are even more explicit in the First Supplement to "Toward Perpetual Peace," where Kant uses a strong teleological language to claim that "nature guarantees perpetual peace." I will argue in what follows that this language should be understood as yet another use of political *Zweckmässigkeit*, and furthermore that this Supplement must also be understood as a part of Kant's nonideal theory, more specifically as providing us with a preliminary political geography that undergirds his proposals for peace.

CHAPTER 5

Political *Zweckmässigkeit* in the First Supplement: On the Guarantee of Perpetual Peace

In this Supplement, Kant will show us that when we employ a regulatively teleological conception of nature within and outside us, we will be able to articulate what at first seems like the arbitrary natural conditions of the world and of ourselves in a purposive manner, that is, in terms of a gradual approximation of universal accord. The teleological account of nature that we find in the First Supplement becomes merely a *supplement* to the ideal institutions that Kant specified in the definitive articles of "Toward Perpetual Peace," and is not meant to serve as a sort of *substitute* for these ideal doctrines. In other words, parallel to the role that it plays in §§82–84 of the third *Critique*, political *Zweckmässigkeit* in the First Supplement of "Toward Perpetual Peace" allows us to articulate an account of human motivation and political progress in less-than-ideal circumstances, such as the ones in which we find ourselves. It therefore enables us to have an additional and important nonidealized perspective that is necessary for showing the feasibility of our political goals in this world. More importantly, in the First Supplement we find another piece of Kant's nonideal theory, what I call Kant's preliminary political geography.

In the First Supplement on the Guarantee of Perpetual Peace, Kant unwaveringly states that nature is the *guarantor* of perpetual peace ("ZeF"/*AA* 8:360–61). This is a puzzling statement, for he seems to claim that we know the final purpose of nature and history, and that it will come about regardless of what we do or how historical events actually unfold.[6] Elisabeth Ellis, the strongest representative of what we may call a *Recht*-based approach to Kant's political theory, explicitly dismisses the teleological language found here. Consistent with her reservations about the role of teleology and teleological language in Kant's politics overall, in her interpretation of "Toward Perpetual Peace" Ellis argues that Kant's dogmatic teleological account of human agency in history and politics in the First Supplement contradicts his account of the pursuit of peace through the public institutions of law. For this reason, she encourages us to omit this section of the essay.[7] However, if we understand political *Zweckmässigkeit* in terms of what Riley calls "weak" teleology, then this teleological view of nature is not really in contradiction with free human agency in history and politics.[8] I will also show that this Supplement is a further case study in Kant's nonideal theory, an exploration and a further test of Kant's political *Zweckmässigkeit*. Furthermore, when read in light of the regulative methodological underpinnings of his nonideal theory of politics that I have developed in previous chapters, we will see that here Kant is reflecting on three sets of natural and geopolitical nonideal conditions pertinent to peace: namely, how our selfish inclinations, the growing "spirit of commerce," and the geographical facilitation and limitations of our mobility each affect our pursuit of peace on earth. While there is no theoretical guarantee, in the strong sense of the word, that peace will come about, Kant's preliminary political geography allows us to say that peace is a feasible and realistic goal.[9]

Kant begins the First Supplement by making the methodological point that in some cases of reflection on nature and history as a whole, we need to supply our understanding with a concept of purpose. Here, he gives an account of teleology similar to the ones found in the first *Critique*, the "Orientation" and "Idea" essays, and the third *Critique* in that he employs a critical and regulative principle of purposiveness.[10] He writes,

> What affords this *guarantee* (surety) is nothing less than the great artist *nature* (*natura daedala rerum*) from whose mechanical course purposiveness [*Zweckmässigkeit*] shines forth visibly, letting concord arise by means of the discord between human beings even against their will; and for this reason nature, regarded as necessitation by a cause the laws of whose operation are unknown to us, is called *fate*, but if we consider its purposiveness [*Zweckmässigkeit*] in the course of the world as the profound wisdom of a higher cause directed to the objective final end of the human race and predetermining this course of the world, it is called *providence*, which we do not, strictly speaking, *cognize* in these artifices of nature or even so *infer* from them but instead (as in all relations of the form of things to ends in general) only can and must *add* it *in thought*, in order to make for ourselves a concept of their possibility by analogy with actions of human art. ("ZeF"/*AA* 8:360–62)

This passage, together with the footnote that follows, makes clear what lies at the heart of the theoretical or epistemic justification for the claim that nature *guarantees* perpetual peace. Such a purposiveness of nature is only a critical or regulative principle for us. Kant says here that we cannot know much about the purposive operations of nature or providence. In order to make sense of the workings of nature as a whole, we have to *add* a concept of purpose *in thought*, and in this way we can represent these operations to ourselves as purposive. In the footnote explaining his concept of providence, a seemingly dogmatic concept, Kant confirms that this purposiveness is a regulative principle for us and not an actual act of providence by saying that it is a foolish presumption for human beings to want to cognize an event as a divine dispensation ("ZeF"/*AA* 8:362). Thus, we can never recognize anything in the world as an act of providence; we must *add* the concept of purpose to our understanding in order to be able to represent nature as a whole to ourselves as purposive. This means that such a representation of a purposive nature is for us an idea, a regulative one for theoretical purposes. It is thus better and more in keeping with the limitations of our finite reason to use the term "nature" rather than "providence" in our analysis of the purposiveness in nature, for our analysis needs to remain within the limits of possible experience with regard to cause-effect relations ("ZeF"/*AA* 8:362).[11]

Claiming that a regulative notion of a purposive nature is indeed a constitutive one for our experience "presumptuously puts [us] on the wings of Icarus in order to approach more closely the secret of [nature's] inscrutable purpose" ("ZeF"/*AA* 8:363). If we say that peace *is* guaranteed by nature or that nature *is* constituted in such a way that it will inevitably lead to peace, it is like flying too close to the sun: just as such arrogance destroyed Icarus, it will annihilate our search for meaning in politics and undermine our efforts as well. After all, if we know that peace will come about regardless of what we say and what we do, what is the point of trying to argue for it or to implement it through our actions, institutions, and policies?

On the other hand, if we are allowed to regulatively assert that nature as a whole is purposive and that its purpose is peace, then we can theorize nature to be coherent with our freely given goals as well. In this respect, there is nothing in "Toward Perpetual Peace" suggesting that our knowledge of the *guarantee of nature* is theoretically, absolutely justified. What is more, Kant denies again and again that such theoretical justification is possible for us. As beings with limited cognitive faculties, we need to make use of regulative principles. The claim about nature's purposiveness or the eventual guarantee of peace on earth is justified only on regulative grounds, and we should not forget that regulative principles are not constitutive of our experience. While these principles make it possible for us to understand nature as a whole in a coherent framework, they nevertheless do not in any way predict that peace *will* come about. This critical or regulative sense of this guarantee, then, should be interpreted as a legitimate hope that we have about the course of nature given that we also have something to do and say about our collective lives.[12]

Ellis writes that the First Supplement makes it sound as if "the hidden hand of nature moves human beings without their knowledge toward providential goals, motivating them naturally by their interests, even as they progress, taken as a whole, toward ideal institutions."[13] This is for her not an acceptable story of political progress, for such progress cannot be achieved by the mechanism of nature but has to be the result of our voluntary actions. The teleological account of nature that Kant gives here, however, is regulative, and as I have argued, it aims to show how we can be minimally assured that nature will support the duties given to us by the principles of practical reason—and thus, nature will ensure that, "without prejudice to our freedom," we will do what we ought to do ("ZeF"/ AA 8:365). According to this view, we are allowed to presume that our political goals are realistic and feasible, though we should not stop thinking about what we ourselves ought to do in order to accomplish them. We are given some kind of assurance "that is still enough for practical purposes and makes it a duty to work toward this (not merely chimerical) end" ("ZeF"/AA 8:368). When in the First Supplement Kant writes that "nature guarantees perpetual peace," this refers to the hypothetical alignment between our purposes and the purposes of nature. Thus, the sense of guarantee here has to be understood in the "weak" sense of political *Zweckmässigkeit* as a useful hypothesis for politics.

The view that Kant is providing in this Supplement does not contradict the imperatives given by the definitive articles, which are based on free human agency and come with a practical necessity. Rather, the Supplement provides a complementary view of nature according to which these imperatives are also seen as *realistic*. This interpretation is later confirmed in the text when Kant writes that the purposive view of nature, a view that hypothesizes that nature is in alignment with our political goal of perpetual peace, is not meant to serve as a theoretical means for predicting our future ("ZeF"/AA 8:368). Because the judgments and view that it affords us are hypothetical, Kant says in the end that these assurances are "admittedly not adequate for predicting [nature's] future (theoretically) but that is still enough for practical purposes" ("ZeF"/AA 8:368). Ellis, therefore, misinterprets both the role and the main contribution of the teleological view provided by Kant in the First Supplement. There is an important theoretical reason why Kant provides a supplement to his proposals for peace and couches it in a teleological view.

What Nature Makes of the Human Being: From Physical to Political Geography

After his methodological remarks, in the First Supplement Kant offers an examination of the current condition (*Zustand*) in which nature has placed human beings. The idea behind this examination seems to be the following: if peace is to be a realistic political goal that we can bring about here on earth, we need to start with an understanding of our current

CHAPTER 5

conditions, as we will need to shape the present state of affairs accordingly. Kant does not start with idealized conditions or idealized human capacities; rather, he starts with the current natural and nonideal conditions in which we find ourselves and traces "what nature makes of the human being" in order to show how this knowledge can be put to use for political purposes. I use the phrase "what nature makes of the human being" as I describe the task of the First Supplement throughout in order to emphasize the parallels between the main argument of this text and Kant's description of the task of physiological knowledge of the human beings in *Anthropology from a Pragmatic Point of View* as well as the task of physical geography, the geographical description of the earth, in his *Physical Geography* (*Anth/AA* 7:119; *PG/AA* 9:157). In brief, I will show that Kant in the First Supplement provides a physical geography oriented by the principle of external purposiveness in order to see how such a view of nature as a whole can aid our political goal, peace on earth. This is the sense in which I place these reflections squarely in a nonideal theory of politics.

In the First Supplement, Kant's goal is twofold: first, "to examine the condition that nature prepared for the persons acting on its great stage, which finally makes its assurance of peace necessary"; and second, to "examine the way nature affords this guarantee [of peace]" ("ZeF"/ *AA* 8:363). In other words, he aims to examine what nature makes of the human being and how nature contributes to our cultural and political goals. Here, we see that a teleological view of nature plays a role at two distinct stages: the first stage is "nature's preparatory arrangement" ("ZeF"/ *AA* 8:363–64), or physical geography; and the second is a stage involving the fitness between nature and the actions of human beings, or political geography ("ZeF"/*AA* 8:365–66). This examination takes a teleological perspective, meaning that it utilizes the regulative guiding principle of political *Zweckmässigkeit* and therefore allows us to presume that nature will be supportive of our goals: indeed, this is what the "guarantee of nature" means.

The task of the First Supplement, then, is quite different from that of the definitive articles: the definitive articles articulate the three proposals that make perpetual peace an unattainable goal (a republican constitution, a federation of free states, and a universal right to hospitality), whereas here Kant gives us an account of how nature within and outside us may *help* or *hinder* the attainment of this goal. This second account resorts to a teleological view of nature as a whole. In other words, while the definitive articles are primarily concerned with what we ourselves can and ought to do in order to achieve perpetual peace, the First Supplement investigates what nature makes of us and whether nature supports our cultural and political goals.

In three statements, Kant summarizes nature's provisional arrangement for human beings, or "what nature makes of the human being": "(1) [Nature] has taken care that people should be able to live in all regions of the earth; (2) by *war* [nature] has driven them everywhere, even into the most inhospitable regions, in order to populate these; (3) by war [nature] has compelled them to enter into more or less lawful relations" ("ZeF"/*AA* 8:363). If we take a regulatively teleological perspective on what nature makes of the human being, we can hypothesize that nature makes sure that we are able to survive even under the worst geographical conditions, that it requires us to come into contact one way or another, and that as a result it will force us to enter into lawful relations. Nature seems to prefer to compel us—almost against our will—by means of war. This preference may strike us as distasteful, to say the least, but note that Kant's overall aim here is to focus on the less-than-ideal circumstances of human life by means of turning what seem to be contingent processes of nature (dispersion and forced contact) into a lawful arrangement. It is not the case that we know that nature's law is war, but we hypothesize it so that we can then begin where we are.

Based on these three hypotheses about nature's provisional and purposive arrangement, Kant then provides examples of what he calls the "evidence of design in nature" and of visible signs of "nature's care": the facts that the shores of the Arctic ocean have furry animals as well as seals and whales to provide food for them, and that nature carried driftwood to treeless regions for the natives to construct boats, weapons, or dwellings ("ZeF"/*AA* 8:363). All of these teleological statements about why seals, whales, or driftwood exist must be read as coming out of a regulatively teleological conception of nature. Kant is providing instances of how the regulative principle of teleology helps us to make sense of these seemingly random occurrences of natural phenomena, instances of how organisms can be thought as a coherent whole, relative to our purposes. The experimental idea that nature as a whole is purposive for us, justified subjectively and as an extension of the inner purposiveness of organisms, proves *useful* for our theoretical inquiries, especially when we are theorizing the current conditions in which we find ourselves. Specifically, such a teleological view of nature as a whole helps us to discern how nature and natural beings can be purposive for the goals of human beings, that is, how nature can be thought to be purposive *in reference to us*. This, as I have shown, is the way in which we are justified to use the principle of political *Zweckmässigkeit*.[14]

The specific ideals of republicanism, the federation of free states, and universal hospitality, *as ideals*, are grounded in and justified by the principle of *Recht*. If we take the First Supplement seriously as an important supplement to what can be established by *Recht*, we see that Kant here gives these ideals a physico-geographical foundation. This is why, therefore, in the midst of a political essay we find him all of a sudden talking about physical geography and nature's purposiveness. The use of the regulative principle of external purposiveness helps Kant to produce both a physical and political geography in line with our political vision: a nonideal theory. Such teleological judgments about nature and human beings as a whole are not justified in absolute terms but only in relative terms, relative to our purposes and interests or *from a pragmatic point of view*.

From such a pragmatic point of view, then, Kant goes on to speculate that it was probably war that drove people to inhabit all kinds of places and that forced them to enter into lawful relationships with one another ("ZeF"/*AA* 8:364). Because human beings could live anywhere on earth, nature must have willed that they ought to live everywhere, for it would go against a purposive nature if there were places on earth that were not conducive to life at all. This "ought" does not come from any compliance with moral law: it is rather a hypothetical "ought" based on a regulatively teleological view of nature. The political question at stake here is how we can interpret natural or geographical processes in relation to our goal of peace, and this question directs us to look at the natural tendencies and inclinations that human beings have.

A teleological consideration of geography comes into play in Kant's political theory, furthermore, in order to bring the seemingly utopian ideal of peace down to earth. First, the principle of *Recht* posits a republican constitution as a necessary condition of achieving peace, as I have shown. Now, reflecting on the natural conditions and our self-seeking inclinations, Kant theorizes that perpetual war or the constant threat of wars will tire us out and make us desire, out of completely self-seeking reasons, lawful and peaceful living conditions. It is therefore not out of moral considerations but for completely selfish reasons that we will eventually begin to promote lawful order and peace. This is a less-than-noble view of human beings, but note that this view at least does not idealize us as rational or free agents. In this view, we will be forced to become the law-abiding citizens of a republican constitution, if not exactly moral people ("ZeF"/*AA* 8:366). The distinction between being a good citizen and being a moral person reveals that Kant is not claiming that nature guarantees that we will become moral. All that his teleological view of nature tells us is that we may assume that out of our own selfishness we will come to live in a lawful order. In short, we will try to become good citizens and we will learn to play nice in order to preserve our lives and properties.

In his exposition of the first definitive article, Kant already gave an argument for why a republican constitution, arising from the pure source of the principle of *Recht*, is the most conducive to peace ("ZeF"/*AA* 8:349–51). Now in the Supplement, he provides more support for this idea, in that even if we were not motivated by practical laws to establish a republican constitution, as is often the case with not-yet-fully rational agents such as ourselves, a constant state of war would motivate us, through our own self-seeking inclinations, to put an end to war and pursue peace ("ZeF"/*AA* 8:366). Once we realize that constant wars are costly for human beings as well as for states, all we need to know is how the mechanism of nature can be put to use by our end-setting capacities for peace and we realize that a republican constitution is the most conducive to this goal ("ZeF"/*AA* 8:366).[15] For less-than-moral agents such as ourselves situated in less-than-ideal external circumstances, the primary political task becomes a matter of knowing how to put an end to ongoing wars, and in this way it becomes a technical task of using political machinery. This is why Kant writes that "the problem of establishing a state is soluble even for a nation of devils (as long as they have understanding)" ("ZeF"/*AA* 8:366).

Second, an ever-growing federation of free states led by an enlightened nation is a necessary condition of peace, as we have seen. However, if the states are indeed a lot like humans in that they also have self-seeking tendencies, then it is also highly likely that each one of them will want to dominate the rest. One way to put a stop to the world-dominating aims of the states would be to appeal to *Recht*; the other would be to point out the seemingly irreconcilable religious and linguistic differences between them. Although every state might want to achieve lasting peace by dominating the entire world, then, Kant tells us that nature uses linguistic and religious differences to separate nations, thus blocking the way for the rise of a single tyrannical power. These differences are often the cause of more wars, but on the larger scale Kant thinks that cultural hostilities can be seen as providing more assurance against the rise of a single totalitarian world government, thus indirectly facilitating the need and desire on the part of states for peaceful relations ("ZeF"/*AA* 8:367).

In his exposition of the second definitive article, Kant already argued against a world-league and for a federation of free states that will maintain peace on earth. This doctrine of a federation of free states was postulated from the perspective of the principle of *Recht* by analogy with individuals leaving a state of war behind and entering into a civil condition ("ZeF"/*AA* 8:357). Here in the Supplement, he further argues that the fact that human beings are geographically separated thanks to religious and linguistic differences can be interpreted as facilitating our goal of perpetual peace, for these differences will help to prevent us from founding a universal monarchy or all-dominating world power, which would be counterproductive for maintaining peace on earth ("ZeF"/*AA* 8:367). We are instead motivated to work out our differences, and attempt to bring about, even if perpetual peace is not immediately possible, then at the very least a universal state of equilibrium ("ZeF"/*AA* 8:367).

Nature will also lead us toward implementing a condition of universal hospitality. Kant writes that while it "wisely separates the nations," nature also unites them by means of their mutual self-interest, because the spirit of commerce cannot exist alongside war and requires peaceful relationships. Nations will therefore be driven to advocate the noble goal of peace, not because of moral motivations, but out of their own self-interest in commerce ("ZeF"/*AA* 8:365–67). In his exposition of the third definitive article, Kant had already given an argument for the cosmopolitan right to universal hospitality based on the right of possession in common of the earth's surface ("ZeF"/*AA* 8:358). Here in the Supplement, he adds to it by saying that because of the spirit of commerce, we will be compelled to promote peace and be hospitable to foreigners, not for moral reasons but in order not to interrupt commerce, for "the spirit of commerce . . . cannot coexist with war and . . . sooner or later takes hold of every nation" ("ZeF"/*AA* 8:368).[16]

In sum, the First Supplement elaborates on the political agenda put forth by the preliminary and definitive articles and produces a nonideal theory of peace by employing the principle of political *Zweckmässigkeit*. It grants us the assumption that, in addition to the requirements of the pure principle of *Recht*, our natural tendencies and cultural activities, when viewed teleologically, will at the very least propel us to gradually solve the problem of perpetual peace. Peace is not only a pure ideal required by the principle of *Recht* but can be rendered feasible by means of the principle of political *Zweckmässigkeit*. Nature guarantees perpetual peace by the actual mechanisms of human inclinations and cultural activities, not through moral considerations. We come to desire peace on earth because we want to preserve our lives and possessions, understanding that wars are brutal, costly, and in the final analysis, useless. As I have shown, this guarantee of nature should not be taken to mean that this is the real purpose of nature or that perpetual peace will necessarily come about. We make such teleological statements about nature by using the principle of political *Zweckmässigkeit* because it is *useful* to conceive of these realms in this way, relative to our purposes, from a pragmatic point of view. The evidence Kant finds in the empirical consideration of human inclinations guided by the regulative teleological understanding of nature makes it theoretically *likely* that perpetual peace will come about, even if the speculative reason is not granted to foretell that perpetual peace *will* come about. This would be to embrace dogmatism, claiming to know what is unknowable within the limits of possible experience. It is, as he claims, "a far-fetched idea in theory" to claim that nature *is* purposive ("ZeF"/ AA 8:362), and if it were a theoretically justified idea that peace will come about regardless of what we do, by means of nature, it would not make sense to claim it as a political goal. That is, if it will necessarily happen we do not need to do anything at all to achieve it. Instead, by positing peace as a regulative political goal and by employing a teleological understanding of nature and history, we can figure out what sorts of policies or institutions should be implemented here and now so that this goal remains within our reach. This is in part granted by the principle of *Recht* and in part by the principle of political *Zweckmässigkeit*.

Recht and *Zweckmässigkeit* as Complementary Principles of Kant's Political Thought

Although what the Supplement accomplishes is not dogmatic, one may still ask if it is indeed really necessary. In Ellis's view, because Kant's notion of judgment is sufficient to demonstrate the practical necessity of perpetual peace, a teleological guarantee of peace is not only dogmatic but also unnecessary.[17] Given both that Kant limits the epistemological status of this guarantee and that we already have a practical necessity originating out of the principle of *Recht* and the doctrines postulated by this principle, Ellis argues that he might as well have omitted it.[18]

In my view, the first Supplement is not only useful but also necessary for complementing the ideal theory of "Toward Perpetual Peace." If all we had in the Kantian framework were the three definitive articles of peace, with no elaboration on their feasibility, we would not know whether we can expect to have real results: all we would know is that we *ought* to implement them. The First Supplement here is taking political *Zweckmässigkeit* one step further to provide a physico-geographical perspective that will support our goal of establishing peace on earth. The principle of political *Zweckmässigkeit* is useful because it allows Kant to orient himself in his inquiry of physico-geographical conditions and human inclinations in order to further explore whether we can reasonably expect to implement a republican constitution, a federation of free states, and universal hospitality—and therefore achieve peace. This teleological consideration is also necessary because, without a consideration of their empirical feasibility, these three ideals remain just that, ideals

CHAPTER 5

originating out of the principle of *Recht*. The principle of political *Zweckmässigkeit*, therefore, gives these ideals a fuller content as well as pragmatic support.

The First Supplement consists of an actual *supplement* (*Anhang*) to the definitive articles of perpetual peace in the form of a series of reflections on the feasibility of his three specific ideals for peace for our less-than-ideal circumstances. In this sense, it *complements* Kant's ideal theory of politics based on the principle of *Recht*. Kant is providing knowledge of what nature makes of the human beings in light of what they ought to make of themselves. Such theorization is a matter of a nonideal theory of politics, which here takes the form of a physical geography from a pragmatic point of view. Although this is not the term that Kant himself uses, we can call this a preliminary political geography.

When Kant turns to pragmatic considerations in responding to political questions, such as the direction of history (in the "Idea" essay), the aim of human natural-cultural development (in the third *Critique*), and the suitableness of nature outside us for our political ambitions (in the First Supplement), he is doing nonideal theory. As I have shown in the previous chapters, in the first case he is providing a political history and in the second a political anthropology, both from the perspective of a cosmopolitan goal. In "Toward Perpetual Peace," especially in the First Supplement, he is providing, through the same nonideal theory approach to politics utilizing the principle of *Zweckmässigkeit*, a preliminary political geography and reminding us that geography matters to politics.

The disregard in the scholarship for the regulative teleology at play in Kant's political writings is partly responsible for the idea that Kant's only relevant political legacy is the ideal theory laid out in the three definite articles of "Toward Perpetual Peace." What we miss when we omit the First Supplement or ignore the teleological language in this essay altogether, however, is that Kant here shows an awareness of physical geographical conditions and their ramifications for our political ideals. He asks how natural conditions may or may not facilitate social, cultural, and political progress. Through his nonideal theory of politics he provides what he himself calls in his lectures on anthropology and physical geography "a knowledge of the world [*Welterkenntnis*]" (*Anth/AA* 7: 119–20; *PG/AA* 9: 157–58). Teleological considerations that appear in Kant's writings on politics, then, remind us that nonideal theory, namely, questions of the historical, cultural, and geographical feasibility of our goals, is a necessary and important part of political thought. This shows us that Kant is more than a mere ideal theorist of politics and that there are more resources in his political thought than we previously thought. In what follows, I show that his particular understanding of the world is also at play in his formulation of a public *Recht* concerning the international—or more accurately, global—relations. A geopolitical consideration provided by a teleological perspective on the current status of the world complements Kant's proposal for the cosmopolitan right, specifying it to be a right of universal hospitality.

6

Peace, Hospitality, and the Shape of the Earth

Commentators such as Höffe, Flikschuh, Ellis, and Ripstein have demonstrated that Kant's political philosophy in *The Doctrine of Right* is not simply an extension of the ideal formal ethics found in his *Groundwork of the Metaphysics of Morals* or the *Critique of Practical Reason* for a number of reasons: ethics is about internal freedom whereas politics is about external freedom;[1] ethical and juridical lawgiving have distinct spheres of moral competence;[2] and duties of ethics are nonrelational whereas those of politics are relational.[3] Simply put, while *Recht* is a branch of morals in the broader sense of the term *Moral*, the principle of *Recht* is not directly derived from the Categorical Imperative, the supreme principle of Kant's moral philosophy. Moreover, Kant argues in the Introduction to *The Metaphysics of Morals* that *Recht* requires us to take into consideration pathological and natural incentives—this is something we should avoid in Kant's ethical theory as it is found in the *Groundwork*, the second *Critique*, and *The Doctrine of Virtue*.

One important thing that the principle of *Zweckmässigkeit* brings to the table in *The Doctrine of Right* is that, as the material principle of politics, it allows us to incorporate a physical-geographical knowledge of the world so that we can conceptualize a specific universal policy of cosmopolitan right: universal hospitality. I will argue first that the consideration of the necessity of bumping up against each other in a limited spherical space that belongs to us all in common is the reason why we must posit a global *Recht* regulating our interactions with one another at this public level in the first place. To this extent, the principle of *Recht*, as a principle requiring incentives, already incorporates an empirical consideration of the shape of the earth in the proposals that it generates, including the proposal of the cosmopolitan right. Second, figuring out the specific form that this interaction must take—namely, its content—requires that we get a deeper knowledge of the real conditions of the world; it requires a more granular theoretical map, as it were. My argument is that in order to arrive at such a theoretical map Kant employs the principle of political *Zweckmässigkeit* and comes to propose universal hospitality as a necessary condition of peaceful commerce. More specifically, I will show that

CHAPTER 6

because Kant formulates this right of hospitality by reflecting on and in response to the colonial injustices of his time, it must be interpreted first and foremost as a pragmatic, realistic, and a concrete solution for the problems that he observes around him.

This interpretation of the cosmopolitan right of hospitality aims to challenge two prevailing ones: Benhabib's reading of hospitality as a universal moral obligation, and Ypi's and Niesen's readings of hospitality as proof of Kant's staunch anticolonialism. My interpretation of the cosmopolitan right of universal hospitality rather highlights its grounding in both *Recht* and political *Zweckmässigkeit* in order to advocate for turning our attention to the nonideal context in which Kant proposes such a right. I will show that none of the prevailing readings are nuanced enough to tease out the concrete basis of Kantian hospitality. When we pay attention to the geopolitical knowledge that Kant incorporates into his formulation of the cosmopolitan right, we will see that hospitality is not just a broad normative and moral ideal. Lastly, I will also show that Kant's formulation of hospitality as a right of possible commerce prioritizes the interests of European commercial states, and as such, his is a Western-specific conceptualization of a purportedly universal political right. However, the fact that he uses the material principle of politics in this conceptualization of the cosmopolitan right to universal hospitality, the principle of *Zweckmässigkeit*, reminds us to pay close attention to a genuine assessment of the geographical and geopolitical conditions that undergird this right. Thus, teleology, or the regulative principle of *Zweckmässigkeit*, does not only provide hope or a comforting prospect for politics. Kant's deployment of this principle in the *Doctrine of Right* further reminds us that spatial considerations, specifically a geopolitical knowledge of the world, matter to the formulation of global or cosmopolitan rights. Focusing on Kant's nonideal theory, then, encourages us to look beyond mere universal norms and leads us to anchor our political theories in more accurate depictions of the world that are informed by history, culture, and geography.

Ethics and Politics in Kant's Practical Philosophy: A Brief Overview

Despite contemporary Kantian liberal political philosophers' tendency to conflate ethics and politics in Kant's thought,[4] these two domains have distinct principles. The domain of ethics has its supreme principle in the Categorical Imperative: "Act only in accordance with that maxim through which you can at the same time will that it become a universal law" (*GMS/ AA* 4:421). The domain of politics, by contrast, has as its universal principle the concept of *Recht*: "Any action is *right* [*Recht*] if it can coexist with everyone's freedom in accordance with a universal law, or if on its maxim the freedom of choice of each can coexist with everyone's freedom in accordance with a universal law" (*MS/AA* 6:230). They might sound similar at first, but the crux of the difference between the two principles is the domains over which they legislate: while the Categorical Imperative is a law of our inner freedom, or the freedom of the will, the principle of right refers to our external freedom, or our "independence from being constrained by another's choice" (*MS/AA* 6:237). As Katrin Flikschuh also argues, then, external freedom is a novel conception of freedom, not to be conflated with the autonomous willing that Kant develops in the *Groundwork* or the *Critique of Practical Reason*.[5] There is a substantial difference between how Kant's ethical and political inquiries are oriented.

Let me note also that *Recht*, the guiding principle of law or politics, is concerned with juridical law or rightful lawgiving, while political duties do not require the sole incentive of dutifulness.[6] In §4 of the Introduction to *The Metaphysics of Morals*, Kant distinguishes between duties of right and duties of virtue. According to this distinction, what underlies our duties of right, or political duties, is a *juridical* (*rechtlich*) *lawgiving*, which is defined as that "which admits an incentive other than the idea of duty itself" (*MS/ AA* 6:219). On the other hand, our moral duties, or duties of virtue are prescribed by *ethical* (*ethisch*) *lawgiving* (*MS/AA* 6:219). This means that for Kant juridical or political duties are directed merely at external actions and their conformity to law, whereas ethical duties require that the laws themselves be the determining ground of actions (*MS/AA* 6:214). He writes,

> Duties in accordance with rightful or juridical [*rechtlich*] lawgiving can be only external duties, since this lawgiving does not require that the idea of this duty, which is internal, itself be the determining ground of the agent's choice; since it still needs an incentive suited to the law, it can connect only external incentives with it. (*MS/AA* 6:219)

The distinction between juridical and ethical lawgiving found in *The Metaphysics of Morals* shows that the domain of *Recht* is not fully reducible to the domain of ethics in the Kantian system because, unlike ethics, politics must deal with pathological, natural, and subjective incentives.

In Flikschuh's terms, the distinction between law and ethics here refers to their respective spheres of moral competence; as she puts it, for

Kant "rightful action need not be ethical."[7] According to Kant's distinction between juridical and ethical lawgiving, a juridical law based on the principle of *Recht* does not require, as ethical lawgiving does, that we do the right thing for the right reasons or with no immediate or mediated incentives other than the idea of duty. To the contrary, a juridical law is often prescribed by taking into account various internal and external incentives, as opposed to an ethical law that requires us to avoid such incentives in its formulation (*MS/AA* 6:219).

Let us recall that in Kant's moral philosophy, actions are moral only when they are done for the sake of duty and to obey the moral law (i.e., the Categorical Imperative). without any reference to an incentive or a desired result (*GMS/AA* 4:397–98). Thus, inclinations, feelings, expectation of reward, or avoidance of punishment cannot enter into moral lawgiving, because such incentives do not originate from a good will; moral law-giving, rather, is solely determined and necessitated by pure practical reason. By contrast, in *The Metaphysics of Morals* Kant proposes that the domain of *Recht* admits of and even *requires* that we take into consideration the context, incentives, and consequences of human interaction.[8] If political prescriptions given by juridical lawgiving necessarily include pathological, natural, and subjective incentives, then we must conclude that the principle of *Recht* in the Kantian system is neither reducible to nor exhausted by the Categorical Imperative.

This means that the grounds of the obligation and law-giving in the juridical-political and the ethical domains in Kant are distinct. If a rightful action is not always necessarily an ethical action, then the problem of a just state, one of the main issues of the principle of right, is subordinated to ethics but not exhausted by it. The point is that one can act justly without at the same time acting virtuously, which means that the domain of *Recht*, the proper domain of politics in Kant, while a part of Kant's moral (*moralische*) or practical philosophy broadly construed, is not simply an off-shoot of the pure principles of Kant's ethics, as Höffe, Flikschuh, Ripstein, and Ellis also contend.[9]

Furthermore, *The Doctrine of Right* already incorporates an account of the human condition, a version of what Otfried Höffe calls "an anthropology of right." Höffe argues that *The Doctrine of Right* practices a specific kind of anthropology, one which asks the fundamental question of "why right is at all needed, given the *conditio humana*."[10] According to Höffe, then, Kant makes two modest assumptions that still have a high degree of generality: that we are finite rational beings and that we must share limited living space with each other.[11] Therefore we see that *Rechtslehre* has quite a concrete understanding of politics. That is, a doctrine of right is not a mere extension of Kant's ethical theory but provides a political discourse that minimally incorporates an account of pathological, natural, and subjective incentives, such as the external and empirical circumstances of our interactions. The assumptions about our finitude and the nature of our habitat are still abstractions or generalizations. However, these assumptions show us that *The Doctrine of Right* operates at a lower level of abstraction than the formal ethical theories of the *Groundwork* or the second *Critique*, and that therefore Kant's political theory is more interested in the empirical and seemingly contingent variables of our collective lives than we might have previously thought.

In what follows I turn to a set of particular incentives that Kant takes to be relevant to his formulation of the three rights in *The Doctrine of Right*, the incentives at stake in how he conceives of the cosmopolitan right of universal hospitality. First, I will show that a consideration of the physico-geographical shape of the earth is already embedded in the general formulation of the principle of *Recht*. Second, I will argue that Kant's proposal of the right of universal hospitality arises as a relevant and necessary pragmatic solution to a contemporary problem, resulting from a reflection—provided by the principle of political *Zweckmässigkeit*—on (some of) the world's inhabitants' growing spirit of commerce as well as on the injustices of colonialism that accompany this spirit. Thus, it is textually and conceptually incorrect to think that the cosmopolitan right of universal hospitality is a moral obligation grounded in the Categorical Imperative, for, as a duty of right, it is a pragmatic precept occasioned by the nonideal circumstances in which Kant finds himself.

A Natural Incentive for the Cosmopolitan Right: The Spherical Shape of the Earth

In "Toward Perpetual Peace" Kant writes that the cosmopolitan right to universal hospitality "belongs to all human beings by virtue of the right of possession in common of the earth's surface on which, as a sphere, they cannot disperse infinitely but must finally put up with being near one another" ("ZeF"/*AA* 8:358). No human being has any original claim to the earth's surface, and thus, the problem of how we ought to interact with each other in a rightful way in an enclosed habitat constitutes the very problem of the cosmopolitan *Recht*. The relevance of our natural obligation to live near one another due to the spherical shape of the earth is reiterated in the postulate of public right in the *Rechtslehre*, a postulate that has its ground in the concept of right in external relations: "When you cannot avoid living side by side with all others, you ought to leave the state of nature and proceed with them into a rightful condition" (*MS/AA* 6:307). Kant clarifies this notion of public right as grounded in external relations a little later in the text, where he writes that, "[s]ince the earth's surface is not unlimited but closed, the concepts of the right of a state and of a right of nations lead inevitably to the idea of a right for a state of nations (*ius gentium*) or cosmopolitan right (*ius cosmopoliticum*)" (*MS/AA* 6:311). Simply put, the spherical shape of the earth necessitates that we implement a cosmopolitan right regulating how we interact with each other as entities bumping into one another in such a limited space. Thus, the physical or geographical fact of the shape of the earth provides an incentive for formulating a cosmopolitan right.

Such spatial considerations or incentives of space are already at work in both private and public right. That is to say, what Otfried Höffe terms an "anthropology of right" in *The Doctrine of Right* presupposes that *Recht* is minimally about embodied human beings and their external freedom in spatial relations. Katrin Flikschuh dwells on the metaphorical resonances of the very image of the earth's spherical surface and suggests that "the abstract but widely accessible image of the earth's spherical surface provides a theoretical context which enables different contributors to explore and discuss issues of globalization and of global justice from a common perspective without in so doing fixing a predetermined policy-making agenda."[12] For Arthur Ripstein, space is more than a useful metaphor for Kant; in his *Force and Freedom*, Ripstein reminds us that Kant's principles of right are meant to

> [govern] *persons represented as occupying space*. The basic case for thinking about your right to your own person is *your right to your own body*; the basic case for thinking about property is property in land, that is, *a right to exclude others from a particular location on the Earth's surface*; the basic case for thinking about contract is the transfer of an object from one place to another; the basic case for thinking about a state involves *its occupation of a particular region of the Earth's surface*.[13]

This formulation of the basic cases for thinking about rights, at various levels, in spatial terms also confirms the difference between right and ethics that I have drawn earlier. As Ripstein puts it, in formulating principles of right, space has a normative significance which "arises from the ways in which separate persons who occupy space can come into conflict in the exercise of their freedom, depending on where they are doing their space-occupying activities and what others happen to be doing in the same location."[14] Along these lines, Jeffrey Edwards develops a spatial understanding of private *Recht*, arguing that the spherical shape of the earth's surface, an objective property of the earth, has to be thought in connection with Kant's justification of the concepts of original possession and acquisition.[15] In sum, all of these authors account for the significance of spatial relations in *The Doctrine of Right* and further confirm that the very notion of *Recht* already incorporates spatial considerations in a way that goes beyond a simple application of the Categorical Imperative to spatially located or embodied beings.

A cosmopolitan right requires a genuine assessment and a successful negotiation of our external conditions; in Onora O'Neill's terms, "our *geographical* situation inevitably raises *political* questions about the forms of association that a plurality of human beings can have, given that they cannot indefinitely continue to lead dispersed and solitary lives."[16] It is not through considerations of ethics or duties of virtue, then, but based on a spatial consideration that Kant concludes that a right must be implemented on a global scale:

> This rational idea of a *peaceful,* even if not friendly, thoroughgoing community of all nations on the earth that can come into relations affecting one another is *not a philanthropic (ethical) principle but a principle having to do with rights.* Nature has enclosed [all nations of the earth] together within determinate limits (by the spherical shape of the place they live in, a *globus terraqueus [globe of earth and water]*). (*MS/AA* 6:352, emphases in the original).

Note here that the cosmopolitan right is *not* justified in terms of ethics or morality; it is not grounded in the duty of treating others as ends in themselves or even in a friendly manner. Kant poses the question at stake here as one of rights, arising out of a consideration of the concrete geographical fact that we live in a spherical and thus limited space, in a *globus terraqueus.*[17] This is a contingent physico-geographical fact that nonetheless requires our lawful compliance. While we do not know exactly why we live on a sphere, having found ourselves in this situation we are now required to find a solution to the problem of navigating this space in a rightful manner. In this way, we see that for Kant a geographical consideration is embedded in the very formulation of a cosmopolitan right.

In sum, if *The Doctrine of Right* incorporates an empirical consideration of space, it does so still in idealized and general terms. A consideration of space or of the shape of the earth leads Kant to formulate a cosmopolitan right, a right possessed by all human beings on account of their living on a limited habitat, without determining in particular what this right should be. In other words, this spatial consideration requires that there be a principle regulating how we interact with each other but it does not immediately tell us about any particular, appropriate principle for such rightful interaction. Complementing and concretizing this spatial consideration, the principle of political *Zweckmässigkeit* will allow Kant to draw a more detailed theoretical map of his current conditions, and from this perspective to propose a more specific principle regulating our global interactions on this earth. The additional specification that narrows the content of the cosmopolitan right down to a principle of universal hospitality originates out of Kant's consideration of commercial relations and colonial injustices, as I show next.

Geopolitical Incentives for the Cosmopolitan Right: Commerce and Colonialism

That we live on a sphere requires that we come into contact with one another: this is a geographical fact. A cosmopolitan right (*Weltbürgerrecht*) further requires that these interactions be peaceful, if not friendly. While the shape of the earth necessitates human interaction, it does not dictate the form that this interaction will take, however. In other words, the fact that the earth belongs to all does not mean that we can move about it freely, expecting to be welcomed by everyone at any time. Kant will proceed to lay out specific provisions for our ability and right to do so: he states that the right to the earth's surface "does not extend beyond the conditions which make it possible to *seek commerce* [*Verkehr*] with the old inhabitants" ("ZeF"/*AA* 8:358). Taking into account the empirical realities of his own sociohistorical circumstances, he posits *commerce* as the preferred form of international relations. What he is proposing is not more porous borders or an unlimited freedom of travel—what is in question here is not an unconditional right of hospitality for vulnerable populations, as we often imagine it to be. Rather, as we will see, it is a very limited right of travel for possible commerce.

A more specific articulation of the cosmopolitan right originates out of Kant's reflections on his own geopolitical context, in which he considers the inhospitable conduct of the civilized states of Europe during his time and finds that under the auspices of hospitality European states proceed to conquer, colonize, and exploit other peoples. As he writes in "Toward Perpetual Peace" concerning the actions of the British Empire: "In the East Indies (Hindustan), they brought in foreign soldiers under the pretext of merely proposing to set up trading posts, but with them oppression of the inhabitants, incitement of the various Indian states to widespread wars, famine, rebellions, treachery, and the whole litany of troubles that oppress the human race" ("ZeF"/*AA* 8:358–59). Kant goes on to argue that it is in order to avoid such evils—wars, famine, and rebellions—that we should aim at instituting the right of universal hospitality as a cosmopolitan right. This right, however, must be limited: it is not the right of a guest to plunder or to be entertained but that of a visitor seeking possible commerce. Such a limited right of universal hospitality is necessary for all the peoples from the distant parts of the world, not so that they can become one global community without borders, but so that they can enter into peaceable commercial relations with one another ("ZeF"/*AA* 8:357). I have shown in my analysis of the cosmopolitan right in "Toward Perpetual Peace" that Kant foregrounds commercial enterprise in his political reflections and his formulation of hospitality. This centering of commerce, as we saw in chapter 5, was also at play in his condemnation of the cruelties of colonial trade in "Toward Perpetual Peace," not only from a purely moral perspective but additionally and importantly from a commercial or pragmatic one.

Another place where we see Kant's emphasis on commerce as a means for peaceful coexistence of the inhabitants of the world is in his pragmatic hope that the spirit of commerce will eventually render wars unnecessary and unprofitable. Flikschuh emphasizes that this naïveté is in part due to his fascination with the growth of overseas commerce and trade, which allows him to develop a preliminary account of economic desiring that becomes a centrally relevant incentive for politics.[18] As Ypi puts it, commercial interaction is in this sense the worldly manifestation of what Kant called in the "Idea" essay our unsociable sociability:[19] although we would rather be left alone, the spherical shape of the earth—a material fact—does not really allow for isolationism.[20] In other words, the shape of the world, purposively viewed, encourages or even requires us to come into contact with others primarily through commerce. In the First Supplement to "Toward Perpetual Peace" Kant writes that while "nature wisely separates the nations," it also unites them by means of their mutual self-interest, because the spirit of commerce "cannot coexist with war and . . . sooner or later takes hold of every nation"; because of their selfish inclinations and "admittedly not through incentives of morality," each nation will eventually be compelled to promote honorable peace ("ZeF"/*AA* 8:368). Here, he claims that we will be compelled to promote peace and to be hospitable to foreigners, specifically to those who are sales representatives or traders, albeit not for moral reasons but in order not to interrupt commerce.[21]

In §62 of *The Doctrine of Right*, Kant reiterates most of the points that he makes in "Toward Perpetual Peace" in more detail. We find once again that the cosmopolitan right to universal hospitality is *not* a call for open borders or an unlimited right to visit anywhere anytime:

> All nations . . . stand originally in a community of possible physical interaction [*Wechselwirkung*] (*commercium*), that is, in a thoroughgoing relation of each to all the others of *offering to engage in commerce* [*Verkehr*] with any other and each has a right to make this attempt without the other being authorized to behave toward it as an enemy because it has made this attempt. This right, since it has to do with the possible union of all nations with a view to certain universal laws for their possible commerce [*Verkehr*], can be called *cosmopolitan right*. (*MS/AA* 6:352)

He again considers a series of questions related to the commercial relations in his contemporary context of colonization and conquest. He asks if the cruelties that go along with the undertakings of the so-called civilized states can in any way be justified in terms of the relations of right, which require a just allocation of space and a principle for navigating that which originally belongs to all in common. Here, he finds nothing that would justify their inhospitable behavior. There can be no justification of the cruel conduct and of the subjugation of these "less civilized nations" to the worst cruelties. Even the so-called civilizing missions or the introduction of Christianity will not make their suffering rightful: as Kant puts it, "all these supposedly good intentions cannot wash away the stain of injustice in the means used for them" (*MS/AA* 6:353). From this, Kant concludes that we must implement the right to hospitable commerce as the basic right of all human beings who have to interact with each other. Making hospitable commerce a global right is therefore the most pragmatic way to negotiate the geographical conditions in which we find ourselves, both in "Toward Perpetual Peace" and in *The Doctrine of Right*.

Note that the cosmopolitanism that Kant espouses in *The Doctrine of Right* as a universal right of hospitality is *not* primarily a moral ideal. As I have argued, it is a consideration arising out of a balancing act among the limited resources that we have on earth, the necessity to put up one another in close proximity, our selfish inclinations, the growing spirit of commerce, and colonialism and its discontents. In his consideration of these material facts Kant employs the principle of political *Zweckmässigkeit*, which provides him with a regulatively teleological view of his circumstances, allowing him to evaluate the actual and possible consequences of these circumstances on a global scale. Based on these reflections, Kant concludes that the spirit of commerce and the injustices of colonialism provide incentives to posit universal hospitality as the legitimate and limited principle of our interaction with foreigners. Universally hospitable commercial relations, the specific cosmopolitan right, are proposed as the primary means of eventually securing perpetual peace on earth.

My interpretation of hospitality as grounded in Kant's nonideal theory of politics, and specifically in his spatial and geopolitical considerations, presents a challenge for the prevailing readings of Kantian hospitality. In contemporary social and political philosophy, Kantian hospitality tends to be taken up in one of two ways: on the one hand, we have ideal theorists of cosmopolitanism, such as Seyla Benhabib, who proposes in *The Rights of Others* that we extend what was originally a circumscribed right to visit for a limited amount of time into a basic human right to permanent residency and citizenship for all disenfranchised others: aliens, refugees, and immigrants.[22] She admits that this goes beyond Kant's original intent; nonetheless, and especially in *Another Cosmopolitanism*, she interprets the right of hospitality as a mark of the capaciousness of the norms of universal morality in an increasingly interdependent world.[23] Benhabib therefore takes Kantian hospitality to be a *prescriptive* term belonging to an ideal and moral theory of politics. On the other hand, we have Peter Niesen, Lea Ypi, and Jeremy Waldron, who each read Kant's restriction of hospitality as his ultimate and definitive condemnation of colonialism. They argue that by shaping the right as a limited right to visit, Kant takes a *normatively* anti-imperialistic stance in a contemporary political debate about whether European commercial states may settle on what they understand to be underinhabited or underused lands.[24] Thus, rather than positioning it as a timeless cosmopolitan ideal to which we should aspire, Niesen, Ypi, and Waldron draw our attention to the specific nonideal context in which the Kantian right to universal hospitality arises. From this context, they conclude that the most important intervention that this right of hospitality makes to political theory is its stance against settler colonialism.

While both positions make important contributions to political philosophy and discussions of hospitality, my contention is that neither is nuanced enough to portray a full and systematic picture of how Kantian hospitality fits in with the rest of Kant's political thought. In my view, their attention to the nonideal context of this right is insufficient and can even be misleading. I have already shown that the universal right to hospitality is not an unconditional moral ideal of cosmopolitanism, but one that is necessarily tied to the specific historical and geopolitical context of European colonialism. Thus, Benhabib's moral interpretation of hospitality is not textually accurate and does a further disservice to Kantian cosmopolitan political thought by hiding from our sight the context and incentives of the social-political interactions that Kant proposed to be pertinent. We are reminded of this context by Waldron, Ypi, and Niesen; however, in contrast to their unequivocal championing of Kant's anticolonialism,

I will show that his anti-colonialist stance is at best ambiguous, for in the end the formulation of hospitality in the text nevertheless privileges the perspective and the commercial interests of the European states, or the Global North. Thus, the normative stance recommended by Kant's policy of universal hospitality is already shaped by a specific geopolitical context and a skewed understanding of this context.

Hospitality as a Universal Moral Obligation:
Benhabib and Human Rights

Seyla Benhabib's formulation of universal hospitality aligns with and even constitutes the background of our widespread usage of the term today. While Benhabib's proposal to extend the meaning of hospitality to a moral ideal that ought to include all disenfranchised populations—specifically aliens, immigrants, and refugees—is a noble one, I will show that it in fact has nothing to do with the way Kant formulates this principle. Furthermore and more importantly, Benhabib's ideal theory argument, which relies on a moral interpretation of "Toward Perpetual Peace" as well as *The Doctrine of Right*, tends to obscure the entanglement of the real state of world affairs in global economic relations, as Bonnie Honig aptly points out.[25]

In her earlier work, *The Rights of Others*, Benhabib takes Kant's construction of the cosmopolitan right of temporary sojourn as a reference point, and proposes that we extend this right to all human beings.[26] In *Another Cosmopolitanism*, she reiterates her Kantianism, as she "follow[s] the Kantian tradition in thinking about cosmopolitanism as the emergence of norms that govern relations among individuals in a global civil society."[27] Here, Benhabib contends that the actual Kantian right of hospitality entails a claim only to temporary residence on the part of the stranger who comes on our land; however, she writes, "hospitality is a right that belongs to all human beings insofar as we view them as potential participants in a world republic."[28] Furthermore, she argues both in *The Rights of Others* and *Another Cosmopolitanism* that hospitality "occupies that space between human rights and civil rights, between the rights of humanity in our person and the rights that accrue to us insofar as we are citizens of specific republics."[29] By "Kantian hospitality," Benhabib refers to "all human rights claims which are cross-border in scope."[30] Despite Kant's own restrictions, therefore, she argues that the right to be a temporary resident must be understood "as a human right which can be justified along the principles of a universalistic morality."[31]

Benhabib's extension of Kantian hospitality revolves around a moral reading of Kant's political philosophy. In this extension, despite the political and economic complications that may arise out of his celebration of commercial and maritime capitalism, she understands Kant to be ultimately committed to our individual moral obligations toward other free and rational human beings. She then frames her view of the right to hospitality as a universal moral duty stemming from each and every person's innate freedom, which includes the freedom to travel:

> Kant wanted to justify the expansion of commercial and maritime capitalism in his time, insofar as these developments brought the human race into closer contact, without condoning European imperialism. The cosmopolitan right of hospitality gives one the right of peaceful temporary sojourn, but it does not entitle one to plunder and exploit, conquer and overwhelm by superior force those among whom one is seeking sojourn. *Yet the cosmopolitan right is a right precisely because it is grounded upon the common humanity of each and every person and his or her freedom of the will which also includes the freedom to travel beyond the confines of one's cultural, religious, and ethnocentric walls.*[32]

Here, Benhabib suggests that the cosmopolitan right of universal hospitality takes the Categorical Imperative, in its formula of humanity, as its major normative principle. From there, she concludes that "the universal right to hospitality which is due to every human being imposes upon us an *imperfect moral duty* to help and offer shelter to those whose life, limb, and well-being are endangered."[33] This is an imperfect duty, meaning that it permits us to make exceptions in cases where other concerns (such as self-defense) would override it.

Benhabib contends that asking questions about how narrowly or widely we must interpret this imperfect duty of hospitality might be anachronistic, since Kant's own motivations for proposing this cosmopolitan right are *not* his "concerns for the needs of the poor, the downtrodden, the persecuted, and the oppressed as they search for safe haven, but rather the Enlightenment preoccupation of Europeans to seek contact with other peoples and to appropriate the riches of other parts of the world."[34] Nonetheless, she immediately drops this contextual consideration and urges us to look at the underlying universal moral obligation. In this way, she adapts the right of hospitality as a human right grounded in a universal notion of morality and argues—inspired by but eventually contra Kant—that "the right to membership of the temporary resident must be viewed as a human right which can be justified along the principles of a universalistic morality."[35]

CHAPTER 6

As she mentions in passing without much elaboration, however, there is a peculiar political economy tied to the context of Kant's own formulation of the right of hospitality. This political economy prioritizes commercial relations and interests over philanthropic concerns; and the ideal of hospitality therefore has a somewhat paradoxical nature. In his playfully titled piece, "Hostipitality," Jacques Derrida warns us about the aporias inherent to hospitality, reminding us of the uneasy affiliation between hostility and hospitality as well as of the always asymmetrical relationship between the host and the visitor that is contained in our very understanding of the term.[36] For Derrida, the problem is that hospitality by definition cannot be disentangled from hostility and therefore can never be truly unconditional. It is not an egalitarian exchange; the guest is always in the house of another and not their own.

Building on Derrida's warning, Bonnie Honig criticizes Benhabib's for her optimism about the universal ideals of humanity being easily extendable to disenfranchised populations and for ignoring the long history of colonialism and xenophobia.[37] Benhabib finds the idea of hospitality helpful, since in her view this idea seems to have anticipated and intimated the evolution of cosmopolitan norms of justice, whose development, she argues, we are witnessing in various areas of international politics. In her account, we see a remarkable evolution, especially in the norms of hospitality (which go far beyond Kant's understanding), in that they are recognized and increasingly protected by the European Convention on Fundamental Rights and Freedoms.[38] Honig argues that Benhabib's ideal theory account is "marked by traces of earlier universalisms that promise *moral guidance from above to a wayward human world below.*"[39] To cast the recent developments in Europe as a welcoming of refugees with open arms on account of a universal morality, as Benhabib does, is dangerous, as this account obscures the fact that there are now new borders within Europe, drawn across lines of culture or ethnicity, that construct a new political order which Balibar has provocatively called an "apartheid in Europe."[40] Honig reminds us that European hospitality has always already been conditional, clearly demarcating those worthy of being included and those who must remain at the threshold.[41]

Additionally, Benhabib's extension of hospitality as a cosmopolitan right follows a *moral* account of political theory; however, Kant's notion of cosmopolitan right is not grounded in his ethics or in the Categorical Imperative, as I have shown. My close reading of the relevant Kantian texts further demonstrates that for Kant political thought is not directly reducible to a universal ethics, consisting of idealized notions of agency or institutions like the ones Benhabib seems to have in mind. This means that political rights are not directly deducible from or reducible to pure moral ideals. Rather, the principle of *Recht*, the governing principle of Kant's political thought, requires us to pay attention to the historical context and actual consequences of human interaction. My earlier analysis of the distinction between Kant's ethical and political thought shows that the cosmopolitan right to universal hospitality belongs to the domain of right, not to that of ethics. Kant does not propose hospitality as an unconditional moral obligation that belongs to all human beings by virtue of their humanity, innate freedom, or free will—or even as an imperfect duty, as Benhabib claims. It is thus incorrect to interpret hospitality as a moral duty, perfect or imperfect, as if it has no historical or contextual resonances. At the very least, it is clear that Kant did not propose or take it to be without such considerations in the first place.

Furthermore and more importantly, what we miss when we read hospitality in exclusively ethical terms, as if it were a moral duty, is the awareness that Kant shows of the concrete geopolitical context in which our political ideals are developed. In his political theory, he frequently asks how external conditions may or may not facilitate the implementation of political duties. His reflections on the contingent elements and circumstances of politics, then, provide what he calls in his lectures on anthropology and physical geography a specific type of "knowledge of the world [*Welterkenntnis*]" (*Anth/AA* 7:119–20; see also *PG/AA* 9:157–58) that should matter to any theory of politics. Thus, Kant has a more robust or concrete understanding of politics than we often give him credit for. His formulation of the cosmopolitan right of universal hospitality is not a mere extension of his moral philosophy, but a principle that is attentive to the actual historical context of our political problems and the incentives of political action. We are reminded of the nonideal context in which Kant proposes universal hospitality as a cosmopolitan right by Niesen, Ypi, and Waldron; however, they downplay to varying degrees the Eurocentric view of commerce that shapes Kant's formulation of peaceful commercial relations, as I show next.

Commerce or "Interaction"

The term "commerce" has multiple valences in German as well as in English. In both languages, commerce may refer simply to "interaction between people and exchange of ideas and goods," or it may refer more specifically to "trade relations." A universal right of hospitality seems to be a communicative right with a broad scope, but it is limited, at least in Kant's imaginary, to commercial interaction. Kleingeld argues that the term *Verkehr* must be read as any type of interaction across borders, such as travel, migration, intellectual exchange, or commercial endeavors.[42] Indeed, Kant in the texts that I mentioned above alternates between two terms that may mean either "interaction or exchange" in a general sense (*Wechselwirkung*) or "the contractual and commercial exchange of property" (*Verkehr*). However, he seems to use these terms interchangeably not only because of the double meaning of the term "commerce," but also because the leading form of human interaction as he sees it takes the shape of actual commercial trade, as his subsequent remarks about trade posts and colonial settlement make clear. A central component of hospitality is that it is extended to those who wish to "engage in commerce" ("ZeF"/*AA* 8:358; see also *MS*/*AA* 6:352); thus, just as we cannot think of hospitality outside of the context of colonialism, we cannot think of it outside of a particular kind of political economy.[43]

Additionally, it remains at best ambiguous if it is a global or reciprocal right, for the typical claimants of hospitality in Kant's imagination are the merchants and colonists of European origin.[44] Niesen points out that because the limiting condition of hospitality is Kant's critique of European colonialism and imperialism, we cannot really take this right to refer to just any kind of exchange, transaction, or communication between two legal entities. He argues that the cosmopolitan right is in fact quite limited on account of the specific context in which it is raised:

> [The right of hospitality] provides people arriving at the borders of a foreign nation with the right to make communicative offers. Broadly speaking, those offers are of two different kinds: they may concern engaging in modes of exchange with the foreign nation's citizens, or they may concern "offering oneself" for community with them.[45]

According to Niesen, when we talk about hospitality we need to consider it not as an extension of one's innate right to freedom à la Benhabib, but more comprehensively as a way to take into account various empirical facts such as Kant's critique of colonial injustices.[46] Similarly, Ypi notes that here Kant is providing a common critique of colonialism such as the ones we find in Adam Smith, but that his account is distinguished by the fact that Kant places this critique in a theory of justice.[47] Thus, both Ypi and Niesen remind us of the importance of the empirical context in which Kant proposes and justifies the right of hospitality.

Along similar lines, in unpacking hospitality Jeremy Waldron urges us to pay more attention to the specific context in which these so-called hospitable interactions or exchanges take place. Waldron notes that although Benhabib's interpretation of Kant's principle of the right to universal hospitality might be a bit of a stretch, "there would be no point in reading these antiquated Prussian tracts if we did not stretch and distort them a bit to throw some light on our current concerns."[48] He raises the worry, however, that this reading fails to capture the unique contribution that the principle of hospitality is supposed to make to Kant's political philosophy, namely, the fact that it is a principle regulating the relations among people and peoples, not the relations among all human beings as potential participants in a world republic.[49] Focusing on the context in which Kant's proposal of a cosmopolitan right to hospitality is located, Waldron joins Niesen and Ypi in reading this moment as a critique of colonial violence, injustice, and exploitation, not only in the actions of states as national conquerors but also in the actions of traders, merchants, and settlers.[50]

In sum, these authors demonstrate that Kant's notion of hospitality is limited and cannot be considered independently of the nonideal context in which he finds himself (i.e., the geopolitical context that gives rise to his critique of colonialism and imperialism in the first place).[51] In other words, in their view, the true or unique theoretical contribution of the cosmopolitan right of hospitality is better brought out when we look at its context. Accordingly, hospitality is a right of those states seeking commerce, which is intended to prevent them from abusing their power during their visits to previously underinhabited lands. Kant is, in effect, telling the commercial states not to overstay their welcome and not to claim any rights or privileges besides those pertaining to peaceful commercial transactions. I would add that he is also telling the noncommercial states to be hospitable to those visitors, as long as these visitors behave themselves and simply trade.[52] Instituting the right of universal hospitality as a cosmopolitan right therefore makes sense in and responds to this specific colonial context as a way to regulate international trade.

While I agree with Waldron, Ypi, and Niesen on the link between hospitality and the critique of colonialism, then, I would additionally urge us to account for the issues of commercial enterprise in discussions of a Kantian cosmopolitan right. As I have shown, in both "Toward Perpetual Peace" and *The Doctrine of Right*, the right of hospitality arises out of Kant's critique of colonialism as well as an emphasis *on commerce*. We have seen that this right is justified as a precaution against colonial conquest and furthermore as an incentive for commerce: lest the merchants overstay their welcome, the right of hospitality must be limited to peaceful trade. Economic trade is clearly the sense of "commerce" that Kant had in mind, especially when we remember his condemnation of the ongoing abuses of hospitality in the case of those pretending to set up trading posts or plunder underinhabited lands, as I discussed above. Thus, I too want us to attend to the historical and empirical context in which Kant formulates this right; however, I would remind us that this context furthermore includes a peculiar political economy with regard to Kantian hospitality. We must conclude that Kant in these texts does not seem to be talking about commerce merely as interaction, communication, or exchange, but more directly as the contractual exchange of goods or property via the erection of trade posts.[53] I insist on the political economy of hospitality or on a formulation of hospitality as empirically grounded in *commercial relations*, because, as I have established above, Kant's discussion of this cosmopolitan right comes in the midst of his criticism of European colonial exploitation, and in this sense commerce provides the crucial context for the right of hospitality. If we take Kantian hospitality to be about a critique of colonial violence, then we must also highlight the significance of commerce in its justification.[54]

Commerce and Eurocentrism in the Cosmopolitan Right of Universal Hospitality

If I am right to interpret the central role of commerce in the content of Kant's cosmopolitan right, we need to ask, furthermore and more importantly, *whose* commercial interests are at stake. This question reveals an even more concrete picture of Kant's view of the commercial relations here. In tracing the genealogy of the idea of cosmopolitanism in European thought, Anthony Pagden connects Kant's cosmopolitan ideal first to what Francisco de Vitoria called "the right of natural partnership and communication," a discourse which proposed "the exchange of goods as an expression of shared humanity," then via Christian Wolff's idea of *civitas maxima* to Emeric de Vattel's formulation of "commerce as the dominant mode of peaceful international relations, something like a common or universal language among people."[55] From this, Pagden concludes that while Kant was in many respects an anti-imperialist, his notion of cosmopolitanism, which emphasizes commerce as the primary example of human interaction, is difficult to separate from the history of European civilization and its various imperial projects.[56] As a result, the Eurocentrism embedded in cosmopolitanism, and particularly in its prioritization of commerce, makes it very difficult to articulate any cosmopolitan ideal as genuinely universal or open.[57] Thus, by giving European-led commerce a central place in his formulation of the cosmopolitan right of universal hospitality, Kant straightwardly privileges the commercial interests of the European world.

In other words, paying particular attention to the context in which hospitality is justified is quite helpful in that it shows Kant taking a side in the colonialism debate by limiting the rights of commercial states to a short-term visit. However, the biased nature of this right becomes clear when we parse out the identities of the visitors and the hosts that he had in mind. Hospitality becomes an issue, a matter of right for Kant, when some nations or representatives of some nations pursue commerce with others. It is a right, then, primarily accorded to those seeking commerce at the time: simply put, we may begin by looking at who in fact is actively *seeking* commerce at the time of Kant's writing, who are the "old inhabitants" in question for him, and what kind of commercial or so-called civilized societies Kant has in mind. Kant's model of economic interaction is a narrow one masquerading as a universal form of communication, for his main focus in these texts remains that of a commercial activity that is mainly led and controlled by Westerners or Europeans. Note that in his famous condemnation of the use of violence or the use of improper contracts against newly discovered lands in *The Doctrine of Right*, Kant characterizes the original settlers or dwellers of these lands as "shepherds and hunters (like the Hottentots, the Tungusi, or most of the American Indian nations) who depend for their sustenance on great open regions" (i.e., the noncommercial peoples), as opposed to the peoples who belong to the "visitor nations" (i.e., the European commercial states) (*MS/AA* 6:353). Thus, in addition to being a very circumscribed right, the cosmopolitan right to universal hospitality formulated here is in effect a one-way street between the visiting nations and the original inhabitants. It is a right of the visiting nations to pursue their commercial interests, albeit for a limited amount of time, without being interrupted. This right is not reciprocated because it is not in the first place a right that applies to the hosts, for instance, unless they also seek travel or commerce.[58]

A fuller and more nuanced contextual reading of Kantian hospitality reveals that the incentive of the "spirit of commerce," the leading motivation behind his formula of the cosmopolitan right, is a specifically European- and Western-led activity, and this makes his view of hospitality a Eurocentric one. The fact that Kant's formulation of the cosmopolitan right prioritizes the interests of the commercial European states means that this right of hospitality is not, and perhaps has never been, a universal or cosmopolitan one. Together with Derrida, we can say that we do not know what hospitality is outside of the system of European right, or that we do not know it beyond this European right.[59] As I have shown in chapters 2 and 4, Kant's philosophy of history has a particularly European bent and his notion of the cosmopolitan aim of history and culture includes a specific view of European cultural production as its leading force.

Similarly, then, we find that his formulation of hospitable commerce as the primary principle undergirding the cosmopolitan right here seems to interpret cosmopolitanism exclusively as pertaining to the commercial interests of the European world.

Physical-Political Geography as a Part of Kant's Nonideal Theory of Politics

Kant's *Rechtslehre* provides a systematic theory of our rights and freedoms based on the fact that we are living in a limited space, with limited resources, inevitably bumping up against one another. It seems that the natural or geographical condition of our habitat is the external incentive for our juridical-political duty of establishing peace on earth by way of the cosmopolitan right to universal hospitality. I have shown that *Rechtslehre* is not a simple extension of Kant's ethics, for it includes a spatial consideration of our collective lives as well as a theory of our physical-natural conditions and our interactions in these conditions. Furthermore, I have argued that a consideration of geography oriented by the regulative principle of *Zweckmässigkeit* constitutes a part of Kant's nonideal theory of politics. Thus, paralleling the teleological view of nature that supplemented his notion of a cosmopolitan right in "Toward Perpetual Peace," we see another instantiation of a theory of our actual world in *The Doctrine of Right*, a nonideal theory of political geography that undergirds his articulation of the cosmopolitan right of hospitality—and this in a work that otherwise largely belongs to his ideal theory of politics.

Because I am mainly interested in how Kant's ideal and nonideal theory fit together systematically, I will not get into the details of Kant's physical and political geography. As Günter Zöller and David Harvey argue, his writings on race and lectures on *Physical Geography* round up his theory of political geography and cosmopolitanism by enumerating the differences and similarities between human beings living in a variety of natural conditions.[60] My point is that if Kant's doctrine of right puts forth the formal structures of justice that need to be in place for the arbitration of human interactions in a given state, internationally, and globally, the flip side of this doctrine is a nonideal theory about the underlying material conditions—historical, cultural, and natural—given by the regulative principle of teleology. Thus, Kant's political thought offers us more resources than we previously thought. It has two complementary parts: first, a discourse on the rights and obligations of human beings living together, considering only the lawful *form* of our interactions, and second, a discourse on the nonideal circumstances that undergird these interactions, considering the contingent *matter* of these interactions in a lawful way.

Reading the right of hospitality in merely normative or prescriptive terms is insufficient and misleading. Informed by my previous analyses of the role of a nonideal theory in Kant's political thought, in this last chapter I have proposed that we pay attention to the geopolitical concerns undergirding Kant's formulation of this right. When we uncover that Kant comes to formulate hospitality as a response most suited to the geopolitical conditions of colonialism, we are able to give Kant's political philosophy a renewed relevance for the present. For instance, formulating an effective solution to a number of current global issues following Kant's lead on nonideal theory would require that we first and foremost come to terms with the geopolitical causes of these issues by situating them in the broader context of the history of colonialism and its contemporary politico-economic legacies.[61]

When we give most of our attention to Kant's ideal theory, we miss the actual historical, cultural, and geopolitical backdrop of the political ideals embedded in this theory. I would like us to pivot toward analyzing how a consideration of history, a view of cultural development and production, and a theorization of physico-natural circumstances pertain to politics as Kant theorizes them—and how these elements might have shaped the specific normative principles of his political philosophy of cosmopolitanism. In this book, I have attempted to present a systematic overview of these considerations, one that I have located in the principle of political *Zweckmässigkeit* and have called Kant's nonideal theory of politics. That Kant paid attention to such nonideal circumstances of the world as history and culture does not make him automatically a multicultural cosmopolitan: as we have repeatedly seen, his views of universal history, culture, and geography are not as universal as we would like them to be. His attention to these matters should, however, make Kant scholars today extra attentive to the underlying assumptions and backdrop of any ideal theory that may come forward as a Kantian one. It should lead us to ask the question of what view of history, culture, and nature are presumed in any given ideal theory of cosmopolitanism and it should require us to be more attentive to multiple narratives, to diverse forms of cultural production, and to a variety of geographical views. I briefly sketch out this point and other conclusions to be drawn from my analysis of Kant's political thought in the conclusion.

Conclusion

Theorizing the Lawfulness of the Contingent in Politics: A Defense of Teleology

Today we abhor and condemn the specifics of Kant's philosophy of history, which include his expectation that Europe will eventually legislate for the entire world; we reject the actual content of his anthropology, which includes a hierarchical theory of race and cultural development; we label as naive and outdated the way in which he dealt with geographical and climatological factors, which includes his claim that nature will eventually force us to interact with each other peacefully for the sake of commerce. However, the very fact that he dealt *at all* with these contingent elements of history, anthropology, and geography, and sought to incorporate a picture of them into his political thought, is an extremely important insight that in fact broadens the very definition of politics. The structural theoretical point here is that political thought must include a nondogmatic account of our current circumstances; therefore, it must have a robust nonideal theory. This is an insight we discover only if we recuperate the role of teleology in Kant's political philosophy, analyze its contribution to politics, and restore it to its systematic place.

Teleological language pops up everywhere in Kant's political writings and seems to accomplish important theoretical work for politics. In this book I have defended teleology—and more specifically, its theoretical contribution to Kant's and Kantian political philosophy—on two grounds. First, systematically speaking, teleology (or more accurately, the regulative principle of purposiveness) constitutes an important part of Kant's thought. Since Kant is a systematic philosopher, we need a better, fuller account of what exactly teleology brings to Kant's political philosophy. Here, I have offered just such an account and shown that the regulative principle of purposiveness is the underlying principle of a nonideal theory of politics. Teleology is both a fundamental part of Kant's overall thought and functions in his political philosophy as the key to a nonideal theory. Second, in the Kantian system, teleological principles are regulative. In Kant's formulation, purposiveness as a regulative principle guides our inquiries into diverse and contingent particulars

CONCLUSION

by means of a hypothetically lawful universal and unifying concept. A principle is regulative when it refrains from positing a thick ontology or a dogmatic epistemology. Instead, it negotiates the gap between a lawfulness that we must presuppose in all theoretical inquiry and a contingency that our intellect cannot render fully meaningful. Kant's use of this principle in his political writings, I have argued, tentatively unifies the diverse elements of history, culture, and nature so that they can be of use to political theory. I have shown, therefore, that by deepening our analysis of the role of teleology in Kant's political writings, we gain access to his philosophy of history, anthropology, and geography—that is, to a nonideal theory that undergirds his formal and ideal political thought. This means that the principle of teleology in Kant's thought offers a bridge to a kind of protointerdisciplinarity in political philosophy in that it leads us to engage with the methods and aims of history, anthropology, and geography.

We employ the principle of purposiveness, as Kant writes repeatedly in the *Critique of Judgment*, to name the relationship between what is objectively *contingent* and what is subjectively *lawful*: teleology refers to *the lawfulness of the contingent* (*KU/AA* 20:204, 20:243, 5:180, 5:184, 5:404). In the language of the *Critique of Pure Reason*, purposiveness is a guiding principle that is needed by an intellect like ours in order to orient itself and to make sense of what remains, to a large degree, objectively contingent.

Because teleology is a regulative principle of the lawfulness of the contingent, the pictures of world history, of cultural values, and of geographical relations that Kant presents do not constitute empirically neutral observations about our world. In the way that he theorizes them, the philosophy of history, cultural anthropology, and physical geography are, as Cohen puts it, "value-embedded disciplines that play a crucial role of providing a map for human beings to orient themselves in the world and realize their purposes."[1] One way to think about the actual content of Kant's nonideal theory of politics is, then, to view this content as nothing other than a pragmatic map to orient our thinking about the world. I have shown that in Kant's political thought this kind of orientation proves crucial for the feasibility of the political goal of a cosmopolitan world order, and that the main principle of such orientation, which Cohen calls our "map-making venture,"[2] is the regulative principle of purposiveness.

Kant's reflections on history, culture, and nature are always normatively oriented by the perspective of a purposive whole. For this reason, his nonideal theory of politics always tells a teleological story and works with teleological arguments. When Kant provides a picture of universal history with a cosmopolitan aim, he does so with the help of the normative orientation provided by the regulative principle of purposive unity. Thus, as I demonstrated in my analysis of the relationship between history and politics in the "Idea" essay in chapter 2, his philosophy of history becomes a part of a cosmopolitan political agenda. When he describes our transition from nonideal circumstances to ideal ones in terms of our cultural development, he does so with the help of the normative orientation provided by the regulative principle of the purposiveness of nature as a whole. As I showed in my analysis of §§82–84 of the *Critique of Judgment* in chapter 4, his cultural anthropology is a transitional political theory of our development. When he formulates the specific dictum of a cosmopolitan right, he does so with the help of the normative orientation provided by the regulative principle of the purposiveness of our interactions in a limited space. Consequently, as I demonstrated in my analysis of the right of universal hospitality in chapter 5 and 6, his physical geography addresses feasibility concerns of his political ideals and furthermore concretizes what a cosmopolitan right should look like.

Because Kant's notion of teleology is regulative and nondogmatic, its hypothetical character furthermore conveys a theoretical humility that we would do well to adopt in political thought. A teleological construction of history, culture, or nature at first seems to render these objects of inquiry too deterministic. Indeed, if the final purposes of history, cultural production, or nature were to come about because they are teleologically determined, there would seem to be no room left for any freely willed human actions. Yet Kantian teleology originates in the idea that our approach to reality will always remain limited by the concepts that we ourselves bring to bear upon it—that is, it originates as an imaginary focal point of systematic inquiry in the *Critique of Pure Reason* and is then rehabilitated as a regulative principle that refers to "the lawfulness of the contingent" in the *Critique of Judgment*. In each case, when Kant proposes a purposive unity of history, culture, or nature, this unity remains tentative, in the sense that it is posited for the sake of our interpretation. Pictures of the whole of history, human nature, culture, or the world, in other words, can only be given in the form of hypothetical or reflective judgments.

A closer look at the methodological assumptions and achievements of teleology in Kant's political thought led me to excavate a nonideal theory of politics in his thought, a theory of a politically salient view of history, human nature and culture, and geography. My analysis has thus identified three main domains of his nonideal theory of politics that utilize regulative teleology: his philosophy of history, which produces a historical narrative; his physico-cultural anthropology, which provides a theory of cultural development; and his physico-political geography, which provides an important reflection on our natural habitat. The first is a theorization of where human history is headed; the second is a theorization of human nature, capabilities, and purposes in this world; and the third is a theorization of geography and its effects on our lives.

Kant's cosmopolitanism is embedded in specific notions of history, culture, and nature. In reflecting on history, Kant tries to tell a story that brings together the seemingly contingent collective actions of people in a lawful narrative with a beginning, a middle, and an end. In reflecting on our cultural existence, he tries to discern the ultimate and final lawfulness, a purpose behind all our seemingly haphazard interactions with each other and nature. In reflecting on our geographical conditions, he tries to come up with lawful connections between our contingent position on earth and the role of nature to attain some sense of assurance that our specific location in this world has a purpose. In all of these inquiries Kant argues that it is only by means of the regulative principle of purposiveness that we can theorize that which seems to be objectively contingent or purposeless instead as lawful, meaningful, and purposive for us.

In directing our attention to the role played by the principle of purposiveness in Kant's political thought, I aimed to show that his most important political insight is not a one-size-fits-all ideal theory of cosmopolitanism. Rather, this insight exists in the systematic emphases that he places on a historical narrative, a theory of cultural production, and a political geography of human interaction. It turns out that a cosmopolitan world order, or the cultural-civil-political end of our existence as Kant sees it, is not an ideal political goal that is devoid of a view of history, nature, or culture, as we often suppose it to be. A theory of cosmopolitanism is better served if it takes into consideration and incorporates a lawful account of these contingent human conditions. In Kant's own version, a theory of cosmopolitanism has foundations in a Eurocentric view of history, culture, and nature; however, I believe that acknowledging teleology's theoretical contribution to Kant's political thought, and thereby uncovering his nonideal theory of politics, will make a more honest and inclusive Kantianism possible.

Advantages of Regulative Teleology for Politics

While the distinction between ideal and nonideal theories of politics is not directly found in Kant, the texts offer plenty of material to justify the distinction as a helpful one. Accordingly, I have drawn a distinction between Kant's ideal theory of politics, which is guided by the principle of *Recht* and is undergirded by idealized notions of human agency and interactions, and his nonideal theory of politics, which, by reference to the principle of *Zweckmässigkeit*, accounts for the historical-cultural-natural embeddedness of human beings. In this way, I have been able to articulate the important role of regulative teleology for politics. A regulatively teleological view reminds us that we should treat political theory not as a mechanistic or mathematical-physical science of rational agents making informed choices but as a study of living, breathing human beings who are situated in—and to a certain extent determined by—various historical narratives, who are equipped with different cultural skills, and who are surrounded by distinct physico-geographical conditions.

My contention is that regulative teleology provided the conceptual means by which Kant was able to grapple with the pressing issues of multiplicity, diversity, and plurality that we, to this day, encounter in the real world. In other words, I defend teleology not in terms of the specific claims that it produces in Kant's own thought, but as a hermeneutic invitation to political thought today to take into account historical narratives, to study and formulate stories of human cultural development, and to develop detailed geographical analyses of our habitats. More specifically, my interpretation of Kant's political thought, which maintains a distinction between ideal and nonideal theory by directing our attention to the use of regulative teleology, offers political thought the following three related yet distinct theoretical benefits.

1. Conceptual Clarity Regarding Cosmopolitanism and Its Various Roles in Kant's Political Writings

Cosmopolitanism takes on different roles in Kant's political thought depending on where he places it any given text. I do not mean that the meaning of cosmopolitanism changes or that Kant's cosmopolitan ideal became more complex over time; that Kant's understanding of what cosmopolitanism means evolved in the course of his career is most certainly true and is clearly established by Kleingeld.[3] And yet Kant's is not just an evolving vision of cosmopolitanism. The very term itself plays different roles, systematically speaking, in each of Kant's political writings. Most importantly, I would suggest that the term "cosmopolitan world order" in Kant's political texts almost never refers to a straightforwardly moral or egalitarian ideal of politics as we would have it today. In the 1784 essay, a cosmopolitan world order names "the aim of universal history," a concept construed by means of the hypothetical use of reason or the regulative

CONCLUSION

principle of purposiveness. Here, it is an umbrella concept that tentatively names the culmination of universal history as Kant sees it. It answers an epistemic question about whether or not we can attribute an overall meaning and aim to history. As I demonstrated in chapter 2, in this instance a universal history with a cosmopolitan aim signifies, for Kant, the history of Europe. In the *Critique of Judgment*, a cosmopolitan world-whole names "the ultimate end of nature," or the final purpose of our actions in civil society, as the culmination of all cultural activity. Once again, it refers to a specific cultural condition, namely, to the European way of life, characterized by work and by the continuous development of a culture of skill, as I showed in chapter 4. In *The Doctrine of Right*, cosmopolitanism is a branch of public right that envelops the right of any given state, as well as the right of states altogether: the cosmopolitan right is a right to universal hospitality encompassing all human interactions. As I showed in chapter 6, the exemplary form of this interaction in Kant's terms, commerce, is tied to the geopolitics of Europe.

The reminder that the term "cosmopolitanism" plays various roles in Kant's political writings further serves to caution us against importing our own contemporary understanding of what a cosmopolitan world means to Kant's political philosophy. For Kant, a cosmopolitan world order is not identical to an egalitarian moral vision; each time the term comes up in his writings it signifies something different, whether in his vision of history, cultural development, or geography. When we use the term today and, in one way or another, attribute it to Kant, we are in fact reading our contemporary signification back into it anachronistically. Systematically considered, cosmopolitanism for Kant is an intermediate political goal, a means for achieving peace on earth and it is not an end in itself. It provides a direction for world history ("universal history with a cosmopolitan aim"); it is the culmination of our cultural activities ("a cosmopolitan world-whole"); and finally, it is the right stemming from the necessity of peacefully interacting with each other on a limited space ("a cosmopolitan right to universal hospitality"). Thus, we should be cautious both of appropriating Kant's cosmopolitanism as merely an abstract moral ideal and of infusing it with just anything that we find useful today.

2. A Broader Definition of Politics in Kant's Thought

I have developed a nonideal theory of politics in Kant's thought, a theory directed by the principle of teleology, in order to demonstrate that Kant has more to offer contemporary political thought than a mere ideal theory of cosmopolitanism. The holistic picture of his political philosophy that I have defended here suggests that the achievement of perpetual peace, the highest political good (*das höchstes politisches Gut*), will require two complementary or simultaneous theoretical endeavors: first, it will require an ideal theory, one which proposes a number of political ideals that will best achieve peace by specifying the right kind of institutions to organize and regulate our interactions at the state, international, and global levels; and second, it will require the production of nonideal theories that give us specialized views of the empirical realities (i.e., the historical, cultural, and geographical circumstances) surrounding us. While the rights, just institutions, and forms of relations named by an ideal theory are necessary conditions for achieving peace on earth, the framework of Kant's political thought that I have provided here reminds us that they are not the sufficient conditions; we must always still reflect on and take into account the empirically contingent factors of history, human nature and culture, and geographical circumstances. Ideal and nonideal theories in Kant work in tandem and together constitute the necessary and sufficient conditions for establishing peace, the highest political good.

When we focus on the role that teleology plays in Kant's political thought, then, we find a political philosophy that is a broad endeavor and which draws on various disciplines, including the philosophy of history, cultural anthropology, and physical geography. In this book, I have limited my analysis to what are commonly considered to be Kant's critical and political works and have located elements of a nonideal theory in his explicitly political writings. In other words, I have developed the historical, cultural, and geographical foundations of his political thought, concluding that we find in Kant the theoretical beginnings of a political history, a political anthropology, and a political geography. Kant's other writings on anthropology, the beginnings of human history, the theory of race, and physical geography are not, strictly speaking, part of the canon, although this view is beginning to change in Kant scholarship. My contention is that Kant's *Anthropology from a Pragmatic Point of View*, "Conjectural Beginning of Human History," "Determination of the Concept of a Human Race," "On the Use of Teleological Principles in Philosophy," and *Physical Geography* lectures can and should be incorporated into his nonideal theory via the principle of regulative teleology. A detailed account of this, however, remains outside the scope of the current study, which has primarily aimed to provide the methodological background for and a systematic overview of what we should delineate as Kant's nonideal theory of politics.

3. A More Honest Kantian Political Philosophy

An additional benefit of systematically dividing up Kant's political thought into its ideal and nonideal theories and exploring its nonideal side is that

CONCLUSION

this approach furthers the conversation about Kant and historical, cultural, and racial diversity. We can now move the conversation regarding Kant's racism and Eurocentrism from debates on whether or not he was just a man of his time, whether or not he changed his mind at some point in late 1780s, and whether or not he was as critical of imperialism as we think, to a different terrain altogether by first acknowledging that Kant's political philosophy is undoubtedly racist and Eurocentric in its formulation of history, culture, and nature.

Such an honest acknowledgement of Kant's cosmopolitanism as anchored in a Eurocentric view of history and cultural development will in the first place allow us to see why we cannot just trust that any idea of cosmopolitanism will be morally universal, egalitarian, and culturally pluralistic. In Kant's body of work, a nonideal theory of who counts as the major leading force of history, culture, and geography undergirds—and thus inflects, if not infects—the way we must hear and understand his political thought. More often than not, and certainly in Kant's case, nonideal theories are implicit in the way we formulate our political ideals and ideal theories. Making them explicit, as I have attempted to do by attending to Kant's use of teleology, allows us to acknowledge that any given political ideal brings with it, or is embedded in, a certain view of the world that may or may not be as palatable, acceptable, universal, neutral, or inclusive as we might at first think. If we pay attention to the role played by teleology in Kant's politics, we stand a better chance of making explicit what were implicit assumptions about history, culture, or geopolitics; we put all our cards on the table, so to speak. This honesty about the influence of nonideal theory on ideal theory is the Kantian insight that we should take with us going forward, and this insight must furthermore be tempered by an acknowledgement of the distorting effect that his racism and Eurocentrism had on his and on related conceptions of cosmopolitanism.

From this point of honest acknowledgement, it is possible to make a distinction between *Kant's* political philosophy and *Kantian* political philosophy: while Kant's own thought and cosmopolitanism is complicit in these issues, a Kantian philosophy stands a chance of not being so *if* it first reckons with the fact that a particular view of reality is embedded in any given ideal theory. This is the Kantian lesson that we need to take more seriously today. The structure of his political thought as I have construed it here will allow us to envision a cosmopolitan world in diverse and multiple ways, but only when we make a distinction between ideal and nonideal theories *and* admit that the latter, at least as it figures in Kant's own thought, is problematic. As a result, there is no need to reinvent Kant himself as a champion of diversity; we need not argue, as

Sankar Muthu does, that Kant did value all cultures or all forms of social life and agency.[4] My account makes clear that this is far from being the case. Instead, we should admit our complicity in a worldview that Kant championed, which, while aspiring to be global, universal, egalitarian, and all-inclusive, ended up being anything but. The real Kant was racist, sexist, and Eurocentric; a real Kantian political philosophy, however, can hope to move beyond racism, sexism, and Eurocentrism and can hope to achieve a diverse cosmopolitanism if only we, the Kantians, first admit and analyze the distorted grounds and consequences of the past formulations in earnest.

In fact, when we admit that Kant did value one particular form of culture, one which he framed as the only relevant culture for a cosmopolitan world order as he saw it, we are liberated to critique the actual content of his anthropology while making visible the structures of his nonideal theory as they informed his ideal theory. Just as Kant's political thought had two parts, a more honest Kantian political thought today can have two complementary parts—one informed by plural constructions of history, culture, and geography, and another informed by ideal theory. Inspired by Kant's attention to the empirical elements of politics and despite his exclusive valuation of one kind of culture, we can then still say that culture did and should matter to political thought.

Producing better nonideal theories than Kant's seems key to achieving peace by means of a truly inclusive and egalitarian global vision today. To elaborate on such a view goes beyond the scope of this book, but a new political vision that is informed by different and plural local histories, that is not exclusively produced by nonwhite, non-Western, nonmale, and non-European people, and that is genuinely open to different cultural values of life and nature—and even different fundamental concepts of history, culture, and geography—might have a better chance of being globally adopted.[5]

Toward a Kantian Political History, Political Anthropology, and Political Geography

A more honest assessment of Kant's nonideal theory allows us to move from Kant's philosophy of history to a Kantian political history, from Kant's cultural anthropology to a Kantian political anthropology, from Kant's physical geography to a Kantian political geography, all while being explicit about what Kant can and cannot do for us. Kant cannot provide us with an actual multicultural cosmopolitanism, although he

CONCLUSION

can provide us with the theoretical structures of a nonideal theory that should inform and aid any ideal theory of politics. An ideal theory of cosmopolitanism, which attempts to incorporate an actual diversity of historical, cultural, and geographical perspectives, might not be exactly what Kant himself had in mind; however, such an ideal would be one that we can hope to construct by taking seriously his insight into the pertinence of history, culture, and geography to politics.

When we pay closer attention to how Kant uses teleology, not only in developing an exclusive concept of civilization but also as a general hermeneutic to produce a perspective of nonideal political theory according to which cultural differences matter, we can begin to move toward a better-informed cosmopolitanism. I disagree with Pagden, therefore, who finds it hard to see how cosmopolitanism can ever be entirely separated from its European and Eurocentric genealogy, concluding that "it is an error to hope that we can ever achieve a truly cosmopolitan vision of the cosmopolis."[6] Against this, I contend that it is not an error to hope for such a truly cosmopolitan vision if we take Kant's political history, anthropology, and geography seriously, understanding their limits and faults so that we do not replicate their Eurocentric construction and yet remaining mindful of the importance of developing nonideal theories of historical, cultural, and geographical difference alongside an ideal theory of politics. Such a theory of human difference and diversity, if elaborated in a nonhierarchical way and with the bottom-up methodology of nonideal theory, would allow for richer and more nuanced political philosophies than a one-size-fits-all ideal theory could. Therefore, when we think of Kant's legacy for political thought today, we are not stuck between a naively idealistic or abstract extension of the Categorical Imperative, a universalistic theory of cosmopolitanism, and a formal theory of force and freedom. Rather, if we deepen our analysis of teleology in Kant's political philosophy, then we also have the option of producing multiple, better, and nuanced nonideal theories of political history, political anthropology, and political geography.

Notes

Introduction

1. Elisabeth Ellis, *Kant's Politics: Provisional Theory for an Uncertain World* (New Haven, Conn.: Yale University Press, 2005), 43.

2. See Robert Louden, *Kant's Impure Ethics: From Rational Beings to Human Beings* (New York: Oxford University Press, 2000); Patrick Frierson, *Kant's Questions: What is the Human Being?* (New York, Routledge, 2013); Holly Wilson, *Kant's Pragmatic Anthropology: Its Origin, Meaning, and Critical Significance* (Albany: SUNY Press, 2006); Alix Cohen, *Kant and the Human Sciences: Biology, Anthropology and History* (New York: Palgrave MacMillan, 2009).

3. Laura Valentini, "Ideal vs. Nonideal Theory: A Conceptual Map," *Philosophy Compass* 7, no. 9 (2012): 654.

4. Valentini, "Ideal vs. Nonideal Theory," 654; Matt Sleat, "Realism, Liberalism, and Nonideal Theory, or Are There Two Ways to Do Realistic Political Theory?" *Political Studies* 64, no. 1 (2016): 28.

5. John Rawls, *A Theory of Justice* (Cambridge, Mass.: Harvard University Press, 1971), 245.

6. Zofia Stemplowska and Adam Swift, "Ideal and Nonideal Theory," in *The Oxford Handbook of Political Philosophy*, ed. David Estlund (Oxford: Oxford University Press, 2015), 380.

7. John Rawls, *The Law of Peoples* (Cambridge, Mass.: Harvard University Press, 1999), especially, 89–91; A. John Simmons, "Ideal and Nonideal Theory," *Philosophy and Public Affairs* 38, no. 1 (2010): 5–36.

8. Charles Mills, "Ideal Theory as Ideology," *Hypatia: A Journal of Feminist Philosophy* 20, no. 3 (Summer 2005): 165–84; Charles Mills, "The Domination Contract," in *Contract and Domination*, ed. Charles Mills and Carole Pateman (Malden, Mass.: Polity Press, 2007): 79–105.

9. Rawls, *A Theory of Justice*, 245–46.
10. Mills, "Ideal Theory as Ideology," 168.
11. Ibid., 166–68.
12. Ibid.
13. John Rawls, *Political Liberalism* (New York: Columbia University Press, 2005), 285.
14. While Rawls is not particularly clear on what he means by nonideal theory, Simmons provides a helpful reconstruction of it in his "Ideal and

Nonideal Theory"; see Simmons, "Ideal and Nonideal Theory," 13; and Rawls, *The Law of Peoples*, 89.

15. Simmons, "Ideal and Nonideal Theory," 12.

16. Ibid., 18.

17. Valentini, "Ideal vs. Nonideal Theory," 654, 661; Sleat, "Realism, Liberalism, and Nonideal Theory," 35.

18. Simmons, "Ideal and Nonideal Theory," 19.

19. Sleat, "Realism, Liberalism, and Nonideal Theory," 35; Valentini, "Ideal vs. Nonideal Theory," 660.

20. Mills, "Ideal Theory as Ideology," 166–68; 173.

21. Ibid., 166–67.

22. Valentini, "Ideal vs. Nonideal Theory," 660.

23. Ibid., 662.

24. Stemplowska and Swift, "Ideal and Nonideal Theory," 385.

25. Unlike Rawls's and Simmons's, my claim is not grounded in insisting on the completeness or the priority of ideal theory, although a version of this claim is valid for Kant's practical thought in general, as I will contend.

26. John H. Zammito, *Kant, Herder, and the Birth of Anthropology* (Chicago: University of Chicago Press, 2002), 349.

27. To this extent, then, I agree with Rawls's claim that nonideal theory is compatible with ideal theory, at least in Kant's version: Rawls, *Political Liberalism*, 285.

28. See note 2 above.

29. Louden, *Kant's Impure Ethics*, 26–28.

30. Cohen, *Kant and the Human Sciences*, xv.

31. Arthur Ripstein, *Force and Freedom: Kant's Legal and Political Thought* (Cambridge, Mass.: Harvard University Press, 2009); Onora O'Neill, *Constructions of Reason: Explorations of Kant's Practical Philosophy* (Cambridge: Cambridge University Press, 1989); Onora O'Neill, *Bounds of Justice* (Cambridge: Cambridge University Press, 2000); Garret Wallace Brown, *Grounding Cosmopolitanism: From Kant to the Idea of a Cosmopolitan Constitution* (New York: Oxford University Press, 2009); Seyla Benhabib, *The Rights of Others: Aliens, Residents, and Citizens* (Cambridge: Cambridge University Press, 2004); Seyla Benhabib, *Another Cosmopolitanism*, ed. Robert Post (New York: Oxford University Press, 2006); Rawls, *A Theory of Justice*; David Held, *Democracy and Global Order: From the Modern State to Cosmopolitan Government* (Cambridge: Polity Press, 1995); Jürgen Habermas, "Kant's Idea of Perpetual Peace, with the Benefit of Two Hundred Years' Hindsight," in *Perpetual Peace: Essays on Kant's Cosmopolitan Ideal*, ed. James Bohman and Matthias Lutz-Bachmann (Cambridge, Mass.: MIT Press, 1997): 113–54; see also the framing and essays in the classic volume *Perpetual Peace: Essays on Kant's Cosmopolitan Ideal*, ed. James Bohman and Matthias Lutz-Bachmann (Cambridge, Mass.: MIT Press, 1997).

32. James Ingram, *Radical Cosmopolitics: The Ethics and Politics of Democratic Universalism* (New York: Columbia University Press, 2013), 23.

33. Habermas, "Kant's Idea of Perpetual Peace," 113.

34. Pauline Kleingeld, "Kant on Historiography and the Use of Regulative Ideas," *Studies in History and Philosophy of Science* 39 (2008): 526n7; Emanuel

Chuckwudi Eze, "The Color of Reason: The Idea of 'Race' in Kant's Anthropology," in *Postcolonial African Philosophy: A Critical Reader*, ed. Emanuel Chukwudi Eze (Oxford: Blackwell, 1997): 103–31; Tsenay Serequeberhan, "Eurocentrism in Philosophy: The Case of Immanuel Kant" *The Philosophical Forum* 27, no. 4 (Summer 1996): 333–56.

35. Günter Zöller, "Kant's Political Anthropology," *Kant Yearbook: Kant and German Idealism* 3, no. 1 (2011): 144; Inder Marwah, "Bridging Nature and Freedom? Kant, Culture, and Cultivation," *Social Theory and Practice* 38, no. 3 (2012): 385–406; Todd Hedrick, "Race, Difference, and Anthropology in Kant's Cosmopolitanism," *Journal of the History of Philosophy* 46, no. 2 (2008): 245–68.

36. David Harvey, *Cosmopolitanism and the Geographies of Freedom* (New York: Columbia University Press, 2009), 26–30; Anthony Pagden, "Stoicism, Cosmopolitanism, and the Legacy of European Imperialism," *Constellations* 7, no. 1 (2000): 3–22; see also chapter 6 in this volume.

37. For the former debate, see Pauline Kleingeld, "Kant's Second Thoughts on Race," *The Philosophical Quarterly* 57, no. 229 (October 2007): 573–92; Robert Bernasconi, "Kant's Third Thoughts on Race," in *Reading Kant's Geography*, ed. Stuart Elden and Eduardo Mendieta (Albany: SUNY Press, 2011); Pauline Kleingeld, "Kant's Second Thoughts on Colonialism," in *Kant and Colonialism*, ed. Katrin Flikschuh and Lea Ypi (New York: Oxford University Press, 2014): 43–67; Charles Mills, "Kant's *Untermenschen*," in *Race and Racism in Modern Philosophy*, ed. Andrew Walls (Ithaca, N.Y.: Cornell University Press, 2005), 169–93. Regarding the latter question of whether Kant's political thought can accommodate non-European cultures, see Sankar Muthu, *Enlightenment against Empire* (Princeton, N.J.: Princeton University Press, 2003): 122–209; Todd Hedrick, "Race, Difference, and Anthropology"; Marwah, "Bridging Nature and Freedom?"; Thomas McCarthy, *Race, Empire, and the Idea of Human Development* (Cambridge: Cambridge University Press, 2009), esp. 42–68.

38. Harvey, *Cosmopolitanism*, 26–30; see also Zöller, "Kant's Political Anthropology," 144–46; Pagden, "Stoicism," 18–20; McCarthy, *Race, Empire, and the Idea of Human Development*, 64–65; Marwah, "Bridging Nature and Freedom?," 395–97; Hedrick, "Race, Difference, and Anthropology," 262–65.

39. Charles Mills, "Occupy Liberalism! Or, Ten Reasons Why Liberalism Cannot Be Retrieved for Radicalism (and Why They Are Wrong," *Radical Philosophy Review* 15, no. 2 (2012): 305–23; and Charles Mills, "Black Radical Kantianism," *Res Philosophica* 95, no. 1 (2017): 1–33.

Introduction to Part I

1. See, respectively, Pauline Kleingeld, "Kant on Historiography"; Henry E. Allison, "Teleology and History in Kant: The Critical Foundations of Kant's Philosophy of History," in *Kant's "Idea for a Universal History with a Cosmopolitan Aim": A Critical Guide*, ed. Amélie Oksenberg Rorty and James Schmidt (Cambridge: Cambridge University Press, 2009): 24–45; and Allen Wood, "Kant's Philosophy

of History," in *Toward Perpetual Peace and Other Writings on Politics, Peace, and History*, trans. David L. Colclasure, ed. Pauline Kleingeld (New Haven, Conn.: Yale University Press, 2006): 243–62.

2. Garrett Wallace Brown, *Grounding Cosmopolitanism: From Kant to the Idea of a Cosmopolitan Constitution* (New York: Oxford University Press, 2009), 23.

3. Ibid.

4. For a sampling of authors who treat cosmopolitanism as a part of Kant's ideal theory of morals and politics, see Brown, *Grounding Cosmopolitanism*; Benhabib, *Another Cosmopolitanism*; Christina Lafont, "Alternative Visions of a New Global Order: What Should Cosmopolitans Hope For?" *Ethics and Global Politics* 1, nos. 1–2 (2008): 1–20; Sharon Anderson-Gold, *Cosmopolitanism and Human Rights* (Cardiff: University of Wales Press, 2011); Onora O'Neill, "A Kantian Approach to Transnational Justice," in *Cosmopolitanism Reader*, ed. Garrett W. Brown and David Held (New York: Polity Press, 2010): 61–79; Martha Nussbaum, "Kant and Cosmopolitanism," in *Cosmopolitanism Reader*, ed. Garrett W. Brown and David Held (New York: Polity Press, 2010): 27–44; Michael Doyle, "Kant and Liberal Internationalism," in *Toward Perpetual Peace and Other Writings on Politics, Peace, and History*, ed. Pauline Kleingeld (New Haven, Conn.: Yale University Press, 2006): 201–42; Axel Honneth, "Is Universalism a Moral Trap? The Presuppositions and Limits of a Politics of Human Rights," in *Perpetual Peace: Essays on Kant's Cosmopolitan Ideal*, ed. James Bohman and Matthias Lutz-Bachmann (Cambridge, Mass.: MIT Press, 1997), 155–78.

5. Pauline Kleingeld, "Kant's Changing Cosmopolitanism," in *Kant's Idea for a Universal History with a Cosmopolitan Aim: A Critical Guide*, ed. Amélie Oksenberg Rorty and James Schmidt (Cambridge: Cambridge University Press, 2009): 171–86.

6. Onora O'Neill, "Orientation in Thinking: Geographical Problems, Political Solutions," in *Reading Kant's Geography*, ed. Stuart Elden and Eduardo Mendieta (Albany: SUNY Press, 2011), 228. Kleingeld has explored the link between the "Idea" essay and the first *Critique* in Kleingeld, "Kant on Historiography"; what I propose to do here is to bring Kant's notion of orientation in thinking to bear on his philosophy of history.

7. In this way, Kant's historical narrative here becomes what Cohen calls "pragmatic history," namely, "knowledge of history that is necessary to further the realization of human purposes in the world"; see Cohen, *Kant and the Human Sciences*, 136–38.

Chapter 1

1. The hypothetical use of reason is what many Kant scholars see as the prefiguration of the reflecting judgments of the *Critique of Judgment*. I think that this connection is right; for a summary and an argument, see Henry E. Allison, "Is the *Critique of Judgment* 'Post-Critical'?," in *The Reception of Kant's Critical Philosophy*, ed. Sally Sedgwick (Cambridge: Cambridge University Press, 2000), 78–92.

2. The idea of God is the imaginary focal point of a purposive unity; the idea of soul is the imaginary focal point of a unified self, "the guiding thread of inner experience as if the mind were a simple substance that (at least in this life) persists in existence with personal identity" (*KrV* A672/B700); the idea of the world-whole is the imaginary focal point of all causal relations (*KrV* A672/B700, A685/B713).

3. Indeed, if this were a constitutive or objective principle of research, its seeming opposite would not be valid; Kant's point here is that there can be two maxims of research here and they need not contradict each other as long as we understand them to be subjective or regulative principles. Note that the other maxim here is the following: never assume that you will find this *a priori* explanation, an existing first unity, or a necessary and unconditional ground, and continue searching for a further cause. As Kant puts it: "[do] not . . . assume any single determination dealing with the existence of things as such a first ground, i.e., as absolutely necessary, but always hold the way open to further derivation and hence always to treat it as still conditioned" (*KrV* A617/B645). Both maxims are legitimate, and furthermore, if we take these maxims to refer to different inquiries and if we think of these two demands only as *subjective* heuristic principles for research, both of these maxims can coexist without contradiction. Critical philosophy tells us that the former is a maxim that we can use when we undertake systematic research. There is therefore no contradiction between the two maxims.

4. In the Transcendental Dialectic, Kant argues that there are three types of possible proofs for the existence of God and that all three boil down to the ontological proof, the deceptive and faulty nature of which Kant explains (*KrV* A592/B620).

5. The so-called *Pantheismusstreit* or "Pantheism Controversy" was a famous eighteenth-century public philosophical debate, mainly between F. H. Jacobi and Moses Mendelssohn, on the nature of the alleged Spinozism (and therefore possible pantheism) in the thought of G. E. Lessing. In Kant's view, Mendelssohn argues for an orientation of thought in rational faith and takes the side of reason, whereas Jacobi favors moral practice, defending Spinozism and therefore a form of pantheism, an "enthusiastic" or a dogmatic view. Kant takes Mendelssohn's side but gives it his own critical twist. I leave aside the details of this important debate to focus solely on what Kant conveys in the essay in terms of orientation in thought in general.

6. O'Neill, "Orientation in Thinking," 217.

7. See also The Canon of Pure Reason in the first *Critique*, where Kant claims that no one can be disinterested in this question (*KrV* A829/B857).

Chapter 2

1. Yirmiyahu Yovel, *Kant and the Philosophy of History* (Princeton, N.J.: Princeton University Press, 1980), 8; Karl Ameriks, "The Purposive Development of Human Capacities," in *Kant's "Idea for a Universal History with a Cosmopolitan*

Aim": A Critical Guide, ed. Amélie Oksenberg Rorty and James Schmidt (Cambridge: Cambridge University Press, 2009), 67. Yovel and Ameriks are not alone. Other interpretations that dismiss the importance of Kant's historico-political writings by deeming them uncritical include Michel Despland, *Kant on History and Religion* (Montreal: McGill-Queen's University Press, 1973); Fritz Medicus, "Kants Philosophie der Geschichte," *Kant Studien* 7, nos. 1–3: 1–22; and Klaus Weyand, *Kants Geschichte Philosophie: Ihre Entwicklung und ihr Verhältnis zur Aufklärung* (Köln: Kölner-Universitätsverlag, 1963). Despland argues that the concept of progress is taken for granted by Kant and thus has dogmatic status in these writings, while both Medicus and Weyand hold that Kant did not have a critical conception of teleology before the *Critique of Judgment*. Rudolf Makkreel also argues that most of Kant's official writings on history and politics operate with a dogmatic notion of teleology, but that it is possible to reinterpret them in light of the regulative principle of purposiveness introduced in the third *Critique*. Thus, he brings the notion of reflective judgment to bear retroactively on the historico-political writings, most of which were written long before the *Critique of Judgment*; he has to do so, because like Yovel and others he does not think that there is a critical notion of teleology in Kant's writings before the *Critique of Judgment*. See Rudolf Makkreel, *Imagination and Interpretation in Kant: The Hermeneutical Import of the "Critique of Judgment"* (Chicago: University of Chicago Press, 1990), 130–53.

2. Kleingeld, "Kant on Historiography," esp. 524–25. Both Riley and Allison agree that there is an underdeveloped notion of purposiveness in the *Critique of Pure Reason*, if not a full-blown critical teleology: see Patrick Riley, *Kant's Political Philosophy* (Totowa, N.J.: Rowman and Littlefield, 1993), 65–67; Allison, "Is the *Critique of Judgment* Post-Critical?," esp. 170–71. Lastly, Allison and Wood also contend that Kant's teleology in the "Idea" essay is not dogmatic but has its critical foundations, albeit in the third *Critique*; see Allison, "Teleology and History in Kant"; Wood, "Kant's Philosophy of History."

3. See Wood, "Kant's Philosophy of History," esp. 247, where he argues that it is question-begging to attempt to base Kant's philosophy of history itself solely on beliefs held purely on practical grounds; and Allison, "Teleology and History in Kant." For interpretations that highlight the moral-practical side of a teleological view of history, see Pablo Muchnik, *Kant's Theory of Evil: An Essay on the Dangers of Self-Love and Aprioricity of History* (Lanham, Md.: Lexington, 2009), esp. 67–69; Kristi Sweet, *Kant on Practical Life: From Duty to History* (Cambridge: Cambridge University Press, 2013), esp. 194–98. Pauline Kleingeld argues that this essay is important both theoretically and practically for Kant: see Pauline Kleingeld, "Kant, History, and the Idea of Moral Development," *History of Philosophy Quarterly* 16, no. 1 (January 1999): 59–80.

4. Wood, "Kant's Philosophy of History," esp. 245–47.

5. Cohen, *Kant and the Human Sciences*, 105–8.

6. Such disorientation is both theoretical and practical: it is not only that we do not know what history as a whole looks like but also that not knowing has practical consequences in that it can lead to nihilism or fatalism. Here I focus on the theoretical disorientation and my reasons for doing so will become clear in the remainder of the chapter.

NOTES TO PAGES 47–56

7. On narratives and story-telling in Kant's philosophy of history, see Cohen, *Kant and the Human Sciences*, 122–26, 178n42.

8. Kleingeld, "Kant on Historiography."

9. Ibid., 527.

10. This antagonism is nothing other than the famous "*unsociable sociability*" [*ungesellige Geselligkeit*] that Kant attributes to an innate predisposition of human beings, that is to say, the inclination to be in a society on the one hand and wanting to break free from anything that will limit their freedom on the other.

11. This is among the ideas later to be developed in Kant's "Toward Perpetual Peace: A Philosophical Sketch." I turn to this essay in chapter 5.

12. He is referring to Europe, which obviously is not and has never been a continent.

13. Note the language of parts-whole that anticipates the analogy between organism and an ideal body-politic; see chapter 3 below on the use of organic language in Kant's political writings.

14. In fact, we *already* make reference to a bigger picture when we account for history: historical facts are meaningless unless given meaning through interpretation that makes use of a teleological account of universal history. On this point, see also Makkreel, *Imagination and Interpretation in Kant*.

15. Kleingeld, "Kant on Historiography," 526.

16. See introduction on Mills' methodological distinction between ideal and nonideal theory.

17. That Kant exhibits a paternalistic or colonialist attitude in this essay is accepted by various scholars; for an overview, see Katrin Flikschuh and Lea Ypi, eds., *Kant and Colonialism: Historical and Critical Perspectives* (New York: Oxford University Press, 2014), esp. 1–18; on Kant and colonialism see Serequeberhan, "Eurocentrism in Philosophy;" 340–42; Marwah, "Bridging Nature and Freedom?," 391–92; Hedrick, "Race, Difference and Anthropology, " 256–59.

18. Kleingeld, "Kant on Historiography," 526n7. Kleingeld retains this argument in her later works, including in "Kant's Second Thoughts on Colonialism," 45. There is near consensus on the point that Kant, at the very least in the 1780s, endorsed a sexist, racist, and Eurocentric agenda of human social and moral development; see also the introduction to Flikshuh and Ypi, *Kant and Colonialism*.

19. On Kant's racially and geographically differentiated and gendered view of development, see also Serequeberhan, "Eurocentrism in Philosophy"; Marwah, "Bridging Nature and Freedom?"; Inder Marwah, "What Nature Makes of Her: Kant's Gendered Metaphysics," *Hypatia: A Journal of Feminist Philosophy* 28, no. 3 (2013): 551–67; Hedrick, "Race, Difference, and Anthropology"; Mark Larrimore, "The Sublime Waste: Kant on the Destiny of the 'Races'" *Canadian Journal of Philosophy* 29 (1999 suppl.): 99–125; Jennifer Mensch, "Caught between Character and Race: 'Temperament' in Kant's Lectures on Anthropology," *Australian Feminist Law Journal* 43, no. 1 (2017): 125–44. I say more about Kant's views on human cultural development in chapter 4.

20. It has of course been acknowledged and developed in various ways by postcolonial and feminist philosophers as well as by philosophers of race: see, for example, Eze, "The Color of Reason"; Robert Bernasconi, "Will the Real Kant

Please Stand Up: The Challenge of Enlightenment Racism to the Study of the History of Philosophy," *Radical Philosophy* 117 (2003): 13–22; Sarah Kofman, "The Economy of Respect: Kant and Respect for Women," in *Feminist Interpretations of Immanuel Kant*, ed. Robin May Schott (University Park: Pennsylvania State University Press, 1997), 355–72; Gayatri Chakravorty Spivak, *A Critique of Postcolonial Reason: Toward A History of the Vanishing Present* (Cambridge, Mass.: Harvard University Press, 1999); Serequeberhan, "Eurocentrism in Philosophy"; Mensch, "Caught between Character and Race."

21. Perhaps Kant changed his mind about the inferiority of nonwhite races and non-European cultures after 1790s, as Kleingeld argues in "Kant's Second Thoughts on Race," but perhaps not; see Bernasconi, "Kant's Third Thoughts on Race." Another approach that advocates for a multicultural Kantian liberalism and cosmopolitanism can be found in Thomas McCarthy, "On Reconciling Cosmopolitan Unity and National Diversity," *Public Culture* 11, no. 1 (1999): 175–208; and Muthu, *Enlightenment against Empire*.

22. Serequeberhan, "Eurocentrism in Philosophy," 347.

23. Serequeberhan, "Eurocentrism in Philosophy," 347–48; Kleingeld, "Kant on Historiography," 526n7.

24. Mills, "Ideal Theory as Ideology," 178.

25. Ibid.

26. For analyses and examples of how teleology is used to support various historical and political visions, see Henning Trüper, Dipesh Chakrabarty, and Sanjay Subrahmanyam, eds., *Historical Teleologies in the Modern World* (New York: Bloomsbury, 2015).

Chapter 3

1. Here I leave aside the formal-objective purposiveness (in geometry) that Kant contrasts with the material-objective purposiveness of organisms and nature as a whole (*KU/AA* 5:362–64).

2. See Henry E. Allison's "Is the *Critique of Judgment* Post-Critical?" for the strongest arguments that emphasize the continuity between the notion of regulative principles in the first *Critique* and the notion of reflective judgments in the third *Critique*; see Rudolf Makkreel's *Imagination and Interpretation in Kant* for an argument that highlights the differences.

3. See previous note.

4. The "recently undertaken fundamental transformation of a great people into a state" may refer to either the French or the American Revolution. Sedgwick takes it to refer to the former: see Sally Sedgwick, "The State as Organism: The Metaphysical Basis of Hegel's *Philosophy of Right*," *The Southern Journal of Philosophy* 39 (2001): 171–88.

5. On the distinctions between machines and organisms, see Hannah Ginsborg, "Kant on Understanding Organisms as Natural Purposes," in *Kant and the Sciences*, ed. Eric Watkins (Oxford: Oxford University Press, 2001), 231–58.

NOTES TO PAGES 73-77

Ginsborg demonstrates that the basis of Kant's argument about the use of teleology in biology is the question of normativity, and that even today we cannot help but judge organisms in terms of normative structures. For a more recent assessment of the status of Kant's regulative teleology in biology, see the special issue on Kantian teleology and the biological sciences in Joan Steigerwald, ed., *Studies in History and Philosophy of Biological and Biomedical Sciences* 37, no. 4 (2006). Whether or not it is possible to interpret an organism today without the language of purposiveness, the question at stake for the purposes of my argument here is *if* and *how* an analogy with organisms might be useful for understanding an ideal body politic.

6. This equivocation of organic and social-political forces would bring Kant closer to Herder's position, of which he was highly critical; see his review of Herder's *Ideas for the Philosophy of the History of Humanity* ("RezHerder"/*AA* 8:55–57). I return to this issue later in the chapter.

7. G. W. F. Hegel, *Elements of the Philosophy of Right*, trans. H. B. Nisbet, ed. Allen Wood (Cambridge: Cambridge University Press, 1991), §256, §258, and §269; see also Sedgwick, "The State as Organism," 181.

8. See chapter 1.

9. As Susan Meld-Shell notes, the metaphor of the body-politic is ancient, with common medieval versions equating the king with the head or the heart of a polity: see Susan Meld-Shell, *The Embodiment of Reason: Kant on Spirit, Generation, and Community* (Chicago: University of Chicago Press, 1996), 155n77.

10. Although the third *Critique* was written approximately five years after the "Enlightenment" essay, I will show that it provides a productive interpretive lens for the essay's reliance on organic language. Thus, my interpretive strategy here is similar to Henry E. Allison's work on "Idea for a Universal History with a Cosmopolitan Intent"; see Allison, "Teleology and History in Kant."

11. See, respectively, Ellis, *Kant's Politics*, 15–17, 62–63; Axel Honneth, "The Irreducibility of Progress: Kant's Account of the Relationship between Morality and History," in *Pathologies of Reason: On the Legacy of Critical Theory* (New York: Columbia University Press, 2009), 1–18. O'Neill considers teleology only in terms of Kant's developmental view of reason: see O'Neill, *Constructions of Reason*, 28, 39. Deligiorgi incorporates a teleological view of history but argues that Kant's view of progress can be understood without it: see Katerina Deligiorgi, *Kant and the Culture of Enlightenment* (Albany: SUNY Press, 2005), 4, 107.

12. I use female pronouns "she" and "her" in referring to the human being in compliance with the *Guidelines for the Nonsexist Use of Language* published in 1986 by the American Philosophical Association. For an excellent assessment of the issues concerning the use of gender-neutral language and female pronouns in Kant's philosophy, see Pauline Kleingeld, "The Philosophical Status of Gender-Neutral Language in the History of Philosophy: The Case of Kant," *Philosophical Forum* 25, no. 2 (1993): 134–50.

13. See O'Neill, *Constructions of Reason*, 33–34; Deligiorgi, *Kant and the Culture of Enlightenment*, 63–65; and Jonathan Peterson, "Enlightenment and Freedom," *Journal of the History of Philosophy* 46, no. 2 (2008): 223–44.

14. It is important to note that while Kant focuses mainly on matters of religion throughout the essay, he concedes that matters of politics and legislation

can also be a part of public discussion ("WA"/*AA* 8:41); see also Peterson, "Enlightenment and Freedom."

15. Kant also discusses the freedom of the public use of reason as the only means for changing our social political condition for the better in the "Orientation" essay ("WDO"/*AA* 8:144).

16. See O'Neill, *Constructions of Reason*; Deligiorgi, *Kant and the Culture of Enlightenment*; Ellis, *Kant's Politics*.

17. On the conception of a regulatively teleological history of philosophy underlying this essay, see also Pauline Kleingeld, *Fortschritt und Vernunft: Zur Geschichtsphilosophie Kants* (Würzburg: Königshausen and Neumann, 1995), 23–24.

18. See also Ginsborg, "Kant on Understanding Organisms."

19. Kant reiterates this point in the "Orientation" essay ("WDO"/*AA* 8:145) and in "On the Common Saying" (*AA* 8:305).

20. I clarify the sense in which a majority of *The Doctrine of Right* represents an expression of Kant's ideal theory of politics in the introduction and chapter 6.

21. On his preference for political reform over revolution, see also Kant's "On the Common Saying" (*AA* 8:299–300).

22. Meld-Shell, *The Embodiment of Reason*, 157–58, emphases added.

23. Howard Williams, "Metamorphosis or Palingenesis? Political Change in Kant," *The Review of Politics* 63, no. 4 (2001): 719–20.

24. Ibid., 714.

25. Ibid.

26. As Jennifer Mensch suggests, what we can call "organic thinking" or "organicism" was pervasive among mid- to late-eighteenth-century European intellectuals and is a suitable response to the problem of political constitution, especially "when grasping the problems and possibilities of an irreducibly living nature." See Jennifer Mensch, *Kant's Organicism: Epigenesis and the Development of Critical Philosophy* (Chicago: University of Chicago Press, 2013), 1.

27. Like Williams, I too am wary of putting forth a concrete interpretation of political change as a natural process. Herder, among others, uncritically resorts to such organicism when describing an ideal state: see Johann Gottfried Herder, *On World History: An Anthology*, trans. Ernest Menze, ed. Hans Alder (New York: M. E. Sharpe, 1997), 288. By contrast, Kant adopts organic language here in a careful way: utilizing the regulative principle of purposiveness, he argues that the similarity between an ideal state and an organism is an analogy *in the way* we judge each of them, as I have shown.

28. Williams, "Metamorphosis or Palingenesis?," 712.

29. Ibid., 719.

30. Ibid., 721, emphasis added.

Chapter 4

1. Zöller, "Kant's Political Anthropology," 133–34.

2. Ibid., 1.

NOTES TO PAGES 89-99

3. Riley, *Kant's Political Philosophy*, 84.
4. Ibid., 96–98.
5. Ellis, *Kant's Politics*, 64–65.
6. Williams, "Metamorphosis or Palingenesis?," 719.
7. Here, I leave aside the latter issues of geography, and focus on the relationship of usefulness between nature in general and human beings. I discuss the issue of physical geography and its significance for Kant's political thought more fully in the next chapters and demonstrate that a consideration of geography in political discourse is still an application of the principle of political *Zweckmässigkeit*.
8. Compare his claim in the "Conjectural Beginning" essay that the first stage of human history consists of a transition from a natural condition of inequality to a cultural condition of civil state (*AA* 8:116–18).
9. Allen Wood, *Kant's Ethical Thought* (New York: Cambridge University Press, 1999), 296–300; see also Hedrick, "Race, Difference, and Anthropology," 256–57.
10. On the differences among the roles played by nature, providence, fate, and reason in history, see Pauline Kleingeld, "Nature of Providence? On the Theoretical and Moral Importance of Kant's Philosophy of History," *American Catholic Philosophical Quarterly* 75 (2001): 201–19.
11. Ellis, *Kant's Politics*, 66.
12. Ibid., 69.
13. Ellis, *Kant's Politics*, 61; Williams, "Metamorphosis or Palingenesis?," 719.
14. Ellis refers to purposiveness as a "mechanism of nature" a number of times, which also suggests a misinterpretation of the relationship between mechanism and teleology; see Ellis, *Kant's Politics*, 48, 61–62, 68, 100.
15. Ibid., 69.
16. Ibid., 48.
17. Note that there is no domain [*Gebiete*] that fills in the gap between nature and freedom, but only a territory [*territorium* or *Boden*]; the bridge, then, has its own territory but not a domain or a doctrine. On Kant's distinction between domain and territory, see the introduction to the *Critique of Judgment* (*KU/AA* 5:75–77). I owe a debt of gratitude to Rudi Makkreel for this insight; according to the distinction between domain and territory there can only be a tentative bridge, a transitional territory, between nature and freedom, not an actual unified domain.
18. See also Henry E. Allison, *Kant's Theory of Taste*, 202. Here I leave aside the various debates on the exact way in which mechanism and freedom are shown to be compatible in the third antinomy.
19. Elsewhere Kant expands on why happiness [*Glückseligkeit*] cannot be an end set by reason and freedom (*GMS/AA* 4:395–97). I return to this point below to show how this assumption also has nonideal theory undertones about what counts as a valuable form of existence.
20. For arguments that highlight the "culture of discipline," see Rachel Zuckert, *Kant on Beauty and Biology: An Interpretation of the "Critique of Judgment"* (Cambridge: Cambridge University Press), 379ff; Makkreel, *Imagination and*

Interpretation in Kant, 139–41; Kristi Sweet, "Kant and the Culture of Discipline: Rethinking the Nature of Nature," *Epoché: A Journal for the History of Philosophy* 15, no. 1 (2010): 121–38. For an argument that both a culture of discipline and skill are valuable for the humanity's progress, see Lara Denis, "Individual and Collective Flourishing in Kant's Philosophy," *Kantian Review* 13 (2008): 94–96.

21. Denis, "Individual and Collective Flourishing," 94.
22. Ellis, *Kant's Politics*, 67.
23. Riley, *Kant's Political Philosophy*, 97.
24. The language here parallels the fourth proposition of the "Idea" essay in terms of the language of the "unsociable sociability" of human nature. In the fourth proposition of the "Idea" essay, Kant had singled out the "unsociable sociability" of human beings as the means by which the development of human capacities can be realized in history, and here in §83 of the third *Critique* he posits, similarly, that inequality among people and the misery of hardship, oppression, and war are the means by which skills can be best developed in the human race ("IaG"/*AA* 8:20; *KU*/*AA* 5:432).
25. Ellis, *Kant's Politics*, 67–68.
26. As such, this political-legal condition constitutes the matrix in which we can *also* start to develop as final ends, moral agents; compare the seventh proposition of the "Idea" essay, where Kant claims that a civil condition is a necessary but not sufficient step toward an ethical commonwealth ("IaG"/*AA* 8:26).
27. In the "Idea" essay, Kant similarly makes a distinction between a moral community and a pathological one ("IaG"/*AA* 8:21).
28. Compare Kant's claim in the "Idea" essay that culture only prepares us for morality and it does so through unsocial sociability or social antagonism ("IaG"/*AA* 8:26–27).
29. See, e.g., Louden, *Kant's Impure Ethics*, 11–12; Cohen, *Kant and the Human Sciences*, 70–71.
30. On how—in this passing remark—Kant seems to exclude the non-European subject from the sphere of rationality, see also Spivak, *A Critique of Postcolonial Reason*, 26–29.
31. Marwah, "Bridging Nature and Freedom?," 400.
32. Zöller, "Kant's Political Anthropology," 144–45, emphases added.
33. Muthu, *Enlightenment against Empire*, 209. I agree with Marwah here that at the very least "Muthu's conceptualization of culture mistakenly imports the contemporary usage of the term, and in so doing, misrepresents Kant's understanding of what culture is at all": Marwah, "Bridging Nature and Freedom?," 387n7.
34. Marwah, "Bridging Nature and Freedom?," 397, emphases added.
35. Pagden, "Stoicism," 18–19.
36. I do not wish to get too much into Kant's hierarchical theory of race and its relation to culture and politics here; for excellent resources on Kant's theory of race and its relationship to his ethical and political thought, see Mensch, "Caught between Character and Race"; Eze, "The Color of Reason"; Kleingeld, "Kant's Second Thoughts on Race"; Robert Bernasconi, "Kant as an Unfamiliar Source of Racism," in *Philosophers on Race: Critical Essays*, ed. Julie K. Ward and Tommy

NOTES TO PAGES 109-120

Lot (Albany: SUNY Press, 2007), 145-66; Bernasconi, "Kant's Third Thoughts on Race"; Mills, "Kant's *Untermenschen*"; Hedrick, "Race, Difference, and Anthropology"; Serequeberhan, "Eurocentrism in Philosophy"; Pagden, "Stoicism"; Larrimore, "The Sublime Waste"; and Marwah, "Bridging Nature and Freedom?"

37. Pagden, "Stoicism," 19-20. I analyze Kant's anticolonialism in the next two chapters.

38. Zöller, "Kant's Political Anthropology."

39. Ibid., 138.

40. Ibid., 137.

41. Ibid., 136-38.

42. Ibid., 134-36.

Introduction to Part III

1. See Gerd-Walter Küsters, *Kants Rechtsphilosophie: Erträge der Forschung* (Darmstadt: Wissenschaftliche Buchgesellschaft, 1988); Bernd Ludwig, *Metaphysische Anfangsgründe der Rechtslehre* (Hamburg: Felix Meiner Verlag, 1986); Bernd Ludwig, *Kants Rechtslehre* (Hamburg: Felix Meiner Verlag, 1988); Allen Rosen, *Kant's Theory of Justice* (Ithaca, N.Y.: Cornell University Press, 1993); Wolfgang Kersting, *Wohlgeordnete Freiheit* (Frankfurt a.M.: Suhrkamp Verlag, 1993); Leslie Mullholand, *Kant's System of Rights* (New York: Columbia University Press, 1991); Jeffrie Murphy, *Kant: The Philosophy of Right* (Macon, Ga.: Mercer University Press, 1994); Thomas W. Pogge, "Is Kant's *Rechtslehre* Comprehensive?," *The Southern Journal of Philosophy* 36, supp. (1997): 161-87; Sharon Byrd and Joachim Hruschka, *Kant's Doctrine of Right: A Commentary* (Cambridge: Cambridge University Press, 2010).

2. Paul Formosa, "The End of Politics: Kant on Sovereignty, Civil Disobedience, and Cosmopolitanism," in *Politics and Teleology in Kant*, ed. Paul Formosa, Avery Goldman, and Tatiana Patrone (Cardiff: University of Wales Press, 2014), 37.

3. Paul Formosa, "The End of Politics," 56.

Chapter 5

1. Ellis, *Kant's Politics*, 97-100.

2. This kind of inquiry that attempts to bridge the gap between ideal and real political circumstances by reference to "what human beings ought to make of themselves" is what in the Kantian schema a pragmatic knowledge of the world looks like (*Anth/AA* 7:119).

3. Pauline Kleingeld demonstrates this most effectively, against Habermas, in her *Kant and Cosmopolitanism: The Philosophical Ideal of World Citizenship* (Cambridge: Cambridge University Press, 2011), 187-99. For alternative accounts of

Kant's rejection of a world government, see also Held, *Democracy and Global Order*; Thomas Mertens, "Cosmopolitanism and Citizenship: Kant against Habermas," *The European Journal of Philosophy* 4 (1996): 328–47.

4. It is rather curious that the spherical shape of the earth—a geographically contingent fact—here provides a basis for formulating a Cosmopolitan Right. This argument is repeated in the conclusion of the Public Right of *The Doctrine of Right*, to which I turn in the next chapter.

5. Seyla Benhabib, for instance, extends the Kantian right of universal hospitality further to long-term stays for immigrants and refugees as well: see Benhabib, *The Rights of Others*. I address Benhabib's interpretation in the next chapter. For a sampling of discussions of any of the proposals found in "Toward Perpetual Peace," see Thomas Mertens, "From 'Perpetual Peace' to the 'Law of Peoples': Kant, Habermas, and Rawls on International Relations," *Kantian Review* 6 (2000): 60–84; and the essays in Bohman and Lutz-Bachmann, *Perpetual Peace*, especially Habermas's "Kant's Idea of Perpetual Peace."

6. That is, it seems as if—whatever actually happens—nothing will have any effect on the course of nature approaching peace. It is clear that there is a moral dilemma here concerning a mechanism of nature bringing about perpetual peace regardless of individual or collective human actions. As important as this moral dilemma is, I will not be focusing on it here, for I am interested first and foremost in how this poses itself as a theoretical dilemma for political thought—if peace is *guaranteed*, how can it be a theoretical *hypothesis*? For a comprehensive analysis of the complicated relationship between moral and historical progress, see Sharon Anderson-Gold, *Unnecessary Evil: History and Moral Development in the Philosophy of Immanuel Kant* (Albany: SUNY Press, 2001); Kleingeld, "Kant, History, and the Idea of Moral Development"; and Lea Ypi, "Natura Daedala Rerum? On The Justification of Historical Progress in Kant's Guarantee of Perpetual Peace," *Kantian Review* 14, no. 2 (2010): 118–48.

7. Ellis, *Kant's Politics*, 97–100.

8. See chapter 3 on the "weak teleology" of political *Zweckmässigkeit*. For additional arguments regarding why a guarantee of perpetual peace does not contradict human freedom, especially with regard to "Toward Perpetual Peace," see Luigi Caranti, "What Is Wrong with a Guarantee of Perpetual Peace?," in *Kant und die Philosophie in weltbürgerlicher Absicht: Akten des XI. Kant-Kongresses*, ed. Stegano Bacin, Alfredo Ferrarin, Claudio La Rocca, and Margit Ruffing (Berlin: Walter de Gruyter, 2013), 611–22; and Ypi, "Natura Daedala Rerum?"

9. On the idea of a "realistic utopia" and the role of nonideal theory, see the introduction.

10. See also my analyses in chapters 1–4.

11. On the distinction that Kant makes between nature and providence, see Kleingeld, "Nature or Providence?"; for an agent-centered defense of the teleology of nature as Kant uses it here, see Ypi, "Natura Daedala Rerum?"

12. On the role of teleology in providing political hope, see also Loren Goldman, "In Defense of Blinders: On Kant, Political Hope, and the Need for Practical Belief," *Political Theory* 40, no. 4 (2012): 497–523.

13. Ellis, *Kant's Politics*, 97.

NOTES TO PAGES 129-140

14. See chapter 3 on external purposiveness and its experimental or hypothetical purchase.

15. Note the similarity to the argument that Kant makes in §83 of the third *Critique* (*KU/AA* 5:432–33; see also *MS/AA* 6:354).

16. I say more about commerce and its connection to universal hospitality in the next chapter.

17. Ellis, *Kant's Politics*, 41–43, 97.

18. Ibid., 100.

Chapter 6

1. Katrin Flikschuh, *Kant and Modern Political Philosophy* (Cambridge: Cambridge University Press, 2000), 80–82.

2. Ibid., 85–91.

3. Otfried Höffe, *Kant's Cosmopolitan Theory of Law and Peace*, trans. Alexandra Newton (Cambridge: Cambridge University Press, 2001), 79–80; Arthur Ripstein, *Force and Freedom*, 356–58; Elisabeth Ellis, *Kant's Politics*, 4.

4. The main representatives of a Kantian philosophy based on Kant's moral theory are John Rawls and Rawls-inspired political thinkers: see Rawls, *A Theory of Justice*; Christine Korsgaard, "Taking the Law into Our Own Hands: Kant on the Right to Revolution," in *Reclaiming the History of Ethics: Essays for John Rawls*, ed. Andrews Reath, Barbara Herman, and Christine Korsgaard (Cambridge: Cambridge University Press, 1997), 297–328; Brown, *Grounding Cosmopolitanism*; Benhabib, *The Rights of Others*; Benhabib, *Another Cosmopolitanism*; Murphy, *Kant: The Philosophy of Right*; Riley, *Kant's Political Philosophy*; and Susan Neiman, *The Unity of Reason: Re-Reading Kant* (New York: Oxford University Press, 1994). For criticism of this conflation, especially in Rawls's work, see Onora O'Neill's "Kant's Justice and Kantian Justice," in her *Bounds of Justice*, 65–80.

5. Flikschuh, *Kant and Modern Political Philosophy*, 85–86.

6. This is why the problem of a just state, the main problem of the principle of right, is subordinated to ethics but not exhausted by it. In Appendix I to "Toward Perpetual Peace," where Kant considers a possible disagreement between morals and politics, he makes clear that politics has to be subordinated to ethics; that is, the art of political governance is not just know-how and its principles must adhere to the highest principle of ethics ("ZeF"/*AA* 8:380). To say that political problems cannot be resolved by immoral means or that "morals cut the knot that politics cannot untie" ("ZeF"/*AA* 8:380) is not the same thing as saying, however, that political problems are reducible to moral ones, as is demonstrated by the distinction between the domain of right and the domain of virtue.

7. Flikschuh, *Kant and Modern Political Philosophy*, 89–90.

8. Thus, I agree with Alix Cohen that *The Metaphysics of Morals* can be called Kant's "applied ethics," albeit one still operating at a somewhat abstract level of generality regarding the human condition; see Cohen, *Kant and the Human Sciences*, 165n34.

9. Here, I do not want to get too much into the relationship between the Categorical Imperative and the principle of *Recht*; I follow Ripstein, *Force and Freedom*, 1–29, 355–388; Ellis, *Kant's Politics*, 1–11; Cohen, *Kant and the Human Sciences*, 84–108; and Höffe, *Kant's Cosmopolitan Theory*, 81–93, in the reading that the doctrine of right is *not* simply a direct application of the Categorical Imperative to specific circumstances of politics or right.

10. Höffe, *Kant's Cosmopolitan Theory*, 102.

11. Ibid., 102–6.

12. Flikschuh, *Kant and Modern Political Philosophy*, 197–98.

13. Ripstein, *Force and Freedom*, 12, emphases added; see also 358–60.

14. Ibid., 12.

15. Jeffrey Edwards, "'The Unity of All Places on the Face of the Earth': Original Community, Acquisition, and Universal Will in Kant's Doctrine of Right," in *Reading Kant's Geography*, ed. Stuart Elden and Eduardo Mendieta. (Albany: SUNY, 2011), 233–63.

16. O'Neill, "Orientation in Thinking," 223, emphasis added.

17. That this right is not a matter of philanthropy is a point Kant also makes in "Toward Perpetual Peace" ("ZeF"/*AA* 8:357).

18. Flikschuh, *Kant and Modern Political Philosophy*, 101–3. This is another aspect of Flikschuh's argument for the distinction between ethics and politics: in politics, we need an account of economic desiring, as this seems to matter to historical and political agency in ways that it did not matter to Kant's notion of ethical agency.

19. Lea Ypi, "Commerce and Colonialism in Kant's Philosophy of History," in Flikschuh and Ypi, *Kant and Colonialism*, 99–126.

20. Note that Kant thinks that focusing on hospitable commerce is a better prospect for bringing humans together than the linguistic and religious differences that tend to separate us and cause wars ("ZeF"/*AA* 8:367).

21. I agree here with Kleingeld's point that the spirit of commerce does not seem to guarantee hospitality for everyone, only those dealing with trade; however, we part ways when she then turns to recent history of U.N. regulations to draw a connection between the spirit of commerce and states' incentive for peace: see Kleingeld, *Kant and Cosmopolitanism*, 87–88. I say more about Kant's prioritization of commerce in international law in what follows.

22. Benhabib, *The Rights of Others*.

23. Benhabib, *Another Cosmopolitanism*.

24. Jeremy Waldron, "Liberal Nationalism and Cosmopolitan Justice," in Benhabib, *Another Cosmopolitanism*, ed. Robert Post (New York: Oxford University Press, 2006), 83–101; Peter Niesen, "Colonialism and Hospitality," *Politics and Ethics Review* 3, no. 1 (2007): 90–108; Ypi, "Commerce and Colonialism."

25. Bonnie Honig, "Another Cosmopolitanism? Law and Politics in the New Europe," in Benhabib, *Another Cosmopolitanism*, ed. Robert Post (New York: Oxford University Press, 2006): 102–27; see 107–8.

26. Benhabib, *The Rights of Others*, 35–36.

27. Benhabib, *Another Cosmopolitanism*, 20.

28. Ibid., 22.

NOTES TO PAGES 148-154

29. Benhabib, *The Rights of Others*, 27; Benhabib, *Another Cosmopolitanism*, 22.
30. Benhabib, *Another Cosmopolitanism*, 37.
31. Benhabib, *The Rights of Others*, 42.
32. Ibid., 20.
33. Ibid., 36.
34. Ibid., 38.
35. Ibid., 42.
36. Jacques Derrida, "Hostipitality," *Angelaki* 5, no. 3 (2000): 3-18.
37. Honig, "Another Cosmopolitanism?," 108.
38. Benhabib, *Another Cosmopolitanism*, 36.
39. Honig, "Another Cosmopolitanism?," 102, emphases added.
40. Honig, "Another Cosmopolitanism?," 109; Étienne Balibar, *We, The People of Europe: Reflections on Transnational Citizenship* (Princeton, N.J.: Princeton University Press, 2004), 122, 162.
41. Honig, "Another Cosmopolitanism?," 113-14; see also Derrida, "Hostipitality," 14.
42. Kleingeld, *Kant and Cosmopolitanism*, 75-77. Höffe also argues that commercium must be taken to refer to transactions in the wide sense and not exclusively in economic terms; see Höffe, *Kant's Cosmopolitan Theory*, 140.
43. Other interpreters who take the term *Verkehr* in the more limited sense of economic or commercial interaction include Kevin Thompson, "Sovereignty, Hospitality, and Commerce: Kant and Cosmopolitan Right," *Jahrbuch für Recht und Ethik* [*Annual Review of Law and Ethics*] 16 (2008): 305-19; Flikschuh, *Kant and Modern Political Philosophy*, 189; Byrd and Hruschka, *Kant's Doctrine of Right*, 7, 207-11.
44. Niesen, "Colonialism and Hospitality," 94; see also Martin Ajei and Katrin Flikschuh, "Colonial Mentality: Kant's Hospitality Right Then and Now," in Flikschuh and Ypi, *Kant and Colonialism*, 237.
45. Niesen, "Colonialism and Hospitality," 92.
46. Ibid., 100.
47. Ypi, "Commerce and Colonialism," 119.
48. Waldron, "Liberal Nationalism," 89.
49. Ibid., 89-90.
50. Ibid., 90.
51. On the importance of trade, see also Kleingeld, *Kant and Cosmopolitanism*, 134-48.
52. Although as Niesen notes, Kant commends China and Japan for restricting even commercial access ("ZeF"/AA 8:359): Niesen, "Colonialism and Hospitality," 96-97. On this and Kant's empirical reasons for allowing China and Japan such restrictions, see Kleingeld, *Kant and Cosmopolitanism*, 80-81.
53. As Anna Stilz notes, for Kant nature's purposiveness with regard to the necessary interaction between peoples does not justify colonial acquisition or plunder of the land of another, for such acquisition takes place not by nature but by a will (*MS/AA* 6:266). This does not mean, however, that people can simply remain in isolation from one another: as we see here, the right to hospitable commerce is grounded in the fact that the spherical shape of the earth or nature

outside us *necessitates* that we interact with each other in one way or another. Kant understands the main form of this interaction to be commerce and the minimal condition of such interaction to be a "universal hospitality." See Anna Stilz, "Provisional Right and Non-State Peoples," in Flikschuh and Ypi, *Kant and Colonialism*, 207.

54. I therefore disagree with Ypi's point that the right to attempt to make commercial contact with distant others is *merely an instance* of universal cosmopolitan relations or "simply another route [rather than war] through which we might explain the emergence of global interdependence and communication." See Ypi, "Commerce and Colonialism," 22, 99. Ypi argues that Kant's later political philosophy (i.e., "Toward Perpetual Peace" and *The Doctrine of Right*) no longer defends commerce from a normative perspective but only in descriptive terms: see Ypi, "Commerce and Colonialism," 99, 113, 122. In my reading, however, first, commerce is not just one way of establishing international communication but is *the* way that Kant has in mind; in both texts, commercial contact is the universal form that cosmopolitan interaction takes. He tells us in "Toward Perpetual Peace" that commerce is a better prospect than cultural means, such as linguistic or religious exchange, since linguistic and religious differences tend to separate us and cause wars whereas commerce brings us together ("ZeF"/*AA* 8:367). Second, my point is that because it is theorized by means of the principle of *Zweckmässigkeit*, commercial relations bear on the way the cosmopolitan right is shaped and formulated.

55. Pagden, "Stoicism."
56. Ibid., 4, 18.
57. Ibid., 3–22.
58. This is not to say that there were no non-European or nonwestern peoples or nations seeking commerce at the time; the point is that in Kant's texts and imagination, European states are the relevant party of the Kantian cosmopolitan right of universal hospitality.
59. Derrida, "Hostipitality," 11.
60. Zöller, "Kant's Political Anthropology," 135–45; Harvey, *Cosmopolitanism*, 24–50.
61. On multiple conceptualizations of space and the idea of a geographically-informed cosmopolitanism, see Harvey, *Cosmopolitanism*.

Conclusion

1. Cohen, *Kant and the Human Sciences*, xiv. While Cohen refers exclusively to the human sciences—namely, to anthropology, biology, and history—I believe that the same can be said of the way in which Kant construes a political geography, as I show in chapters 5 and 6.
2. Cohen calls anthropology and philosophical history "map-making ventures": see Cohen, *Kant and the Human Sciences*, 105–8, 139–40, 146, 182.
3. Kleingeld, "Kant's Changing Cosmopolitanism."
4. Muthu, *Enlightenment against Empire*, 209–10.

5. A few scholars have already indicated intriguing possibilities for this line of inquiry: on diverse uses of teleology for histories of the world, see Trüper et al., *Teleologies in the Modern World*; on the possibility of multiple geographically-informed theories of cosmopolitanism, see Harvey, *Cosmopolitanism*; on cosmopolitanisms from below or "vernacular cosmopolitanism" that problematizes the notion of culture in traditional theories of cosmopolitanism in various ways, see Homi Bhabba, "Unsatisfied: Notes on Vernacular Cosmopolitanism," in *Text and Nation*, ed. Laura Garcia-Morena and Peter C. Pfeifer (London: Camden House, 1996), 191–207; and Walter Mignolo, "The Many Faces of Cosmo-polis: Border Thinking and Critical Cosmopolitanism," *Public Culture* 12, no. 3 (2000): 721–48; and the essays in Pnina Werbner, ed., *Anthropology and the New Cosmopolitanism: Rooted, Feminist, and Vernacular Perspectives* (New York: Bloomsbury, 2009).

6. Pagden, "Stoicism," 20.

Bibliography

Ajei, Martin, and Katrin Flikschuh. "Colonial Mentality: Kant's Hospitality Right Then and Now." In *Kant and Colonialism: Historical and Critical Perspectives*, edited by Katrin Flikshuh and Lea Ypi, 221–50. New York: Oxford University Press, 2014.

Allison, Henry E. "Is the *Critique of Judgment* 'Post-Critical'?" In *The Reception of Kant's Critical Philosophy*, edited by Sally Sedgwick, 78–92. Cambridge: Cambridge University Press, 2000.

———. *Kant's Theory of Taste*. Cambridge: Cambridge University Press, 2001.

———. *Kant's Transcendental Idealism: An Interpretation and Defense*. New Haven, Conn.: Yale University Press: 2004.

———. "Teleology and History in Kant: The Critical Foundations of Kant's Philosophy of History." In *Kant's Idea for a Universal History with a Cosmopolitan Aim: A Critical Guide*, edited by Amélie Oksenberg Rorty and James Schmidt, 24–45. Cambridge: Cambridge University Press, 2009.

Ameriks, Karl. *Kant and the Historical Turn: Philosophy as Critical Interpretation*. Oxford: Clarendon Press, 2006.

———. "The Purposive Development of Human Capacities." In *Kant's "Idea for a Universal History with a Cosmopolitan Aim": A Critical Guide*, edited by Amélie Oksenberg Rorty and James Schmidt, 46–68. Cambridge: Cambridge University Press, 2009.

Anderson-Gold, Sharon. *Cosmopolitanism and Human Rights*. Cardiff: University of Wales Press, 2001.

———. *Unnecessary Evil: History and Moral Development in the Philosophy of Immanuel Kant*. Albany: SUNY Press, 2001.

Arendt, Hannah. *Lectures on Kant's Political Philosophy*. Edited and Translated by Ronald Beiner. Chicago: University of Chicago Press, 1982.

Balibar, Étienne. "Is there a 'Neo-Racism'?" In *Race, Nation, Class: Ambiguous Identities*, translated by Chris Turner, edited by Immanuel Wallerstein and Étienne Balibar, 17–28. New York: Verso, 1991.

———. *We, The People of Europe: Reflections on Transnational Citizenship*. Princeton, N.J.: Princeton University Press, 2004.

Beck, Lewis White. *Selected Essays on Kant*. Edited by Hoke Robinson. Rochester, N.Y.: University of Rochester Press, 2002.

Beiner, Ronald, and Booth William James, eds. *Kant and Political Philosophy: The Contemporary Legacy*. New Haven, Conn.: Yale University Press, 1993.

Benhabib, Seyla. *Another Cosmopolitanism*. Edited by Robert Post. New York: Oxford University Press, 2006.
———. *The Rights of Others: Aliens, Residents, and Citizens*. Cambridge: Cambridge University Press, 2004.
Bernasconi, Robert. "Kant as an Unfamiliar Source of Racism." In *Philosophers on Race: Critical Essays*, edited by Julie K. Ward and Tommy Lott, 145–66. Albany: SUNY Press, 2007.
———. "Kant's Third Thoughts on Race." In *Reading Kant's Geography*, edited by Stuart Elden and Eduardo Mendieta, 291–318. Albany: SUNY Press, 2011.
———. "Who Invented the Concept of Race? Kant's Role in the Enlightenment Construction of Race, In *Race*. Edited by Robert Bernasconi, 11–36. Oxford: Blackwell, 2001.
———. "Will the Real Kant Please Stand Up: The Challenge of Enlightenment Racism to the Study of the History of Philosophy." *Radical Philosophy* 117 (2003): 13–22.
Bhabba, Homi. *The Location of Culture*. New York, Routledge, 2004.
———. "Unsatisfied: Notes on Vernacular Cosmopolitanism." In *Text and Nation*, edited by Laura Garcia-Morena and Peter C. Pfeifer, 191–207. London: Camden House, 1996.
Bohman, James, and Lutz, Bachmann Matthias, eds. *Perpetual Peace: Essays on Kant's Cosmopolitan Ideal*. Cambridge, Mass.: MIT Press, 1997.
Brown, Garrett W. *Grounding Cosmopolitanism: From Kant to the Idea of a Cosmopolitan Constitution*. New York: Oxford University Press, 2009.
Brown, Garrett W., and David Held, eds. *The Cosmopolitanism Reader*. New York: Polity Press, 2010.
Brown, Wendy. *Politics Out of History*. Princeton, N.J.: Princeton University Press, 2001.
Byrd, Sharon, and Joachim Hruschka. *Kant's Doctrine of Right: A Commentary*. Cambridge: Cambridge University Press, 2010.
Caranti, Luigi, ed. *Kant's Perpetual Peace: New Interpretive Essays*. Rome: LUISS University Press, 2006.
———. "What Is Wrong with a Guarantee of Perpetual Peace?" In *Kant und die Philosophie in weltbürgerlicher Absicht: Akten des XI. Kant-Kongresses*, edited by Stegano Bacin, Alfredo Ferrarin, Claudio La Rocca, and Margit Ruffing, 611–22. Berlin: Walter de Gruyter, 2010.
Cassirer, Ernst. *Kant's Life and Thought*. Translated by James Haden. New Haven, Conn.: Yale University Press, 1981.
Chakrabarty, Dipesh. *Provincializing Europe: Postcolonial Thought and Historical Difference*. Princeton, N.J.: Princeton University Press, 2008.
Cohen, Alix. *Kant and the Human Sciences: Biology, Anthropology, and History*. New York: Palgrave MacMillan, 2009.
Deligiorgi, Katerina. *Kant and the Culture of Enlightenment*. Albany: SUNY Press, 2005.
Denis, Lara. "Individual and Collective Flourishing in Kant's Philosophy." *Kantian Review* 13 (2008): 82–115.
Derrida, Jacques. "Hostipitality." *Angelaki* 5, no. 3 (2000): 3–18.

BIBLIOGRAPHY

Despland, Michel. *Kant on History and Religion, with a Translation of Kant's "On the Failure of All Attempted Philosophical Theodicies."* Montreal: McGill-Queen's University Press, 1973.

Doyle, Michael. "Kant and Liberal Internationalism." In *Toward Perpetual Peace and Other Writings on Politics, Peace, and History*, edited by Pauline Kleingeld, 201–42. New Haven, Conn.: Yale University Press, 2006.

Edwards, Jeffrey. "'The Unity of All Places on the Face of the Earth': Original Community, Acquisition, and Universal Will in Kant's Doctrine of Right." In *Reading Kant's Geography*, edited by Stuart Elden and Eduardo Mendieta, 233–63. Albany: SUNY Press, 2011.

Elden, Stuart, and Eduardo Mendieta, eds. *Reading Kant's Geography*. Albany: SUNY, 2013.

Ellis, Elisabeth, ed. *Kant's Political Theory: Interpretations and Applications*. University Park: Pennsylvania State University Press, 2012.

———. *Kant's Politics: Provisional Theory for an Uncertain World*. New Haven, Conn.: Yale University Press, 2005.

Eze, Emanuel Chukwudi. "The Color of Reason: The Idea of 'Race' in Kant's Anthropology." In *Postcolonial African Philosophy: A Critical Reader*, edited by Emanuel Chukwudi Eze, 103–31. Oxford: Blackwell, 1997.

Flikschuh, Katrin. *Kant and Modern Political Philosophy*. Cambridge: Cambridge University Press, 2000.

Flikschuh, Katrin, and Lea Ypi, eds. *Kant and Colonialism: Historical and Critical Perspectives*. New York: Oxford University Press, 2014.

Formosa, Paul. "The End of Politics: Kant on Sovereignty, Civil Disobedience, and Cosmopolitanism." In *Politics and Teleology in Kant*, edited by Paul Formosa, Avery Goldman, and Tatiana Patrone, 37–58. Cardiff: University of Wales Press, 2014.

Frierson, Patrick. *Freedom and Anthropology in Kant's Moral Philosophy*. Cambridge: Cambridge University Press, 2003.

———. *What Is the Human Being?* New York: Routledge, 2013.

Galston, William A. *Kant and the Problem of History*. Chicago: University of Chicago Press, 1975.

Ginsborg, Hannah. "Kant on Understanding Organisms as Natural Purposes." In *Kant and the Sciences*, edited by Eric Watkins, 231–58. Oxford: Oxford University Press, 2001.

———. "Kant's Teleology and Its Philosophical Significance." In *The Blackwell Companion to Kant*, edited by Graham Bird, 455–70. Oxford: Blackwell Publishing, 2006.

———. *The Normativity of Nature: Essays on Kant's "Critique of Judgment."* Oxford: Oxford University Press, 2015.

Goldman, Loren. "In Defense of Blinders: On Kant, Political Hope, and the Need for Practical Belief." *Political Theory* 40, no. 4 (2012): 497–523.

Guyer, Paul. *Kant's System of Nature and Freedom: Selected Essays*. New York: Oxford University Press, 2005.

Habermas, Jürgen. *The Divided West*. Translated by Ciaran Cronin. Cambridge: Polity Press, 2006.

BIBLIOGRAPHY

———. "The Entwinement of Myth and Enlightenment: Re-Reading Dialectic of Enlightenment." *New German Critique* 26, Critical Theory and Modernity (1982): 13–30.
———. "Kant's Idea of Perpetual Peace, with the Benefit of Two Hundred Years' Hindsight." In *Perpetual Peace: Essays on Kant's Cosmopolitan Ideal*, edited by James Bohman and Matthias Lutz-Bachmann, 113–53. Cambridge, Mass.: MIT Press, 1997.
———. *The Philosophical Discourse of Modernity*. Cambridge, Mass.: MIT Press, 1987.
———. *Theory and Practice*. Translated by John Viertel. Boston: Beacon Press, 1988.
Harvey, David. *Cosmopolitanism and the Geographies of Freedom*. New York: Columbia University Press, 2009.
Hedrick, Todd. "Race, Difference, and Anthropology in Kant's Cosmopolitanism." *Journal of the History of Philosophy* 46, no.2 (2008): 245–68.
Hegel, G. W. F. *Elements of the Philosophy of Right* [*Grundlinien der Philosophie des Rechts*]. Translated by H. B. Nisbet, edited by A. W. Wood. Cambridge: Cambridge University Press, 1991.
———. *Lectures on the History of Philosophy* [*Vorlesungen über die Philosophie der Geschichte*]. Translated by E. S. Haldane and F. H. Simson. London: Routledge Kegan Paul, 1896.
———. *Sammtliche Werke*. Edited by H. Glockner. Stuttgart: Fromman, 1927.
Held, David. *Democracy and Global Order: From the Modern State to Cosmopolitan Government*. Cambridge: Polity Press, 1995.
Herder, Johann Gottfried. *On World History: An Anthology*. Translated by Ernest Menze, edited by Hans Alder. New York: M.E. Sharpe, 1997.
Höffe, Otfried. *Kant's Cosmopolitan Theory of Law and Peace*. Translated by Alexandra Newton. Cambridge: Cambridge University Press, 2006.
———. "Kant's Principle of Justice as Categorical Imperative of Law." In *Kant's Practical Philosophy Reconsidered*, edited by Yirmiyahu Yovel, 149–67. Dordrecht: Kluwer, 1989.
Honig, Bonnie. "Another Cosmopolitanism? Law and Politics in the New Europe." In Benhabib, *Another Cosmopolitanism*, edited by Robert Post, 102–27. New York: Oxford University Press, 2006.
Honneth, Axel. "The Irreducibility of Progress: Kant's Account of the Relationship between Morality and History." In *Pathologies of Reason: On the Legacy of Critical Theory*, translated by James Ingram, 1–18. New York: Columbia University Press, 2009.
———. "Is Universalism a Moral Trap? The Presuppositions and Limits of a Politics of Human Rights." In *Perpetual Peace: Essays on Kant's Cosmopolitan Ideal*, edited by James Bohman and Matthias Lutz-Bachmann, 155–78. Cambridge, Mass.: MIT Press, 1997.
Horstmann, Rolf Peter. *Bausteine kritischer Philosophie: Arbeiten zu Kant*. Berlin: Philo, 1997.
———. "Why Must There Be a Transcendental Deduction in Kant's *Critique of Judgment*?" In *Kant's Transcendental Deductions: The Three 'Critiques' and the*

BIBLIOGRAPHY

'*Opus Postumum*'," edited by Eckart Förster, 157–77. Stanford, Calif.: Stanford University Press, 1989.

Ingram, James. *Radical Cosmopolitics: The Ethics and Politics of Democratic Universalism.* New York: Columbia University Press, 2013.

Kelly, George Armstrong. *Idealism, Politics, and History: Sources of Hegelian Thought.* Cambridge: Cambridge University Press, 1969.

Kersting, Wolfgang. *Wohlgeordnete Freiheit.* Frankfurt a.M.: Suhrkamp Verlag, 1993.

Kerszberg, Pierre. *Critique and Totality.* Albany: SUNY Press, 1997.

Kleingeld, Pauline. "Approaching Perpetual Peace: Kant's Defense of a League of States and His Ideal of a World Federation." *European Journal of Philosophy* 12, no. 3 (2004): 304–25.

———. "The Conative Character of Reason in Kant's Philosophy." *Journal of the History of Philosophy* 36 (1998): 77–97.

———. *Fortschritt und Vernunft: Zur Geschichtsphilosophie Kants.* Würzburg: Königshausen und Neumann, 1995.

———. *Kant and Cosmopolitanism: The Philosophical Ideal of World Citizenship.* Cambridge: Cambridge University Press, 2011.

———. "Kant, History, and the Idea of Moral Development." *History of Philosophy Quarterly* 16, no. 1 (January 1999): 59–80.

———. "Kant on Historiography and the Use of Regulative Ideas." *Studies in History and Philosophy of Science* 39 (2008): 523–28.

———. "Kant on the Unity of Theoretical and Practical Reason." *The Review of Metaphysics* 52, no. 2 (1998): 311–39.

———. "Kant's Changing Cosmopolitanism." In *Kant's Idea for a Universal History with a Cosmopolitan Aim: A Critical Guide*, edited by Amélie Oksenberg Rorty and James Schmidt, 171–86. Cambridge: Cambridge University Press, 2009.

———. "Kant's Second Thoughts on Colonialism." In *Kant and Colonialism: Historical and Critical Perspectives*, edited by Katrin Flikshuh and Lea Ypi, 43–67. New York: Oxford University Press, 2014.

———. "Kant's Second Thoughts on Race." *The Philosophical Quarterly* 57, no. 229 (October 2007): 573–92.

———. "Nature or Providence? On the Theoretical and Moral Importance of Kant's Philosophy of History." *American Catholic Philosophical Quarterly* 75 (2001): 201–19.

———. "The Philosophical Status of Gender-Neutral Language in the History of Philosophy: The Case of Kant." *Philosophical Forum* 25, no. 2 (1993): 134–50.

———, ed. *Toward Perpetual Peace and Other Writings on Politics, Peace, and History.* New Haven, Conn.: Yale University Press, 2006.

Kofman, Sarah. "The Economy of Respect: Kant and Respect for Women." In *Feminist Interpretations of Immanuel Kant*, edited by Robin May Schott, 355–72. University Park: Pennsylvania State University Press, 1997.

Korsgaard, Christine. "Taking the Law Into Our Own Hands: Kant on the Right to Revolution." In *Reclaiming the History of Ethics: Essays for John Rawls*, edited

by Andrews Reath, Barbara Herman, and Christine Korsgaard, 297–328. Cambridge: Cambridge University Press, 1997.
Kuehn, Manfred. *Kant: A Biography*. Cambridge: Cambridge University Press, 2011.
Kukla, Rebecca, ed. *Aesthetics and Cognition in Kant's Critical Philosophy*. Cambridge: Cambridge University Press, 2006.
Küsters, Gerd-Walter. *Kants Rechtsphilosophie: Erträge der Forschung*. Darmstadt: Wissenschaftliche Buchgesellschaft, 1988.
Larrimore, Mark. "The Sublime Waste: Kant on the Destiny of the 'Races.'" *Canadian Journal of Philosophy* 29 (1999 suppl.): 99–125.
Lafont, Christina. "Alternative Visions of a New Global Order: What Should Cosmopolitans Hope For?" *Ethics and Global Politics* 1, nos. 1–2 (2008): 1–20.
Longuenesse, Beatrice. *Kant and the Capacity to Judge: Sensibility and Discursivity in the Transcendental Analytic of the "Critique of Pure Reason."* Translated by Charles T. Wolfe. Princeton, N.J.: Princeton University Press, 1998.
———. *Kant on the Human Standpoint*. Cambridge: Cambridge University Press, 2005.
Louden, Robert. *Kant's Impure Ethics*. New York: Oxford University Press, 2000.
Ludwig, Bernd. *Kants Rechtslehre*. Hamburg: Felix Meiner Verlag, 1988.
———. *Metaphysische Anfangsgründe der Rechtslehre*. Hamburg: Felix Meiner Verlag, 1986.
Makkreel, Rudolf. *Imagination and Interpretation in Kant: The Hermeneutical Import of the "Critique of Judgment."* Chicago: University of Chicago Press, 1990.
Marwah, Inder. "Bridging Nature and Freedom? Kant, Culture, and Cultivation." *Social Theory and Practice* 38, no. 3 (2012): 385–406.
———. "What Nature Makes of Her: Kant's Gendered Metaphysics." *Hypatia: A Journal of Feminist Philosophy* 28, no. 3 (2013): 551–67.
McCarthy, Thomas. "On Reconciling Cosmopolitan Unity and National Diversity." *Public Culture* 11, no. 1 (1999): 175–208.
———. *Race, Empire, and the Idea of Human Development*. Cambridge: Cambridge University Press, 2009.
McFarland, John. *Kant's Concept of Teleology*. Edinburgh: Edinburgh University Press, 1970.
McLaughlin, Peter. *Kant's Critique of Teleology in Biological Explanation: Antinomy and Teleology*. Lewiston, N.Y.: Mellen, 1990.
Medicus, Fritz. "Kants Philosophie der Geschichte." *Kant Studien* 7, nos. 1–3 (1902): 1–22.
Mehta, Pratap Bhanu. "Cosmopolitanism and the Circle of Reason." *Political Theory* 28, no. 5 (2000): 619–39.
Meld Shell, Susan. *The Embodiment of Reason: Kant on Spirit, Generation, and Community*. Chicago: University of Chicago Press, 1996.
Mensch, Jennifer. "Caught between Character and Race: 'Temperament' in Kant's Lectures on Anthropology." *Australian Feminist Law Journal* 43, no. 1 (2017): 125–44.
———. *Kant's Organicism: Epigenesis and the Development of Critical Philosophy*. Chicago: University of Chicago Press, 2013.

Mertens, Thomas. "Cosmopolitanism and Citizenship: Kant against Habermas." *The European Journal of Philosophy* 4 (1996): 328–47.
———. "From 'Perpetual Peace' to the 'Law of Peoples': Kant, Habermas, and Rawls on International Relations." *Kantian Review* 6 (2000): 60–84.
Michalson, Gordon E. *Historical Dimensions of a Rational Faith: The Role of History in Kant's Religious Thought.* Lanham, Md.: University Press of America, 1977.
Mignolo, Walter. "The Many Faces of Cosmo-polis: Border Thinking and Critical Cosmopolitanism." *Public Culture* 12, no. 3 (2000): 721–48.
Millán-Zaibert, Elizabeth. *Friedrich Schlegel and the Emergence of Romantic Philosophy.* Albany: SUNY Press, 2007.
Mills, Charles. "Black Radical Kantianism." *Res Philosophica* 95, no. 1 (2017): 1–33.
———. "The Domination Contract." In *Contract and Domination*, edited by Charles Mills and Carole Pateman, 79–105. : Malden, Mass.: Polity Press, 2007.
———. "Ideal Theory as Ideology." *Hypatia: A Journal of Feminist Philosophy* 20, no. 3 (Summer 2005): 165–84.
———. "Kant's *Untermenschen*." In *Race and Racism in Modern Philosophy*, edited by Andrew Walls, 169–93. Ithaca, N.Y.: Cornell University Press, 2005.
———. "Occupy Liberalism! Or, Ten Reasons Why Liberalism Cannot Be Retrieved for Radicalism (and Why They Are Wrong)." *Radical Philosophy Review* 15, no. 2 (2012): 305–23.
———. *The Racial Contract.* Ithaca, N.Y.: Cornell University Press, 1997.
Muchnik, Pablo. *Kant's Theory of Evil: An Essay on the Dangers of Self-Love and the Apriroicity of History.* Lanham, Md.: Lexington, 2009.
Mullholand, Leslie. *Kant's System of Rights.* New York: Columbia University Press, 1991.
Munzel, G. Felicitas. *Kant's Conception of Moral Character: The "Critical" Link of Morality, Anthropology, and Reflective Judgment.* Chicago: University of Chicago Press, 1998.
Murphy, Jeffrie. *Kant: The Philosophy of Right.* Macon, Georgia: Mercer University Press, 1994.
Muthu, Sankar. *Enlightenment against Empire.* Princeton, N.J.: Princeton University Press, 2003.
Narayan, Uma. *Dislocating Cultures: Identities, Traditions, and Third World Feminism.* New York: Routledge, 1997.
Neiman, Susan. *The Unity of Reason: Rereading Kant.* New York: Oxford University Press, 1994.
Niesen, Peter. "Colonialism and Hospitality." *Politics and Ethics Review* 3, no. 1 (2007): 90–108.
Nussbaum, Martha, ed. *For the Love of Country: Debating the Limits of Patriotism.* Boston: Beacon Press, 1996.
———. "Kant and Cosmopolitanism." In *Cosmopolitanism Reader*, edited by Garrett W. Brown and David Held, 27–44. New York: Polity Press, 2010.
———. "Kant and Stoic Cosmopolitanism." *Journal of Political Philosophy* 5 (1997): 1–25.
Nuzzo, Angelica. *Kant and the Ideal of Embodiment.* Bloomington: Indiana University Press, 2008.

BIBLIOGRAPHY

———. *Kant and the Unity of Reason*. West Lafayette, Ind.: Purdue University Press, 2005.
O'Neill, Onora. *Bounds of Justice*. Cambridge: Cambridge University Press, 2000.
———. *Constructions of Reason: Explorations of Kant's Practical Philosophy*. Cambridge: Cambridge University Press, 1989.
———. "Historical Trends and Human Futures." *Studies in History and Philosophy of Science* 39 (2008): 529–34.
———. "A Kantian Approach to Transnational Justice." In *Cosmopolitanism Reader*, edited by Garrett W. Brown and David Held, 61–79. New York: Polity Press, 2010.
———. "Orientation in Thinking: Geographical Problems, Political Solutions." In *Reading Kant's Geography*, edited by Stuart Elden and Eduardo Mendieta, 215–32. Albany: SUNY Press, 2011.
Pagden, Anthony. "Stoicism, Cosmopolitanism, and the Legacy of European Imperialism." *Constellations* 7, no. 1 (2000): 3–22.
Peterson, Jonathan. "Enlightenment and Freedom." *Journal of the History of Philosophy* 46, no. 2 (2008): 223–44.
Piche, Claude. *Das Ideal: Ein Problem der Kantischen Ideenlehre*. Bonn: Bouvier Verlag, 1984.
Pinkard, Terry. "How Kantian was Hegel?" *The Review of Metaphysics* 43 (June 1990): 831–38.
Pippin, Robert. *Hegel's Idealism: The Satisfactions of Self-Consciousness*. Cambridge: Cambridge University Press, 1989.
———. *Kant's Theory of Form: An Essay on the "Critique of Pure Reason."* New Haven, Conn.: Yale University Press, 1982.
Pogge, Thomas W. "Is Kant's *Rechtslehre* Comprehensive?" *The Southern Journal of Philosophy* 36, supp. (1997): 161–87.
Rawls, John. *The Law of Peoples*. Cambridge, Mass.: Harvard University Press, 1999.
———. *Political Liberalism*. New York: Columbia University Press, 2005.
———. *A Theory of Justice*. Cambridge, Mass.: Harvard University Press, 1971.
Rescher, Nicholas. *Kant and the Reach of Reason: Studies in Kant's Theory of Rational Systematization*. Cambridge: Cambridge University Press, 2000.
Riley, Patrick. *Kant's Political Philosophy*. Totowa, N.J.: Rowman and Littlefield, 1993.
Ripstein, Arthur. *Force and Freedom: Kant's Legal and Political Philosophy*. Cambridge, Mass.: Harvard University Press, 2009.
Robinson, Hoke, ed. *System and Teleology in Kant's Critique of Judgment* [*Southern Journal of Philosophy* 30, supp.]. Memphis, Tenn.: Memphis State University, 1992.
Rosen, Allen. *Kant's Theory of Justice*. Ithaca, N.Y.: Cornell University Press, 1993.
Schiller, Friedrich. "What Is Universal History and Why Must One Study It?" In *Poet of Freedom*, translated by the Schiller Institute, https://archive.schillerinstitute.com/transl/Schiller_essays/universal_history.html.
Schott, Robin May, ed. *Feminist Interpretations of Immanuel Kant*. University Park: Pennsylvania State University Press, 1997.
Sedgwick, Sally. "The State as Organism: The Metaphysical Basis of Hegel's *Philosophy of Right*." *The Southern Journal of Philosophy* 39 (2001): 171–88.

BIBLIOGRAPHY

Sedgwick, Sally, ed. *The Reception of Kant's Critical Philosophy*. Cambridge: Cambridge University Press, 2000.
Serequeberhan, Tsenay. "Eurocentrism in Philosophy: The Case of Immanuel Kant." *The Philosophical Forum* 27, no. 4 (Summer 1996): 333–56.
Sikka, Sonia. *Herder on Humanity and Cultural Difference*. Cambridge: Cambridge University Press, 2011.
Simmons, John. "Ideal and Nonideal Theory." *Philosophy and Public Affairs* 38, no. 1 (2010): 5–36.
Sleat, Matt. "Realism, Liberalism, and Nonideal Theory, or Are There Two Ways to Do Realistic Political Theory?" *Political Studies* 64, no. 1 (2016): 27–41.
Spivak, Gayatri Chakravorty. *A Critique of Postcolonial Reason: Toward A History of the Vanishing Present*. Cambridge, Mass.: Harvard University Press, 1999.
Steigerwald, Joan, ed. *Studies in History and Philosophy of Biological and Biomedical Sciences* 37, no. 4 (2006).
Stemplowska, Zofia, and Adam Swift. "Ideal and Nonideal Theory." In *The Oxford Handbook of Political Philosophy*, edited by David Estlund, 373–90. Oxford: Oxford University Press, 2015.
Stilz, Anna. "Provisional Right and Non-State Peoples." In *Kant and Colonialism: Historical and Critical Perspectives*, edited by Katrin Flikshuh and Lea Ypi, 197–220. New York: Oxford University Press, 2014.
Strawson, Peter. *The Bounds of Sense: An Essay on Kant's "Critique of Pure Reason."* New York: Routledge, 1975.
Sweet, Kristi. "Kant and the Culture of Discipline: Rethinking the Nature of Nature." *Epoché: A Journal for the History of Philosophy* 15, no. 1 (2010): 121–38.
———. *Kant on Practical Life: From Duty to History*. Cambridge: Cambridge University Press, 2013.
Thompson, Kevin. "Sovereignty, Hospitality, and Commerce: Kant and Cosmopolitan Right." *Jahrbuch für Recht und Ethik [Annual Review of Law and Ethics]* 16 (2008): 305–19.
Trüper, Henning, Dipesh Chakrabarty, and Sanjay Subrahmanyam, eds. *Historical Teleologies in the Modern World*. New York: Bloomsbury, 2015.
Valentini, Laura. "Ideal vs. Nonideal Theory: A Conceptual Map" *Philosophy Compass* 7, no. 9 (2012): 654–64.
Varden, Helga. "Kant and Women." *Pacific Philosophical Quarterly* 97, no. 2 (2015): 1–42.
Waldron, Jeremy. "Liberal Nationalism and Cosmopolitan Justice." In Benhabib, *Another Cosmopolitanism*, edited by Robert Post, 83–101. New York: Oxford University Press, 2006.
Walsh, W. H. *Kant's Critique of Metaphysics*. Edinburgh: Edinburgh University Press, 1975.
Watkins, Eric, ed. *Kant and the Sciences*. Oxford: Oxford University Press, 2001.
Werbner, Pnina, ed. *Anthropology and the New Cosmopolitanism: Rooted, Feminist, and Vernacular Perspectives*. New York: Bloomsbury, 2009.
Weyand, Klaus. *Kants Geschichtsphilosophie: Ihre Entwicklung und ihr Verhältnis zur Aufklärung*. Köln: Kölner-Universitätsverlag, 1963.

Williams, Howard. *Kant's Political Philosophy*. New York: St. Martin's Press, 1983.
———. "Metamorphosis or Palingenesis? Political Change in Kant." *The Review of Politics* 63, no. 4 (2001): 693–722.
Wilson, Holly. *Kant's Pragmatic Anthropology: Its Origin, Meaning, and Critical Significance*. Albany: SUNY Press, 2006.
Wood, Allen. *Kant*. Malden, Mass.: Blackwell Publishing, 2005.
———. *Kant's Ethical Thought*. New York: Cambridge University Press, 1999.
———. "Kant's Philosophy of History." In *Toward Perpetual Peace and Other Writings on Politics, Peace, and History*, translated by David L. Colclasure, edited by Pauline Kleingeld, 243–62. New Haven, Conn.: Yale University Press, 2006.
———. *Kant's Rational Theology*. Ithaca, N.Y.: Cornell University Press, 1978.
Yovel, Yirmiyahu. *Kant and the Philosophy of History*. Princeton, N.J.: Princeton University Press, 1980.
———, ed. *Kant's Practical Philosophy Reconsidered*. New York: Kluwer, 1988.
Ypi, Lea. "Commerce and Colonialism in Kant's Philosophy of History." In *Kant and Colonialism: Historical and Critical Perspectives*, edited by Katrin Flikschuh and Lea Ypi, 99–126. New York: Oxford University Press, 2014.
———. "Natura Daedala Rerum? On The Justification of Historical Progress in Kant's Guarantee of Perpetual Peace." *Kantian Review* 14, no. 2 (2010): 118–48.
Zammito, John. *The Genesis of Kant's "Critique of Judgment."* Chicago: University of Chicago Press, 1992.
———. *Kant, Herder, and the Birth of Anthropology*. Chicago: University of Chicago Press, 2002.
Zöller, Günter. "Kant's Political Anthropology." *Kant Yearbook: Kant and German Idealism* 3, no. 1 (2011): 131–62.
Zuckert, Rachel. *Kant on Beauty and Biology: An Interpretation of the "Critique of Judgment."* Cambridge: Cambridge University Press, 2007.

Index

Absicht, 41, 49–50. *See also* aim
activity, 103–6. *See also* passivity
aim, 13–15, 22–27, 34, 41–42. See also *Absicht*
Allison, Henry, 21, 171n1, 172n2, 174n3, 176n2, 177n10, 179n18
Ameriks, Karl, 43, 173n1
analogy, 63–64, 67–73, 74–83, 91, 95, 109, 175n13, 177n5, 178n27
Anlagen, 48, 101. *See also* predispositions
anthropology, 18, 64–66, 87–89, 103–12, 134, 140–42, 15; cultural, 65, 88, 108–10, 160–61, 165–67; political, 64–66, 87–89, 103–4, 108, 110, 134
Anthropology from a Pragmatic Point of View, 128, 165
anticolonialism, 138, 147. *See also* colonialism
antinomy, 97, 179n18
apodictic use of reason, 29
Appendix to the Transcendental Dialectic, 14, 17, 27–28, 35–37, 43, 70

Balibar, Étienne, 150, 185n40
Benhabib, Seyla, 12, 138, 147–52, 170n31, 182n5, 183n4, 184nn22–35, 185n38
Bernasconi, Robert, 171n37, 175n20, 176n21, 180n36
Bildungsroman, 51, 58
biology, 11, 73, 89–90, 177n5
body politic, 64, 67–69, 71–75, 78–79, 81, 91, 109, 177n5. *See also* state

Brown, Garret W., 12, 21–23, 170n31, 172n2, 172n4, 184n4

Caranti, Luigi, 182n8
categorical imperative, 115, 137–141, 143, 149–50, 168, 184n9. *See also* moral law
civil society, 6, 49, 56, 80, 83, 87–88, 94, 100–103, 112, 148, 164
Cohen, Alix, 11, 44, 160, 169n2, 170n30, 172n7, 174n5, 175n7, 180n29, 183nn8–9, 186nn1–2
colonialism, 115, 122, 141–44, 146–47, 150–53, 155–57, 175n17, 175n18. *See also* anticolonialism
commerce, 115, 121–22, 125, 132, 137–38, 141, 144–46, 151–56, 184nn20–21, 185n43, 185nn53–54, 185n58
complementarity of right and purposiveness, 3, 9–11, 16, 19, 85, 110–11, 114, 127, 133–34, 156, 167
cosmopolitanism: as aim of history, 17–18, 24–25, 51–55, 58–60, 63, 162; as a cultural goal, 87, 100, 103, 154–56; various meanings of, 163–68; as a universal moral ideal, 12, 13, 16, 22, 57, 108, 146–48
cosmopolitan right, 15, 19, 113–16, 121–23, 134–35, 137–38, 141–56, 161, 164, 182n4, 186n54. *See also* hospitality
cosmopolitan world order, 4, 9, 12–17, 22–24, 27, 34, 41, 43, 35–36, 50, 55–59, 66, 85, 87–88, 93, 100–104, 108, 111, 160, 163–64

199

INDEX

Critique of Judgment, 3, 9, 18, 43, 63–70, 73–74, 88, 96–97, 160–61, 164, 172n1, 173n1, 176n2, 179n17
Critique of Practical Reason, 137–39
Critique of Pure Reason, 21, 23, 27–29, 33, 36–37, 41–43, 53, 70, 97, 160–61, 174n2
Critique of Teleological Judgment, 14, 64, 69, 85–87, 109–12
culture, 66, 83, 88, 92, 99–108, 110–12, 157, 161–62, 167, 171n37, 176n21, 179n20, 180n28, 180n33, 180n36, 187n5. See also *Kultur*
culture of skill, 66, 99–107, 164. See also *Geschicklichkeit*

Denis, Lara, 180nn21–22
Derrida, Jacques, 150, 155, 185n36, 185n41, 186n59
determinism, 67, 82, 93, 111
Doctrine of Right, 4, 6–8, 11–13, 18–19, 64, 68–69. 79–82, 108–9, 113–17, 124, 137–48, 153–56, 164, 184n9. See also *Rechtslehre*
dogmatism, 36, 39–42, 47, 132–33
duty, 120, 122–23, 127, 139–41, 143, 149–51, 156; ethical vs. political, 138–141

Ellis, Elisabeth, 3, 75, 89, 91–93, 95–96, 99–102, 117, 124–27, 133, 137, 140, 169n1, 177n11, 178n16, 179n5, 179nn11–14, 180n22, 180n25, 181n1, 182n7, 182n13, 183n3, 183n17, 184n9
enjoyment, 104–8.
enlightenment, as a goal, 52, 74–80
epoch of nature versus epoch of freedom, 92, 102–3
ethics and politics, 11, 115, 137–51, 183n6, 183n8, 184n18
eurocentrism, 15–16, 44, 55–61, 66, 89, 103–9, 138, 148, 154–56, 166–68, 171n37, 176n21, 180n30, 186n58; in Kant's anthropology, 66, 89, 103–9; in Kant's geography, 138, 148, 154–56; in Kant's philosophy of history, 44, 55–61
Europe, not a continent, 175n12
external purposiveness, 69, 87–93, 102, 109, 128–30

feasibility (of political ideals), 5, 7, 8–12, 19, 113–18, 120–24, 133–34, 160–61
federation of free states, 11–12, 49, 114, 117–123, 129, 131–32. See also league of nations
final end of nature, 98
Flikschuh, Katrin, 137, 139–40, 142–45, 171n37, 175n17, 183n1, 183n5, 183n7, 183n12, 183nn18–19, 185nn43–44, 186n53
focus imaginarius, 30
freedom, 6, 48–49, 52, 64–67, 74–81, 85, 92–94, 96–97, 99–103, 111–13, 118, 120, 127, 137, 139, 142, 144, 149, 151–52, 156, 175n10, 178n15, 179nn17–18, 182n8; innate right of, 151–52; internal vs. external, 137, 139–42; of public use of reason, 64–66, 74–81; to travel, 144–49

gender, 10, 59, 175n19, 177n12; and sexism, 56, 59, 175n18, 177n12
geography, physical and political, 19, 110–11, 113–17, 123–24, 125–28, 130, 134, 151, 156–57, 165
geopolitics, 19, 115, 116, 121, 125, 138, 144–48, 151, 153, 157, 164–66
Geschicklichkeit, 66, 98–100, 103–4, 107–8, 112. See also culture of skill
Ginsborg, Hannah, 177n5, 178n18
globus terraqueus, 143
Groundwork of the Metaphysics of Morals, 12, 104–5, 137–39
guarantee of nature, 114, 117, 123–33, 182n6, 182n8

INDEX

guiding principle, 9, 32, 53, 91, 102, 11, 128, 139
guiding thread, 14, 23–24, 27–29, 32, 41–42, 45–51, 53, 60, 71, 173n2. See also *Leitfaden*

Habermas, Jürgen, 12–13, 170n31, 170n33, 181n3, 182n5
happiness, 98–99, 103–8, 179n19
Harvey, David, 156, 171n36, 171n38, 186nn60–61, 187n5
Hegel, G. W. F., 73, 84, 177n7
Herder, Johann G., 84, 106, 177n6, 178n27
hermeneutic of hope in politics, 41–42, 47, 52, 56, 82, 103, 126, 138, 145, 167–68, 182n12
highest good, 38, 98; highest political good, 6, 8, 11–13, 117, 165
history, 9–11, 13, 15–18, 21–25, 27, 40–61; narrative of, 17, 20, 24–25, 41–49, 51–54, 56, 58–61, 162, 172n7, 175n7; philosophy of, 21–24, 36, 42–47, 49, 53–59, 160–61, 172n6, 174n3, 175n7; political, 52–55, 63–64, 92, 164, 167–68. See also universal history
Höffe, Otfried, 137, 140–42, 183n3, 184nn9–10, 185n42
Honig, Bonnie, 148, 150, 184n25, 185n37, 185nn39–41
hospitality, 15, 19, 113–18, 121, 129, 132–35, 137–38, 141, 144–57, 161, 164, 182n5, 184n21, 185n53, 186n58. See also cosmopolitan right
human rights, 122, 147–49
hypothetical use of reason, 20, 23–25, 27–29, 38–43, 45, 47, 49–50, 59–61, 73, 163, 172n1

"Idea for a Universal History with a Cosmopolitan Aim," 17, 21, 23–24, 34, 40–41, 43–58, 61, 91–92, 106, 108, 134, 145, 172n6, 180n24, 180nn26–28

idealized social ontology, 5–7, 18, 63, 83, 95, 112, 128, 143, 150, 163
ideal theory and nonideal theory, 4–12; distinction in Kant's thought, 6–10, 4–12, 22–25, 55, 57–61, 66, 80, 83–85, 88–89, 96, 98, 100–104, 110–18, 130–35, 147, 156–57, 160–68
idea of God, 27, 29–33, 35, 38–40, 47, 61, 73, 173n2, 173n4
idea of world-whole, 173n2
ideas of reason, 29–30, 33–34, 38
incentives, 103, 137, 139–42, 144–45, 147, 151.
inequality, 101–3, 108, 180n24
internal purposiveness, 88, 103

justice, 7, 12, 22, 59, 66–68, 82–85, 103, 111–13, 142, 150–56; and injustice, 77, 115, 138, 141, 144, 146, 152–53

Kantian political thought, 12, 14, 57, 60–61, 109, 115–17, 159, 165–67
kingdom of ends, 12, 84
Kleingeld, Pauline, 21, 43, 48, 54, 56, 61, 151, 163, 170n34, 171n1, 171n37, 172nn4–6, 174nn2–3, 175n8, 175n15, 175n18, 176n21, 176n23, 177n12
knowledge of the world, 28, 113, 117, 134, 137–38, 151, 181n2. See also *Welterkentniss*
Kultur, 99–100. See also culture

lawfulness of the contingent, 3, 9, 63, 68–70, 159–61. See also purposiveness
league of nations, 10, 113, 117, 120–21, 131. See also federation of free states
Leitfaden, 47, 90. See also guiding thread
Louden, Robert, 11, 169n2, 170n29, 180n29

INDEX

Makkreel, Rudolf, 173n1, 175n14, 176n2, 179n17, 179n20
Marwah, Inder, 106–7, 171n35, 171nn37–38, 175n17, 175n19, 180n31, 180nn33–34, 181n36
maxims of reason, 33, 35–38, 173n3
mechanism of nature, 69–72, 75, 87, 90–92, 94–95, 99, 105, 126–27, 131–32, 179n14, 179n18, 182n6; versus freedom, 94–97, 99, 132
Meld Shell, Susan, 81–82, 177n9, 178n22
Mensch, Jennifer, 175n19, 176n20, 178n26, 180n36
metamorphosis, 18, 68, 79–83, 85, 109; vs. palingenesis, 68, 79–83, 85, 109
Metaphysics of Morals, 12, 137–40, 183n8
methodology of ideal and nonideal theory, 4–6, 8, 23–24, 54, 58–60, 67, 168
Mills, Charles W., 5–8, 16–17, 54, 59–60, 169n8, 169n10, 170n20, 171n37, 171n39, 175n16, 176n24, 180n36
morality and politics, see ethics and politics
moral law, 130, 140. *See also* categorical imperative
Muchnik, Pablo, 170n3
multiculturalism, 107, 157, 167, 176n21
Muthu, Sankar, 107, 167, 171n37, 176n21, 180n33, 186n4

nature and freedom, 65, 94–96, 100, 11, 179n11
Niesen, Peter, 147, 151–53, 184n24, 185nn44–45, 185n52

O'Neill, Onora, 12, 143, 170n31, 172n4, 172n6, 183n4
organism, 63–65, 67–85, 87–91, 104, 129, 176n5; human beings as, 94–98, 109, 112

orientation, 20, 23–24, 27, 35–43, 45–46, 49–50, 53, 55, 59–61, 123, 160l, 172n6, 173n5; in history, 37, 40–41, 172n6; in thinking, 23–24, 27, 35, 38–40, 45, 50, 172n6, 173n5

Pagden, Anthony, 108–9, 154, 168, 171n36, 171n38, 180n35, 181nn36–37, 186n55
passivity, 103–8. *See also* activity
peace, 6–8, 11–13, 19, 102, 107–8, 110, 113–130, 135, 145–47, 156, 164–67, 182n6, 182n8, 184n21
"Perpetual Peace," 8, 13, 19, 113–14, 116–19, 122–29, 121–24, 141, 144–48, 153, 156, 182n5, 182n8, 183n6, 184n17, 186n54
Physical Geography, 128, 151, 156, 165
practical reason, 11, 97, 104, 110, 127, 140
predispositions, 46, 48–49, 83, 101, 175n. See also *Anlagen*
private use of reason, 64, 68, 75–78
progress, 18, 27, 41, 47, 50, 53, 57, 63, 68, 72, 74–79, 82, 85, 88, 92, 94, 101, 108, 124, 126, 134, 174n1, 177n11, 182n6; historical, 27, 41, 47, 50–53, 57, 174n1, 177n11, 182n6; moral, 88, 92, 180n6, 180n20; political, 18, 50, 63, 68, 72, 74–79, 82, 85, 92, 94, 101, 108, 124–26, 134
providence, 24, 41, 125–26, 179n10, 182n11
public use of reason, 64, 75–80, 178n15
purposiveness, principle of, 3, 8–10, 17, 19–20, 23–24, 27, 30–35, 39–41, 43, 45, 47–50, 53, 63–72, 78–79, 84–85, 88–94, 97, 100, 102, 109–12, 125–26, 128–31, 151–61, 174nn1–2, 176n1, 177n5, 178n27, 179n14, 185n53. *See also Zweckmässigkeit*; lawfulness of the contingent

INDEX

race, Kant's writings on, 10, 156, 159, 165; Kant's theory of, 159, 165, 180n36; and racism, 175n20
rational agents, 18, 67, 80, 88, 93, 95–96, 98, 131, 163
rational belief or faith (*Vernunftglaube*), 38–39, 173n5
rational hypothesis, 23–24, 33, 35, 39–41, 43, 47, 53
Rawls, John, 4–5, 7, 12, 169n5, 169n7, 169n9, 169nn13–14, 170n25, 170n27, 170n31, 182n5, 183n4
Rechtslehre, 9, 141, 156. See also *Doctrine of Right*
reform, political, 18, 68, 79–82
regulative principles, 10–11, 31, 35, 39–40, 60–61, 64–67, 69–71, 73, 79, 85, 88, 94, 110–11, 125, 129–30, 138, 156, 159–62, 164, 174n1, 178n27
republican constitution, 114, 117–121, 130–31, 133
revolution, political, 68, 79–82, 178n21; Copernican, 41
Right (*Recht*), principle of, 3–4, 9–13, 15, 85, 112–16, 118–21, 123–24, 129–43, 151, 163, 184n9
Riley, Patrick, 43, 89, 100, 124–25, 174n2, 179n3, 180n23, 183n4
Ripstein, Arthur, 12, 137, 140, 142, 170n31, 183n3, 184n9, 184n13

Sedgwick, Sally, 73, 172n1, 176n4, 177n7
Serequeberhan, Tsenay, 57, 171n34, 175n17, 175n19, 176n20, 176nn22–23, 181n36
Simmons, John, 5, 7, 169n7, 169nn14–15, 169n18
skepticism, 32, 36, 39–42, 46–47
Spivak, Gayatri Chakravorty, 176n20, 180n30
state, 64, 66–68, 71–85, 94–95, 101–2, 109, 118–122, 131, 140, 142, 178n27, 179n8, 183n6; as body with a soul; 68, 74–75; as hand mill, 68, 74, 95; as machine, 64, 68–69, 72–81, 91, 109, 131; organic theory of, 73; as organism, 63–65, 67–91, 109, 175n13. See also body politic
Stemplowska, Zofia, 5, 8, 169n6, 170n24
Sweet, Kristi, 174n3, 180n20
Swift, Adam, 5, 8, 169n6, 170n24

teleological judgment, 69, 73, 84–85, 87, 90, 93, 100, 109, 112
teleology, 23, 25, 27, 35, 43, 48, 55, 59–61, 66–68, 70–73, 75, 83–96, 108–9, 111, 114, 117, 124–25, 129, 134, 138, 156, 159–68, 174nn1–2, 176n26, 177n5, 177n11, 179n14, 182n8, 182n12, 187n5; and politics, 3–4, 9–10, 17, 19–21, 23, 55, 60–61, 64, 68, 73, 83, 85, 87–94, 109, 111, 114, 117, 124, 134, 138, 156, 159–68, 176n26, 182n8; as a way of thinking (*Denkungsart*), 18–10, 87, 94, 97, 111; weak and strong, 89–91, 124–27, 182n8. See also *Zweckmässigkeit*; purposiveness
theoretical or speculative reason, 31, 36, 97, 127
transitional theory or theory of transition, 5, 7, 9, 20, 22, 67, 80, 83–84, 87–88, 92–94, 108, 161

ultimate end of nature, 94–95, 97–103, 105, 107, 110, 114, 164
unity, of reason, 4, 27–28, 173n3; hypothetical, 27, 29–31, 34; organic, 73, 79; purposive, 30–33, 35, 38–40, 45, 50, 53, 161, 173n2; systematic, 29, 33, 40, 91
universal history, 21–25, 34, 41–42, 44–51, 53–61, 63–64, 175n14. *See also* history
unsociable sociability, 92, 99, 101, 145, 175n10, 180n24, 180n28

INDEX

Valentini, Laura, 5, 8, 169nn3–4, 170n17, 170n19, 170n22

Waldron, Jeremy, 147, 151–53, 184n24, 185n48
war, 11, 101–2, 108, 114, 119–21, 123, 129–32, 145, 180n24, 186n54
Welterkenntnis, 134, 151. *See also* knowledge of the world
"What Does It Mean to Orient Oneself in Thinking?," 14, 17, 21, 27, 35
"What Is Enlightenment?," 18, 68–69, 72, 75
Williams, Howard, 81–84, 89, 93, 178n23, 178nn27–28, 179n6, 179n13
Wilson, Holly, 11, 169n2
Wood, Allen, 21, 92, 102, 171nn1–4, 177n7, 179n9

Yovel, Yirmiyahu, 43, 173n1, 174
Ypi, Lea, 138, 145, 147, 151–53, 171n37, 175nn17–18, 182n6, 182n8, 182n11, 184n19, 184n24, 185n44, 185n47, 186nn53–54

Zammito, John H., 9, 170n26
Zöller, Günter, 89, 106, 110–11, 156, 171n35, 171n38, 178n1, 180n32, 181n38, 186n60
Zweckmässigkeit, regulative principle of, 3, 9–12, 19–20, 31, 40, 69–71, 73, 85–91, 93, 95, 109; political, 63, 65, 68, 87–90, 92–95, 99–100, 109–16, 123–28, 132–34, 137–38, 141, 144, 146, 156–57, 179n7, 182n8, 186n54. *See also* lawfulness of the contingent; purposiveness; teleology